BRADY

Public Information Officer

Philip Politano
Training Specialist – U.S. Department of Homeland Security's
Federal Emergency Management Agency
International Association of Emergency Managers
National Information Officers Association
Emergency Medical Technician – Paramedic

Upper Saddle River, New Jersey 07458

Library of Congress Cataloging-in-Publication Data

Politano, Philip.
Public information officer / Philip Politano.—1st ed.
p. cm.
Includes index.
ISBN-13: 978-0-13-171923-1
ISBN-10: 0-13-171923-8
1. Public relations. 2. Chief information officers. 3. Publicity—Management. 4. Information resources management. I. Title.
HD59.P65 2009
659.2—dc22 2008004892

Publisher: Julie Levin Alexander
Publisher's Assistant: Regina Bruno
Executive Editor: Marlene McHugh Pratt
Senior Acquisitions Editor: Stephen Smith
Associate Editor: Monica Moosang
Editorial Assistant: Patricia Linard
Director of Marketing: Karen Allman
Executive Marketing Manager: Katrin Beacom
Marketing Specialist: Michael Sirinides
Managing Production Editor: Patrick Walsh
Production Liaison: Julie Li
Production Editor: Puneet Lamba
Media Product Manager: John Jordan
New Media Project Manager: Stephen J. Hartner
Manufacturing Manager: Ilene Sanford
Manufacturing Buyer: Pat Brown
Senior Design Coordinator: Christopher Weigand
Interior Designer: Lee Goldstein
Cover Designer: Blair Brown
Composition: Aptara, Inc.
Printing and Binding: Edwards Brothers
Cover Printer: Phoenix Color Corporation

Pearson Education LTD
Pearson Education Singapore, Pte. Ltd
Pearson Education Canada, Ltd
Pearson Education—Japan
Pearson Education Australia PTY, Limited
Pearson Education North Asia Ltd
Pearson Educacíón de Mexico, S.A. de C.V.
Pearson Education Malaysia, Pte. Ltd
Pearson Education, Upper Saddle River, New Jersey

10 9 8 7 6 5 4 3 2 1
ISBN13 978 0-13-171923-1
ISBN10 0-13-171923-8

Contents

Chapter 2 The Media 17

Chapter 3 The Interview 31

Preface

The pager sounds at 3:00 A.M. The tiny screen indicates that a message has been left on the media line's voice mail. I shake myself awake, dial in the access codes, and retrieve the information from the new overnight producer at a local TV station.

She's called to find out if anything is happening—and to chat. I have nothing to tell her; it was a quiet night. The conversation is cordial. I roll over and try to go back to sleep.

This scenario is repeated for three nights in a row when it becomes apparent that this producer thinks that I am sitting in my office, waiting for calls from the media. We clear up the misunderstanding. She learns to trust me and that I'll let her in on any major happenings.

This brief story defines a small part of a public information officer's life. Constant customer service for the media, the public, and the agency makes the public information officer a special breed within an agency.

Of course, many agencies, public, private, governmental, or nongovernmental choose to shut out the media because it is often easier to ignore a phone call than answer difficult questions. Changing this narrow-minded thinking is a driving force that led me to write this text. I have learned through experience and many mentors that worrying about a "bad" news story may cause us to forget the main mission of a public information officer: to save lives through the dissemination of accurate and timely information.

This book is written both for college students learning a profession and for public safety and emergency management personnel, who are professionals at something other than media relations. It is intended to be a reference tool for use well after you've used it in a formal course. The book can also serve as a stand-alone guide for the working public information officer.

Coupled with an instructor's guide, an introductory public information officer's course can be delivered in a formal educational setting, as in-service training for public safety professionals and as career development classes for executives and administrators of governmental and nongovernmental entities.

There are no trade secrets in this text—no magic wands for effective media relations. Instead, there are practical, proven ideas and techniques that have allowed me to be successful as an information officer. These techniques are applicable in today's rapidly changing media environment. They are adaptable to the National Incident Management System's Joint Information System concepts and are practical for many disciplines of public safety, emergency management, and even business and industry.

The text is presented in a specific order to allow a beginning public information officer to learn a logical approach to developing the skills necessary for developing a successful public information program. It begins with the role of a public information officer, and then subsequent chapters dovetail off this presentation, allowing the reader to expand his or her knowledge and skill sets.

Within each chapter are case studies, review questions about those case studies, and key terms relating to the content. Objectives start each chapter, and summaries review the information presented to meet the objectives. Chapters end with review questions designed to challenge the reader to grasp the "must remember" points of the text.

An entire chapter is devoted to case studies presented by working public information officers. The experiences presented in these case studies reinforce the material presented elsewhere in the book.

What makes me qualified to write this book? The humble side of me says I am not qualified, but colleagues tell me I have a gift. I choose to believe there is some luck to the path my life has taken. The twists have put me in contact with great mentors: some of the foremost journalism educators at Syracuse University's Newhouse School and hometown reporters who have made it to the network stage. I've worked with media members and their varied agendas, and with citizen groups of all ages, and have been fortunate enough to have my work recognized by several organizations. Perhaps the most rewarding part of my career has been working with students of public information. I have witnessed them in the "hot seat" and have seen them developing public information programs that have made a difference in the communities they serve. What I found missing for these students was a guide. I believe this text serves that purpose.

About the Author

Phil Politano has worked as an award winning public information officer, field paramedic, field training officer, and college professor. He is currently working for the U.S. Department of Homeland Security's Federal Emergency Management Agency as a training specialist. He has a bachelor's degree in emergency management from State University of New York Empire College and has been a certified paramedic since 1987.

Working as a journalist, field paramedic and public information officer as well as training incident command teams and emergency managers provides Phil with a unique perspective into the real world facing today's emergency personnel.

His passion for building strong relationships with local media perhaps contributed to his being recognized by the Syracuse Press Club as News Source of the Year twice—the only person to have earned that distinction.

Phil has spoken at local, state and national conferences on the subject of media relations and public information.

Phil now resides in Hanover, Pennsylvania, with his wife Carol, their dog Casey and father-in-law Frank Engelhardt. His hobbies include model railroading and traveling in the family motorhome.

Acknowledgments

When I think back to the many sleepless nights and interrupted family events I've experienced over my years as a public information officer, I can't help but think that the pages and phone calls are only a small part of the story. When the pager goes off, sometimes five or six times a night, I'm not alone. My wife Carol, a registered nurse, is also there trying to sleep. She is the woman I affectionately say had the courage to marry me—a lot of courage!

I cannot adequately express how much Carol's support has meant to me through my years as a public information officer. She is still patiently waiting for me to finish that three-year-old "to-do" list. She has also been a major factor in the development of this text, assisting with the editing and making sure that I made my deadlines. She fully supported my recent job change and is, above all, my best friend.

I would be remiss if I didn't thank Jim and Doris Hammer from Goldstar Ambulance in Houston, TX for allowing me the opportunity to start working as a public information officer. During the eighties, my partner Jon Curtis and I wrote articles for a rural weekly newspaper about emergency medical services and the company we worked for.

In 1991 when Marty Yenawine and Bob Barnes hired me at Syracuse, New York's Eastern Paramedics, I had no idea that in less than two years I would begin a new public information program. That program allowed me to meet some of the most dedicated individuals in journalism, public safety, education, and community service. Marty and Bob, along with Bob Reilly, and Kurt Krumperman all deserve kudos for their role in my personal and professional development.

To the members of the Syracuse Press Club, thank you for recognizing my work as a public information officer and for working with me to educate countless community members in the importance of partnerships with the media. Those members bestowed the Club's "Best News Source" award on me, and I'm humbled to say that I'm the only public information officer to have received the award twice. They've also recognized my work on Web sites and public affairs programs promoting various health and safety messages. Perhaps most valuable is the confidence the membership had in electing me to various directorships and officer positions on the Club's board of directors.

Thank you to Jerry Payne, Deputy Chief of the Liverpool, NY Fire Department, and his English prowess. He assisted with the segment of this book that reminds us all about the rules of proper grammar.

Dr. Marley Barduhn is perhaps one of the most passionate people I know when it comes to the issues of critical incident stress and how it affects emergency responders as well as the media. Her chapter on critical incident stress and the public information officer is one of the most important in this book. Everyone should all read it and heed its advice.

The National Information Officers Association has been a significant partner in this effort as well. The group continues to contribute to my education and performance as a public information officer.

Several other people deserve credit in the development of this text. Dr. Tom Phelan of Strategic Teaching Associates has always been a mentor as well as a colleague, and I cherish the professional and personal relationship we have. Tom Olshanski, Director of External Affairs for the United States Fire Administration, continues to motivate and influence me. His public information expertise, as well as instructional style, has helped guide my personal and professional development. Through the years, Rich Flanagan, director of the Public Safety Training Center (PSTC) at Onondaga Community College (Syracuse, New York), has demonstrated the importance of partnership—including partnerships with the media—in effective emergency management. The public information officer courses supported by the PSTC have enhanced the region's ability to provide effective public information.

Finally, a special thanks to the New York State Emergency Management Office Training Section Chief Bill Campbell. Bill and his staff are at the top of their game. Working with them on the New York State Incident Management Assistance Team has been both rewarding and educational. I am honored to call them friends.

Thank you to the following reviewers of this text, who took the time to help me make the book better, proving once again the value of networking and partnerships:

Christopher Black
EMS Director
Eastern Arizona College
Thatcher, AZ

John J. Cannon
Fire Brigade Chief
Johns Manville Corp.
Waterville, OH

Wynn B. Gordy, B.S., L.P.
San Antonio, TX

J. Robert Griffin, City of Asheville
Asheville, NC

David Gurchiek, M.S., NREMT-P
Paramedic Program Director
Montana State University–Billings
Billings, MT

Chris Hafley
EHOVE Adult Career Center
Milan, OH

John J Heiser, IV
FF/EMT-P
Fort Lauderdale Fire Department
Broward Community College

Scott Karr, M.Ed., NREMT-P
ATN Center Director
Jasper, AL

Mark Martin, Division Chief (Retired)
City of Stow Fire Department
Stow, Ohio

Brian O'Keefe
Public Information Officer
Des Moines Fire Department
Des Moines, IA

Don Wollenbecker
EMS Captain
Oregon Fire Department
EMT Program Coordinator
Oregon City Schools

Stephen L. Wortham, NREMT-P, MBA
Chief
Shelby County EMS
Shelbyville, KY

Finally, thank you to all those who take the time to become educated public information officers. I hope this book becomes a valuable starting point for your career. Learn from every interview, news release, and public appearance.

You must never stop learning, because our work saves lives.

CHAPTER 1

The Public Information Officer

Objectives

- Describe the responsibilities of the public information officer to the public, the media, the public information officer's agency, and responding agencies
- Define what is meant by public information
- Name the skills needed to be an effective public information officer, and explain their relevance to the role
- Define the importance of proactive public information

CASE Study

Black smoke billows into the morning sky. Hoses stretch for blocks, while ambulances are ferrying the injured to hospitals. Firefighters struggle to contain the blaze. As the sleepy city wakes, citizens hear public information officers from the fire and police departments outline alternate commuting plans while providing assurance that no toxic chemicals are being released into the air.

Case Study Questions

1. What key messages were provided by these public information officers?
2. How would these messages potentially save lives?
3. What skills do these public information officers need in order to provide this information to the public?

Introduction

After the terrorist attacks of 2001, the U.S. Department of Homeland Security was created, bringing a number of government agencies under one cabinet level department. In order to more effectively manage incidents of national significance, as well as smaller incidents affecting local communities, the **National Incident Management System (NIMS)** was developed. From this system came the **National Response Plan (NRP)**, integrated into which is the **Incident Command System (ICS)**. The NRP has now been replaced by the National Response Framework (NRF).

The advent of NIMS has placed a new emphasis on the importance of public information in the overall scope of incident management. At the focal point of this information is the **public information officer (PIO)**.

Slightly more than a decade ago, the PIO was simply the person at a major incident assigned to work with the media. Training for PIOs was limited, their experience was minuscule, and expectations were low, partly because the media were seen as a nuisance rather than a partner in public safety response. The news media rarely respected the PIO. The public did not identify a face with an agency and a reputation. The agencies put little importance on the role of the PIO, who was often looked at as unavoidable—someone to simply divert attention away from what was going on instead of someone who could actually assist in making an incident run smoother.

"In any community, the role of a PIO's as important as that of frontline responders."

Today the PIO is a vital member of the emergency response community. Whether working for a police, a fire, an **emergency medical services (EMS)** agency, or as a member of the emergency management department, the PIO's role is at least as important as the front line responders in any community. The PIO can engage the media on scene, prompting them to provide the public with important information about the hazards they might face, or perhaps even use the incident as a teachable moment so that future incidents do not occur.

KEY TERMS

- American Ambulance Association (AAA), p. 3
- Assisting Agency, p. 9
- Chief Executive Officer (CEO), p. 5
- Community Relations, p. 4
- Constituencies, p. 6
- Cooperating Agency, p. 9
- Crisis Communications plan, p. 8
- Emergency Public information Annex, p. 8
- Emergency Medical Services (EMS), p. 2
- Emergency Response plan, p. 8
- Equal Access, p. 8
- Federal Emergency Management Agency (FEMA), p. 3

Freedom of Information Laws (FOIL), p. 10

Government Relations, p. 15

Incident Command System (ICS), p. 2

Incident Commander (IC), p. 9

International Fire Service Accreditation Congress (IFSAC), p. 3

Media Kits, p. 4

Media Relations, p. 3

Media Relations Plan, p. 5

News Conferences, p. 11

National Highway Traffic Safety Administration (NHTSA), p. 3

National Incident Management System (NIMS), p. 2

National Information Officers Association (NIOA), p. 4

National Response Plan (NRP), p. 2

Public Information Officer (PIO), p. 2

Recovery, p. 6

Relations, p. 6

Response, p. 6

History of Public Information

Training of PIOs

The PIO position has grown from one box in an organization chart into a full-fledged profession. Training programs and professional organizations are elevating the profession. In 1994, the **National Highway Traffic Safety Administration (NHTSA)** developed a PIO's seminar for law enforcement officers. The course was a complete and comprehensive course, designed to be delivered over a period of a few days. The NHTSA course was designed to get police officers working with the media toward achieving better traffic safety practices in their communities.

The U.S Department of Homeland Security's **Federal Emergency Management Agency (FEMA)** has been training PIOs for many years, with its Basic PIO Course aimed at helping PIOs prepare people for disasters, as well as providing information on how to prevent them.

The **International Fire Service Accreditation Congress (IFSAC)** has since developed standards and a training program for PIOs, and the **American Ambulance Association (AAA)** frequently conducts training sessions on **media relations** and public information. In Figure 1-1, a reporter is helping FEMA deliver an important message.

In 2006, the NIMS Integration Center released draft documents outlining credentialing for emergency responders. Included are new national standards for PIOs. As of this writing, the proposed standards are still open for review. When the standards are finalized, those credentialing documents will be found in the National Incident Management section of the FEMA Web site at http://www.fema.gov/emergency/nims.

FIGURE 1-1

The National Information Officer's Association

In 1989, the **National Information Officers Association (NIOA)** was born, formed out of the realization that no matter where a PIO practiced, the issues were the same. The organization has developed into a true professional association for PIOs. Many PIOs also belong to local press clubs and chapters of the Public Relations Society of America. These associations and the PIO's affiliations with them are helping to bring increased professionalism to the field of public information. There is now a realization that PIOs perform a broad base of activities, many under extremely stressful or dangerous situations.

The Public Relations Specialist

The Bureau of Labor Statistics refers you to "Public Relations Specialist" for information about the PIO. It also points to "Police and Detectives" working in **community relations**. In a way, the "public relations specialist" is a very accurate description of the modern PIO. The fact that there is no specific job description does not accurately reflect the increasing number of PIOs working full or part time in America's public safety and emergency management organizations. The NIOA boasts 600 members (as of November 2005), and that number is low in comparison to the number of people engaged in public information activities.

While many people function as PIOs, they do not retain the title and have little formal training to perform the tasks required of the job.

Duties of the PIO

Characteristics of a PIO

Many people often joke that the most performed task in any job description is the line "all other duties as assigned." For the PIO, this may be the rule rather than the exception. The characteristics set forth next help make someone a good PIO. The person must be flexible because the job itself is ever changing. The PIO must be someone who can adapt to many changing situations. During the course of a day, the PIO will be engaged in many activities. The PIO will be an educator, teaching staff members interviewing techniques or providing information about the **media relations plan**. Training might also include a short course in what the media are all about. Later in the day, that same PIO may provide emergency information about a hazardous materials incident, a crime in progress, or a major motor vehicle crash. When that excitement has died down, the PIO might be writing a presentation for the **chief executive officer (CEO)** of the organization. That presentation might be delivered to a civic organization or perhaps to other stakeholders such as city council members or county legislators.

"Personal Traits of a PIO:
- Professional
- Objective
- Courteous
- Positive
- Cooperative
- Accessible"

For PIOs to be able to perform all these tasks, the person has to be well rounded, be organized, and possess strong leadership skills. The candidate must understand modern computers, have the ability to develop relationships with coworkers, superiors, and community members. The PIO will often interact with community members during their worst tragedies, so the ability to understand, empathize, and function with compassion is of paramount importance.

"PIOs often work with the public during their worst moments."

Emergency Management and the PIO

"Public information can be used to cause people to take actions to save lives, prevent harm, and protect property."

FEMA, an agency within the U.S. Department of Homeland Security, defines public information as information used by the public to make decisions to take action to save lives, reduce injury and harm, and protect property. Traditionally, we think of this as information given during an emergency or disaster, but today much of the public information work is actually done ahead of time.

Information that saves lives, reduces injury, and protects property does not have to be given out once a disaster occurs or when an emergency is in process.

Before the emergency, a PIO can tell area residents to install smoke detectors in their homes to prevent fires, put together a disaster preparation kit, or make sure that they have plenty of lighting on their property to ward off criminals. Public information can be used to change human behavior or attitudes. It can also be used to create positive impressions of a public safety agency.

A PIO will provide information to the news media and the public during an emergency, whether it is a short-lived hour-long structure fire or a natural disaster, which may take days, weeks, or longer to play itself out.

"A watch means conditions are right for situation to occur. A warning means the situation is occurring."

Before a large-scale disaster occurs, the PIO will provide emergency public information such as evacuation announcements or **watches** and **warnings** of floods, tornados, or hurricanes. During these disasters, much of the information provided will be related to **response** and **recovery**, such as information about emergency shelters, drinking water safety, or low-interest loans. All this information is designed to fulfill the primary mission of saving lives, reducing injuries, and protecting property.

The PIO's Constituencies

"PIOs serve the public, the media, their agency, and other responding agencies."

PIOs have four primary **constituencies** that must be served in order to effectively fulfill the PIO's mission: the public, the media, their agency, and other responding agencies. Figure 1-2 illustrates the PIO's mission.

The Public

The main focus of a PIO is to provide information to the public, the largest constituency. PIOs strive to keep the public safe using emergency and educational messages, watches and warnings, and evacuation notices. However, reaching the public is not possible unless PIOs are able to work with another important constituency, the media.

The Media

Public information and **media relations** go hand in hand, but they are not the same thing. Media relations are complex, to say the least. The key word to remember is "**relations**." Strong media relationships are built over time. It takes knowing reporters, editors, photographers, and assignment editors, as well as understanding what news agencies are all about and what these outlets are looking for. The relationships are built on trust. The media must trust the PIO and the PIO must trust the media.

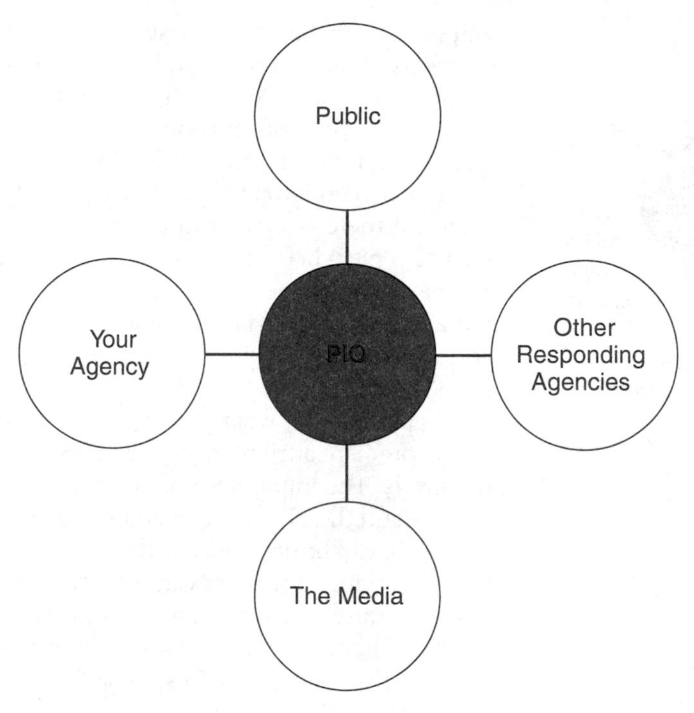

FIGURE 1-2

With a strong working relationship, providing public information through the media is easy. Once developed, the PIO's credibility allows the media to make better news decisions about the various messages it is asked to share with the public.

Many PIOs make regular beat calls, checking in with local newsrooms and reporters. Some arrange exchange tours among media outlets and the public safety or emergency management agency. This serves as a way to bring media members into your organization, as well as providing your employees an entrance into media outlets.

These relationships can also bring important publicity to an agency, and when things go wrong, soften the blow because of better-informed reporters.

The PIO's Agency

Often the PIO does not think that his or her home agency is a constituent, but it is a very important constituent. If the people that you work with do not understand the agency's media relations policy, or even how the community's media work, they will not be able to help spread important messages. Knowledge is power, and knowledgeable employees can be powerful allies in public information pursuits. The members of your agency can play an important role in helping get important information out to those who need to hear it. These colleagues can provide you with tips on things that are going on within your organization; tips that can be turned into news releases.

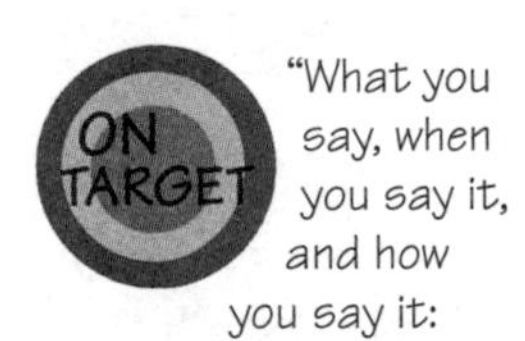

"What you say, when you say it, and how you say it: every comment attributed to a PIO affects the agency either positively or negatively."

It is also important to keep members of your agency informed about events. If there is a major disaster in your community, chances are that many people who work for your agency will be affected by the disaster. You have to keep them informed not only about emergency information, but about what everybody else in your agency is doing. Forgetting that your agency is one of your constituencies can be the biggest mistake that any PIO makes.

Depending on what you say, when you say it, and how you say it, every comment attributed to a PIO affects the agency either positively or negatively. The importance of positive relationships between other employees and the PIO must be emphasized as a priority. One way this relationship can be developed is through training of personnel by the PIO. In-house training services can include a review of the standard operating procedures, media relations, and a **crisis communications plan**. (This would include reviewing the **Emergency Public Information Annex and the Emergency Response Plan**, as well as other items.)

ON TARGET

"Training agency personnel on the media policy will give them confidence to do the right thing when approached by reporters in the field."

Teach field personnel what you know. They are the agency's best ambassadors, and this training can help head off conflicts at scenes. This training should include a discussion about what information can be shared, what should be withheld, and why. An explanation about potential media mistakes and how they will be handled should be included in the training. Further discussion should include information about the media relations policy. Personnel should understand **equal access** and not play favorites. The policy explanation should include a discussion about **exclusives**, and employees should understand this policy.

Supervisors also need training so that they understand the media relations policy as well as the field providers do. They must buy into and fully support that policy. Supervisory personnel often forget that the issues they are dealing with or the decisions they make may harm the agency's image. As a service to the agency, a PIO should be continually evaluating public opinion, sharing this with the CEO, and suggesting image adjustments.

Other Agencies

PIOs serve more than just the public when it comes to providing information. Other responding agencies are of extreme importance. This constituency, often called "mutual aid," is among those who need to be kept informed. This information can help keep the responders safe and give them peace of mind that their families are safe. The ICS system divides these mutual aid companies into assisting and cooperating agencies. An **assisting agency** is one that directly contributes tactical resources to an incident.[1] A **cooperating agency** is one supplying resources other than tactical resources.[2]

Roles and Responsibilities

ON TARGET "The primary function of the PIO is to collect, verify, and disseminate information."

The primary function of the PIO is to collect, verify, and disseminate information to the public through effective communication with the media that will help citizens make decisions about their health, safety, and welfare.

In the ICS, the PIO reports directly to the **incident commander (IC)**. (See Figure 1-3) The IC is the CEO for an incident, and the public image about the incident rests firmly on the shoulders of the PIO.

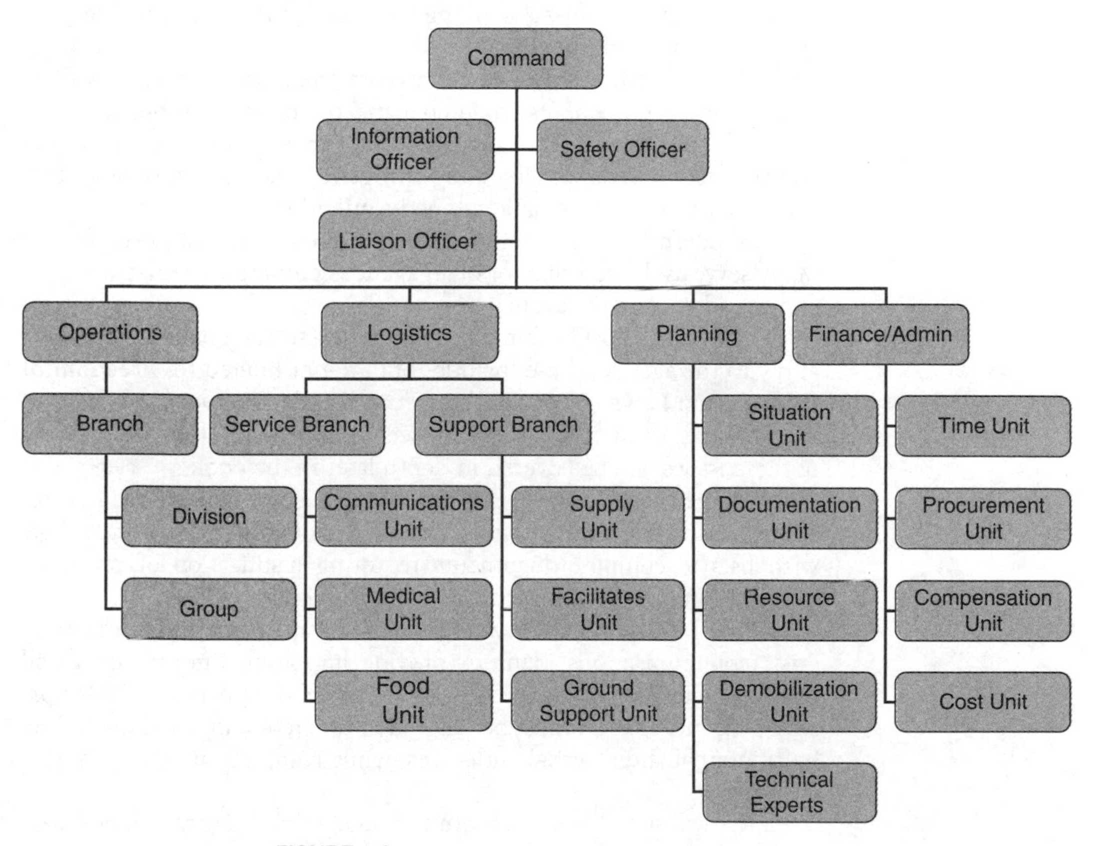

FIGURE 1-3

"Media summaries help track an agency's public image."

PIOs saddled with layers of bureaucracy between themselves and the CEO of an incident or agency will be far less effective than those with direct ties. It is imperative that in an organization's structure, the PIO report directly to the CEO. This could be the fire chief, police chief, emergency manager, or the chief elected official of a governmental jurisdiction. Above all, the PIO must be a trusted guide for the CEO.

Daily Operations

In day-to-day operations, the PIO may function as the agency's and CEO's representative, acting as the public face and voice of the agency. The PIO may speak on behalf of the CEO, or may be a PIO in name only when the CEO always acts as the spokesperson. (This is most common when elected officials are the CEO.)

The PIO will often provide the CEO with regular media summaries indicating positive and negative coverage of the agency. These can be obtained by recording television and radio newscasts, reviewing daily and weekly newspapers, or subscribing to a service that will provide your agency with this information for a fee.

A PIO must be ready to switch gears when an emergency occurs, meet critical requirements when challenged, and issue public information in all situations. The PIO has to be prepared to function on the "world stage" because as technology progresses, so does the chance that a local story will receive national media attention.

A modern PIO will answer dozens of media inquiries every week. Many serve as the coordinator of an agency's **community relations** programs and oversee the agency image.

Today's PIO must be familiar with local, state, and national laws that apply to the agency. These include, but are not limited to, **Freedom of Information Laws (FOIL)**, public records and open meeting laws, and any laws regulating media access to scenes or certain information. Many of these issues will be covered in depth later in the book.

In some agencies, the PIO is part of the management team and is responsible for preparing an annual budget. This can range from simple wish lists to complex documents requiring justification of proposed spending and line-by-line analysis of expenses.

Often PIOs prove their worth when it comes to a crisis. Preparing crisis communications plans to provide important information to all constituencies can be the most stressful, yet least tapped skill PIOs possess. This information must be tailored to different audiences, including both internal and external audiences, while being sensitive to potential legal pitfalls.

PIOs will spend a good amount of time writing. There will be emergency press releases to issue, newsletters for the community and agency to be prepared and published, and health and safety material to be developed. There are **news conferences** to prepare for and **media kits** to design for those news conferences, along with reports on activities, media relations policies and procedures, and speeches for key members of the agency.

If a PIO is lucky to have a well-funded department, there may be a video production division. This division can prepare **"B" roll video** for news outlets. Such video consists of generic footage about your service that can be supplied for use during newscasts. Some media outlets might use the footage when they are unable to assign a videographer to get the necessary footage. A "B" roll can also be supplied to the media when it is unsafe for the media to obtain it themselves.

A PIO will have daily contact with the public, the news media, and members of the public safety community. This can be overwhelming, and a PIO may require assistance to provide the requested information. In a busy agency, the PIO may develop policies about information release and have others authorized to respond to requests for information. The PIO will supervise the release of this information and, perhaps, photographs. Care must be exercised when discussing agency policy information, training practices, and program information. The PIO will often be requested to develop statistics related to the agency. While statistics can be used to show great progress of an agency, some can be interpreted with the opposite meaning. The PIO must always look at statistics from several points of view, to be aware of the various interpretations there might be.

"A PIO must be available 24-hours a day, 7 days a week. There is no substitute for availability."

After a hard day in the office, the PIO must understand that there is no substitute for availability. Whether through an on-call rotation system, a network of PIOs, or a single person charged with carrying out this responsibility, there must be a PIO available 24 hours a day, 7 days a week.

What Makes a Good PIO?

Agency History

The strengths necessary to become a PIO are many. The PIO should obtain an authentic history of the organization and understand the strengths and weaknesses of that history. This historical knowledge can make or break a PIO's performance in certain crisis settings. The reporters doing a story on your agency have access to all agency history, and when or if the moment is right, that history may find itself becoming the story.

History can bring you perspective on an organization, helping you understand attitudes of the public or press. Understanding the history of public and media opinion about your agency's mission and past performance can help you craft messages for the future. History can teach

"Where to find your agency's history:
- Your local or agency library
- The historical society archives
- Organization veterans
- Old documents, newspapers, photos, and videos
- Local reporters
- The Internet
- Trade journal archives
- The back storage closet"

you about mistakes, so they are not repeated. It can also provide you with a basis for many story ideas. News stories with a historical perspective often appeal to a broad audience. These stories are nostalgic for long-time residents and show progressiveness to a younger audience. The good, the bad, and the ugly are in our history, and we should embrace all of these in our role as PIO.

Relationships

A progressive PIO will cherish good relationships with the media, but cannot forget the importance of strong relationships with all constituents. Coworkers and those in related organizations must be kept in the loop at major incidents, as well as during day-to-day activities.

Every organization has a skeleton in the closet, strong and timid personalities, and the right and wrong way of doing things. It is this understanding, that makes it ever more important that a PIO develop strong internal and external relationships. When the bad news comes, these relationships are the basis for preplanning and can help minimize the negative impact of the event.

One popular way to provide coworkers with information is through an agency newsletter. A newsletter can provide important operational information, as well as stories about the good work people are being recognized for. However, never assume that internal newsletters remain internal. These circulate through other agencies and the public. If you do not want certain information out in the public, you should not put it in writing.

"Typical software used by PIOs:
- Word processing
- Spreadsheets
- Databases
- Presentation programs
- Photo editing software
- Web page design software
- Incident management software
- E-mail and electronic calendars"

Personal Traits

PIOs should not be shy. Rather, a PIO should have a progressive and appropriately aggressive nature. A PIO will become both a strategist and trusted advisor to the CEO. To reach this level of trust, the PIO must be a person of exceptional character and judgment, and must be able to take criticism. A successful PIO projects candor, honesty, integrity, and respect, as well as an understanding of the media.

In order to perform all the tasks of a PIO, the person must be motivated, enjoy the work, and be publicity oriented and politically astute. When the phone rings, the PIO should welcome inquiries from the media and the community. When responding to questions, the PIO must be sensitive to the community and its concerns.

While a good PIO could become a community celebrity and the face of the agency, a fine line should never be crossed. A PIO should never become a credit grabber and should give credit where credit is due. The PIO should exhibit likable human qualities, which will help in developing

long-term relationships with the media and other constituencies. PIOs are not perfect. Don't try to be.

A PIO must be schooled in many things, but cannot know everything. It is okay to tell the media you have to "look it up." If you make a mistake, admit it! If you promise to look it up, look it up! Keeping promises improves integrity.

Patience is a virtue, and a PIO must have it and must be able to handle stress and pressure while maintaining an even temperament.

Community Relations Skills

If it were not for the community, the PIO would not have anyone to inform. Community relations is, perhaps, the most important part of a PIO's job. It is incumbent on the PIO to know and understand the demographics of the agency's service area. One way to learn the demographics is to become involved with community organizations. Many of these organizations are microcosms of the neighborhoods they serve, or the community as a whole. These groups can help provide valuable information to the PIO about community education needs, the value of the agency to the community, and trends within the community.

An effective community relations program includes an explanation of the agency's programs, special projects, and policies. The community includes interested persons, legislative officials, businesses, and civic organizations. Presentations to the community can include exhibits and visual displays that promote an understanding of the agency and highlight special programs.

Community education programs can be enhanced with speaker's bureaus. Perhaps the best spokesperson an agency has is the person in the field, the one that relates one-on-one with those in the community. These personnel often make exceptional presenters, and they can pass your message to community groups with front-line experience and compassion.

Strong relationships with other PIOs can also bolster a community relations program, as well as benefit the community during an emergency.

In some organizations, the PIO will be responsible for writing speeches and preparing presentations to be used by the CEO or other officers. These could be specific to an incident or topic, but are often generic. The generic speeches and presentations can be archived and used for different community organizations.

Brochures, Web sites, and other printed material may be on the PIO's daily agenda. These are just more tools the PIO can use to achieve the agency's community relations goals.

Many PIOs work with organizations such as Safe Kids (www.safekids.org), the local traffic safety committee, neighborhood watch, and other community associations. These relationships help enhance the image of the agency. The affiliations can also bring additional advocates for certain causes the PIO wants brought to the forefront.

The PIO should attend any public meeting where the agency is a player, especially if there will be media attention. These include city council meetings and town and county government meetings, as well as others.

Media Relations Skills

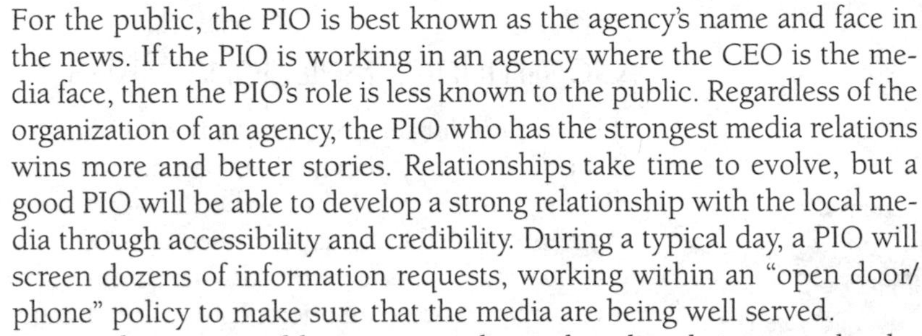

For the public, the PIO is best known as the agency's name and face in the news. If the PIO is working in an agency where the CEO is the media face, then the PIO's role is less known to the public. Regardless of the organization of an agency, the PIO who has the strongest media relations wins more and better stories. Relationships take time to evolve, but a good PIO will be able to develop a strong relationship with the local media through accessibility and credibility. During a typical day, a PIO will screen dozens of information requests, working within an "open door/phone" policy to make sure that the media are being well served.

"The PIO with the best media relations wins more and better stories!"

Just being accessible is not enough; good media relations are also developed when the PIO provides good information and easy access (where it makes sense). Part of this relationship is an understanding of the needs of the media, their operations, and their deadlines. It requires a continuing, open dialog between reporters and the PIO. This is accomplished by cultivating and nurturing contacts with various media organizations. The relationship with the media can be enhanced through regular meetings, which will help the PIO better understand the local media "political" implications. (A reporter may have to ask questions and portray stories a certain way because the boss says so.)

Be the information source. If a media member calls with a question that is not in your area of expertise, the best practice is to refer the caller to someone who can answer the question, even if that person is outside of your agency. Knowing whom to refer them to will paint the PIO in a good light with the reporters. It establishes the PIO as a good source of information. It shows connections with the community and, more importantly, a willingness to share this knowledge with the media.

The PIO should become the "news detective" for the agency. What is routine to you or your colleagues is often "news" to the public. The baby delivered by a dispatcher using telephone instructions is big news; however, the dispatcher may consider it to be "all in a day's work." Coaching agency employees to cue you in on happenings can greatly increase the number of stories you can feed the media.

When an emergency occurs, the PIO will develop a **media relations plan** for the incident. This plan will follow agency media policy and be approved by the IC. To develop the plan, the PIO must know what issues to avoid and what issues take priority in emergency messages.

Writing Skills

"Good writing must become second nature to a PIO. Oral as well as verbal communication skills will be used daily."

While many PIOs are emergency response veterans, they often find themselves in a strange land when they have to write something that isn't full of abbreviations, acronyms, and industry slang. While news releases containing these idioms may be factually accurate, they will not provide a message that can be understood by the reporter or public. Strong writing skills include being able to organize clear thoughts on paper, using proper grammar, spelling, formats, and writing styles. Modern word processing computer programs provide these tools, but there is no substitute for a desktop thesaurus and dictionary set. You should also arm yourself with a glossary of terms commonly used in your industry, as well as Department of Transportation hazardous materials guidebooks.

Government Relations

PIOs should also understand how to maintain good **government relations** at the local, regional, state, and national levels of government. These individuals can influence laws, which the PIO must abide by, as well as be influential when a specific agency agenda is being forwarded. Political leaders like to "hitch their wagon" to good causes. The PIO must be able to convince politicians which agendas are "good causes."

Miscellaneous Skills

While the PIO has a lot to do simply developing news stories and handling media inquiries, there are other skills important to good job performance. These include public speaking and the development and delivery of audiovisual presentations. The PIO should have a strong understanding of emergency management principles: preparedness, response, recovery, and mitigation.

Communications Abilities

Certainly, anyone attempting to establish a relationship must be able to communicate with others. As a PIO, an individual must be able to communicate effectively not only orally in front of a microphone or crowd, but also in writing. The ability to communicate honestly includes an understanding that a PIO is not obliged to tell everything just because he or she knows it. Some things are better left unsaid. The PIO should develop the communication skills necessary to avoid appearing hesitant or unhelpful. An adversarial attitude arouses suspicion. The media frequently view themselves as "guardian of the public interest." You should understand and accept the often adversarial role of the media. Expect tough, provocative, and skeptical questions. Remember, the PIO's response determines the course of the interview.

Summary

The modern PIO must master a significant number of skills to be effective. These skills range from developing and maintaining interpersonal relationships to researching and writing news releases. These abilities must be coupled with a firm commitment from the agency employing the PIO, or success will be limited.

The importance of a PIO in providing information to the public cannot be understated. This information will allow the public to take actions that will save lives and property.

REVIEW QUESTIONS

Complete the sentence:

1. Public information is used by people to make decisions and take actions to _______________.

2. Public information can be used to _______________.

3. In an ideal structure, the PIO reports to _______________.

True or false?

4. The PIO should always attempt to stage a show for the press at the scene of an emergency.

5. The PIO should determine which reporters are trouble and ban them from the organization.

ENDNOTES

1. *Firescope Field Operations Guide, 2004*, p. 19-2.
2. *Ibid.*, p. 19-4.

CHAPTER 2

The Media

Objectives

- Differentiate between electronic, print, and other media formats
- Demonstrate an understanding of media needs
- Compare media needs with the functions of a PIO

CASE Study

The local fire department has taken delivery of a new ladder truck. The media have been invited to a news conference. Television stations will carry the dedication ceremony during the 5:00 p.m. news. Several media outlets will assemble in the fire department's parking lot to broadcast live. A newspaper reporter requests historical information on past equipment purchases, and the radio stations request recordings of the ladder truck extending its ladder. The PIO works with the various media members to fulfill requests, and the fire department receives front-page newspaper coverage and **lead story** coverage on radio and television.

Case Study Questions

1. What are the differing needs of the media to deliver a story?
2. Does the PIO benefit from assisting the media in getting the story?
3. What is the importance of lead story coverage?

Introduction

There are basic needs for life—water, food, companionship, clothing, housing, and so on. Often we receive help to fulfill those needs. If we want to make a sandwich, we go to a deli. The clerk assists us with purchasing our desired product, perhaps even suggesting something special, or provides us with a unique cheese for our meal. Once the product is purchased, there is a brief stop at the bakery for our favorite bread, and then we can proceed to making our sandwich.

Like all of us, the media have needs. In fact, there are basic needs for every profession. In public safety, when a paramedic, police officer, or firefighter arrives at an incident, each requires tools to perform his or her duties. In an emergency management office, emergency program managers use a variety of tools, job aids, and guidebooks to perform their duties. The deli clerk–customer relationship is similar to the one between a PIO and the media.

The Centers for Disease Control, which regularly communicate life-saving information to the public through the media, say that there are 70,000 media outlets in the U.S. that cover the **news** 24/7.[1]

KEY TERMS

Archive, p. 25
Beat Reporter, p. 29
Briefing, p. 27
Broadcast Media, p. 00
Dispatcher, p. 19
Emergency Manager, p. 28
Emergency Medical Services (EMS), p. 23
Freedom of Information Laws (FOIL), p. 27
General Assignment Reporter, p. 28
Investigative Reporter, p. 28
Lead Story, p. 17
Live Truck, p. 24
Media Advisory, p. 27
Media Kit, p. 27
Media Plan, p. 26
News, p. 15
Personal Data Assistant (PDA), p. 20
Police Beat, p. 28
Print Media, p. 00
Public Affairs Programs, p. 20
Scoop, p. 22
Sound Bite, p. 24
Spot News, p. 24
The Big Three plus One, p. 18
Trade Magazine, p. 23
Web Surfer, p. 26

Where Do People Get Their News?

Before we can comprehend the needs of the media, we must understand the media. FEMA, the Federal Emergency Management Agency, has described the media as "**the big 3 plus one**."

"Knowing where the public gets news will help the PIO deliver messages."

"The Internet has made it more difficult for PIOs to get accurate messages out in a timely manner."

This refers to radio, television, newspapers, and the latest entry onto the scene, web-based news. In early 2004, a collaborative effort between the Syracuse, New York, press club and WCNY, the local public television brought members of the press and community together to discuss the often-burning issue of public trust in the media. One glaring revelation gleaned from this meeting was the wide definition of media. When asked where audience members got their news, the answer shocked many panel members because it ranged from the then-popular MTV (Music Television) and ESPN (an all sports network) to syndicated entertainment shows. Some did mention the mainstream media, but all soon realized that defining the media continues to become more complex. The Internet has also changed the way people look at the media, newsgathering, and news reporting. There are more and more sources of information for people to review, making it increasingly difficult for PIOs to deliver their messages.

How the Media Work

One thing is clear, regardless of which type of medium, or "news" organization, we are discussing, they all have the same basic needs. Perhaps the easiest way to understand the needs of the media is to gain a basic understanding of how the media work and their relationship to how public safety organizations respond to emergencies.

When a medical emergency occurs, a call for assistance is placed. Emergency Medical **Dispatchers** will send the appropriate assistance to the scene. Once crews arrive, they assess the scene and report to their dispatchers information on the situation. Crews treat the patient, then transport the patient to the proper medical facility where that staff continues to work with the patient before a final report on the patient's condition is presented to family members.

In a typical newsroom, events are very similar. When an incident occurs, the assignment editor sends the correct crews to cover the incident. These crews report to the assignment editor and determine how the story is going to be handled (treatment). Once they return to the newsroom with their material, the media crews work with a producer/editor to create the final story that we see on television, hear on the radio or read in the newspaper. Figure 2-1 illustrates what goes on in a newsroom.

Why Do the Media Need Stories?

Understanding the media also means understanding why the media need stories, thus making the PIO an important tool in the media's toolbox. To

FIGURE 2-1

recognize this, one only has to add up the number of daily hours and column inches TV, radio, and newspapers must fill in order to satisfy a public that seems to want continual news.

By now, most of us have viewed the national all-news television channels and heard the news/talk-based radio stations. There are even local all news television stations popping up in many markets. Aside from the more traditional TV and radio, the Internet has become a constant source of news for people using cell phones, **personal data assistants (PDAs)**, or computers.

Aside from the regular news broadcasts, there are **public affairs programs** that can devote an entire 30 minutes to one topic. Both commercial and noncommercial radio and television stations produce a variety of news programs. Newspapers can range from dailies, to daily multiedition large-circulation papers, to the smaller weekly neighborhood papers. Some major newspapers are combining the major paper large-area coverage with local neighborhood-based editions.

The dynamics of the Internet continue to change some 15 years after it was born. The Internet itself has changed the way many people communicate and get information. There are now many local web-based newspapers as well as traditional news organizations using the Internet to showcase their stories. Perhaps the best way to understand the media in your market is to review the major media outlet Web sites on a certain day. Look at the lead stories, as well as the others. Do this randomly over time and you should begin to see a pattern develop. This should help you determine what the news philosophy of that news organization would be.

Knowing Your Market

In Chapter 1 of this text, we talked about the importance of a PIO understanding the demographics of the public being served. Armed with this information, we will be better equipped to understand that the public will ultimately affect the news media's decision about what constitutes news. Never forget that the media constitute a business, and business decisions can have an impact on news organizations. (Just don't ask a journalist to admit this.)

ON TARGET

"Study the media in your market to be the most effective in your job."

ON TARGET

"News 1. a: a report of recent events b: previously unknown information <I've got news for you> 2. a: material reported in a newspaper or news periodical or on a newscast b: matter that is newsworthy (http://www.m-w.com/dictionary/news")

We often hear people complain that what they watch on television is not news, but it would be difficult for you to find two people with the same definition of news. To work effectively with the media in your market, you need to study the media. Building strong relationships with journalists will help you understand changes in the local "news" landscape. Trends in the industry, changes in set design, story choices, and presentation style can be indicators of how your stories will be handled.

Typically, news is considered to reflect conflict or controversy, is timely, and has some significant impact on the community. The news, or potential newsmakers' prominence, or uniqueness as well as the human interest of the story can also influence what is printed or broadcast.

If you want to be successful with television stations, you have to think visually. While it should go without saying that TV stations need video to enhance the story telling, many people remain surprised when a camera appears for an interview. Successful radio interviews will include some type of sound, and newspaper stories will often include additional background material.

While all journalists are protected by the First Amendment, there have been differences between print and electronic media. In 1966, the Federal Appeals Court said, "A newspaper can be operated at the whim or caprice of its owner; a broadcasting station cannot." This case referred to the Fairness Doctrine, which mandated balanced coverage of politics. The doctrine was repealed in 1987, and this repeal is said to have given birth to talk radio and its varied political biases. Some of these biases may influence news reporting of a media outlet.[2]

Regardless of the media you encounter, reporters need common items from you. You should always be prepared with the basics: who, what, when, where, why, and how. In this chapter, we will review the characteristics of the various types of media. Understanding these characteristics will help you provide better information and tailor that information to the various media needs.

Print Media

Newspapers

In many communities, the newspaper is still considered the historic record. When people research information about a community, newspapers are often where they start. Whether daily, weekly, or monthly, newspapers reflect the important issues of the time. It is said that one should never argue with someone who buys ink in 55-gallon drums, an indication of the power of the newspapers' influence. Figure 2-2 shows a newspaper reporter doing her job.

Daily newspapers in smaller communities often struggle to fill their pages with news, while larger market papers have many stories to tell and often have competing papers to "**scoop**." Those same struggling dailies may be the ones breaking the best local stories. There is plenty of space to allow for more in-depth articles and focus on local controversies. Even with limited staff sizes, many of these papers regularly produce award-winning stories for readers.

Some newspapers, often with only weekly or monthly distribution, target specific audiences such as parents, business leaders, and professionals, and some are written for non-English-speaking subscribers. These specialty newspapers are ideal for placing audience-specific stories. You can tailor messages to the audience served by the newspaper.

Weekly, regional, and specialty papers will often publish news releases exactly as they are received. These papers need content, but rarely have the staff to develop it originally.

FIGURE 2-2

Magazines

Sometimes it seems like there is a new magazine published every day. Often targeting the "issue of the day," these magazines pose unique opportunities for reaching specific audiences; however, they can also, like newspapers, allow reporters to dig deeper into stories for more details. Some specialty magazines use nothing but freelance writers to fill the pages, therefore, your efforts to place story ideas will have nowhere to go. Perhaps the most popular place for PIOs to run stories about their agencies are **trade magazines**, or those magazines targeted toward the specific trade audience (police, fire, **emergency medical services** [EMS]).

Both newspaper and magazine organizations need similar services from PIOs. The most important service is responsiveness, followed closely by details. Even though newspaper and magazines have deadlines hours or days in advance of publication, there is the need for early contact to give the PIO time to prepare the requested data and completely answer the in-depth questions. Remember, newspaper reporters often paint a picture with their words. While photographs can enhance the news story, the written word provides the reader with the basis for decision making and actions to take, as well as the judgment of actions depicted in the story. Print stories contain far more details than radio or television stories. These details will often be in "side-bar" stories, or stories that tell a related aspect of the main story.

A PIO will often be asked to provide background on previous events at the location of the current event, or, may even be asked to look for similar events that have occurred. If the PIO has these ideas up front, then unexpected questions can be presented.

Electronic Media

Broadcast Media—Radio

By simply touching the "seek" button on your car radio, the number of radio stations available in your home market will be readily apparent. The number of these stations that are important to the PIO varies from area to area. There probably are few that offer a delivery of day-to-day news and information, but most will become very important for delivery of emergency public information. Each of these stations serves a specific audience; an audience that may not turn to "news" stations on a regular basis. The PIO must track these various stations, have access information ready for them, and understand that many belong to groups and that one phone call can reach several stations. Of particular importance could be non-English stations, which could reach minority audiences that may be in harm's way. Figure 2-3 shows a radio reporter at work.

FIGURE 2-3

Radio news organizations gravitate toward stories that have sound, or look for sound when they arrive at an incident, news conference, or promotional event. When being interviewed, keep your answers short; generally, 10 to 15 seconds is sufficient. These short, concise answers become "**sound bites**" in the larger story.

Broadcast Media—Television

The television news landscape is changing. There is more competition among stations for audiences, and yet in some unique markets where some stations have determined that being number three is good enough, they have scaled back their news operations and moved on. These dynamics are important to understand when a television reporter comes to interview you. Some reporters are more seasoned than others, and some stations have a more aggressive approach than others, but the common theme with television is the undeniable fact that it is a visual medium, and stories will be told by pictures. When **spot news** occurs, PIOs should expect **live trucks** to appear. These vehicles will send instant live video back for broadcast or archiving. Many stations are using existing structures and towers to place cameras for long-distance views. Emergency responders are often seeing the next call they will respond to because these stations broadcast stories immediately, before the facts are all out. Driving this need for instant news is the increasing demand of the public for information, the increasing number of information sources,

FIGURE 2-4

and competition for the audience between news outlets. Figure 2-4 shows a reporter interviewing a CEO after a ceremony.

The players in the broadcast world are many. The producer is the manager of content in a television program. In radio, a producer may work the control board as well as develop content. The executive producer typically manages all content of all shows at a television station. The program director handles the same duties at a radio station.

For a television newscast, the producer often writes copy, determines program visuals, and works with the talent on program content. The PIO's job is to hook up the producer with the person making the news. Producers have the responsibility to make sure that the PIO sends the person who presents best on camera. Producers of most long format shows do not have to be objective because they are usually not news programs.

Electronic Media Technical Needs

The modern media are an electronic showcase of innovative tools to gather and report the news and then **archive** the results. When the media "army" descends upon an incident, they bring vehicles capable of operating around the clock on their own power, with telescoping booms containing microwave transmission antennas, and cameras for obtaining long-range and high-vantage video feeds. Many are also equipped with satellite dishes used for long distance transmission of material from an incident. Some trucks are even designed with mini-broadcast studios. The proliferation of cellular phones with digital cameras (still and video) and portable computers allow instant broadcast of scene information. The arrival of these high-tech vehicles will cause additional problems for a PIO. These vehicles, ranging in size from a large van to a vehicle 40 feet in length, require parking spaces and vertical clearance for the elevating masts and satellite dishes. Figuring one vehicle for each television media outlet in your service area adds up to significant space needed on even the smallest incident. As the incident grows in significance or complexity, the space needed will also increase.

Regardless of the type of end product produced by a journalist, there are common needs for all news organizations:

- Rapid response to questions, even if the response is "I don't know the answer now, but I'll get back to you.
- Access to the scene, even if it is only for a moment, so that photos and video can be obtained
- Interviews with policy makers, response workers, victims, and survivors
- Meeting the deadlines

Web-Based Media

The Internet continues to be an often-used source for news. The traditional news organizations are using the Internet to provide news to **web surfers** and promote their main newscasts. Newspapers are increasingly using Internet news sites to update stories already published, or preview stories planned for future publication. There are an increasing number of web-only news outlets, and reporters from these outlets will seek access to information from PIOs just as the reporter from a local TV station. Many of these will also print news releases just as they receive them.

The question remains, however, how do we determine who is a representative from a legitimate news organization, or just someone interested in the big story of the day. **Media plans** should address credentialing to avoid problems at an incident.

Function of the PIO

A PIO's relationship with the media, predicated on understanding the needs of the media, will allow for an efficient collection, verification, and dissemination of information to the public. This information will

ON TARGET

"Contacting the Media
- Establish a Media Contact List
- Keep it on paper or in an electronic organizer.
- Obtain the list through
- Phone Calls
- Media guides produced by
- The Chamber of Commerce
- Press Clubs
- Communication Organizations
- Update the information FREQUENTLY"

subsequently be used by the public to help people make decisions about their health, safety, and welfare.

If this isn't enough of a reason to work with the media, there are certainly other valid reasons to keep strong relationships with the press and understand its changing needs. Aside from citizen safety, the First Amendment, our constitutional right to freedom of the press, provides strong encouragement for public safety organizations to work with the media. If you do not want to talk with the media, **Freedom of Information Laws (FOIL)** and acts at federal and state levels may force you to release certain information. If you work for a government entity, you may be working under one or more open meeting laws.

Working with specialized segments of the media can assist communities in recovering from a disaster to maintain their cultural cohesiveness. You could be providing information to varied cultures about shelters, available emergency assistance, or other issues of interest to that community.

Above all, a strong relationship with the media can help mold the perception of your agency. That does not mean you will be able to avoid negative or inaccurate news stories, but strong media relations will increase the visibility of your organization, improving and maintaining a positive perception about your agency.

"The allure of working with the major networks can be overwhelming as well as tempting."

During a time of disaster or high-profile events, information can flow quickly, and the public will be constantly looking for updated information. News reporters will arrive from long distances, and the allure of working with "the networks" can be overwhelming. The PIO must avoid the temptation to cater to the network and out-of-town reporters. Treat them with the same courtesy as local reporters. You should always remember that the local reporters will be talking with you tomorrow, and you will be pitching stories to them. Just as you do not enjoy being ignored on a personal level, your local reporters do not want to be ignored either.

The benefits of working with local reporters are many and varied. Establishing strong relationships with them will allow you to have a better understanding of their needs. You will get to know them as a "person." The personal relationship may help them to understand the issues that your agency may face. Of course, this type of relationship is not developed in the middle of an emergency.

"Building a relationship with the media starts with the first contact."

Building a relationship can start by simply making contact with news editors or reporters. Sending regular press releases will also establish you as a credible source. Couple these news releases with **briefings** and **media advisories**. You can also mail out **media kits**, containing information about your agency, its personnel, and the mission they undertake every day. These kits should contain fact sheets about your organization, including information about department officers, equipment, personnel certifications, call volume, response area, and any special capabilities. An organizational history should also be included in the packets, and, if possible, so should photos or digital art of the agency logo and chief officers.

The media can play a vital role in emergency management activities. They can also assist in finding suspects of criminal activities, spreading the word about emergency public health concerns, or warning the public about critical roadway incidents.

The media can have a great role in assisting emergency service personnel, including **emergency managers**, before, during, and after an emergency.

Before the emergency, the media can help provide the public with prevention and preparation information. During the emergency, the media have a role in warning and alerting the public to the imminent or present danger, providing accurate information to reduce or eliminate panic, and describing the emergent actions the public can take to protect themselves.

Who Are Reporters?

Now that we have a better understanding about the needs of the media, we need to spend some time talking about the human resource aspect of the media. The people a PIO will interface with are often young. Many reporters start on the "**police beat**," and while some enjoy the interaction and excitement of the emergency scenes, others are looking at the assignment as a means of climbing the journalism ladder, perhaps seeking the glory of an **investigative reporter**. Regardless of the motivation of a reporter, a PIO must remember they are just people, and like every other person, they have reasons for doing what they do. While reporters are often thought to be vindictive troublemakers, they view themselves as protectors of the pubic interest—a part of the checks-and-balances system. It is also important to remember that journalism is virtually the only profession protected by the First Amendment to the Constitution.

"Journalism is protected by the First Amendment to the Constitution."

When developing relationships with reporters, a PIO should always keep in mind the possibility of turnover within the market. Reporters often move from radio to television or from newspaper to radio. Sometimes they even work for multiple media outlets. Smaller markets suffer from fast turnover, which will force the PIO to aggressively track changes within the market so that new relationships can replace those lost to turnover.

Journalism has become a revered and, at some times, reviled profession. Journalists are trained to ask questions, verify sources, and report the news. Journalism schools rarely have difficulty filling classes with eager students, ready to break the next big story. Most learn that there is a lot more to journalism than simply breaking the big story. It has to do with cultivating sources, developing credibility, and earning the trust of the public. Those who have not learned this lesson can be a PIO's worst nightmare.

The newsroom's reporters work out of can be organized in different ways. Some are organized by beats, others organized with **general**

assignment reporters. Still other newsrooms are organized as a hybrid of these two styles.

Beats are specific subjects reporters are assigned to. They include police, courts, health, or government. A general assignment reporter is expected to be the master of all trades. In a day, these reporters may cover a trial, a structure fire, or an award ceremony and then be live at a community festival during the 6 P.M. news.

A debate can rage on about which organizational style is best. Arguments can be made on both sides and argued from many points of view. General assignment reporters are used to receiving many different assignments. During a disaster response, there are seldom normal beat stories to cover. Legal proceedings take on a less important priority than emergency response or recovery operations. Court reporters may be assigned to cover a family assistance center, emergency scene, or an emergency operations center. They may be less accustomed to their new environment than a reporter used to covering many different subjects. However, the **beat reporter** may see another side of a story because of his or her expertise in the subject matter. For instance, a heath reporter may be keenly attuned to health issues and ask questions related to health issues while covering the family assistance center. Understanding the baseline knowledge a reporter has about the subject at hand can be a distinct advantage for a PIO facing a crowd of reporters.

"Avoiding reporters is detrimental to a PIO's success."

"Knowing a reporter's experience can be an asset to a PIO."

Some public safety agencies still believe that the media are better seen than heard and do all they can to avoid interacting with reporters. This is naïve, and such an attitude should be avoided at all costs. Understanding the needs of the media can make interacting with the media easier and more beneficial to the ultimate mission of a PIO, which is saving lives and limiting the suffering of citizens.

Summary

The media have basic needs that must be met. If the PIO does not understand or chooses to ignore those needs, the media will fulfill them somewhere else.

REVIEW QUESTIONS

1. The media are referred to as **the big three plus one**. This means
   a. ABC, CBS, NBC, and Associated Press
   b. Radio, Television, Newspaper, and the Internet

c. CNN, FOX, MSNBC, and C-SPAN
d. Cable, Print, Over-the-air, and Blogs

2. Public affairs programming
   a. Often provides a longer interview to better tell a story
   b. Deals with politics
   c. Allows broadcast outlets to editorialize
   d. Is run by FEMA during disasters
3. The Internet now has many web-only newspapers
   a. True
   b. False
4. Reporter deadlines
   a. Are of no consequence to a PIO
   b. Should be observed whenever possible
   c. Can be changed by reporters
   d. Do not apply to public information
5. The definition of news is the same for everyone
   a. True
   b. False

ENDNOTES

1. http://www.cdc.gov/communication/emergency/features/f009.htm
2. Nancy Gibbs, "Blue Truth, Red Truth," *Time* magazine, Sept. 27, 2004.

CHAPTER 3

The Interview

Objectives

- Identify the skills needed to participate in various styles of interviews
- Classify the styles of questions used by reporters
- Name the various aspects of news conferences and how a proper setup can dictate success

CASE Study

After a tornado has destroyed several residences and damaged a school, the media are seeking information from the PIO. In order to accommodate all the media, the PIO schedules a news conference. During the questioning, reporters begin to turn the topic from the current emergency to past failures in other states. The PIO recognizes the direction of questioning and determines whether it is time to close the news conference. He thanks the reporters, sets a time for the next briefing, and exits the room.

Case Study Questions

1. When should a PIO schedule a news conference?
2. What types of questions should a PIO expect reporters to ask during an interview?
3. When should a PIO end a news conference?

Introduction

The best part about an interview with the news media is that you get to tell your story. The worst part about an interview is that the media can edit your storytelling. Like it or not, this is the way of the world, and until you own your own network and interview only yourself, you will be subject to the perils of the cutting room floor. However, you should remember, many of the Oscar winning movies contained scenes left on the cutting room floor, making the movie better. Likewise, many an interview has been saved by the edit.

A PIO will be interviewed almost daily. These interviewers could be from the local newspaper, a community group, or a student journalist. Each interview is extremely important, as it may affect attitudes about your agency or provide vital "get it right the first time" messages to the public.

KEY TERMS

- Chroma Key Effect, p. 34
- Exclusives, p. 37
- Industry-Specific Jargon, p. 38
- Joint Information Center, p. 43
- Media Advisory, p. 45
- "Mult" Box, p. 44
- News Release, p. 44
- Package, p. 34
- Position Statements, p. 33
- Remote Site, p. 37
- Sidebar Story, p. 36
- Talking Points, p. 00

Key Points for Successful Interviews

"Keys to a successful interview:
- Visualize you success
- Know your subject matter
- Position Statements
- Dress the part"

To be successful at interviews, it is important to understand several key points. The first is simply to *visualize your success*. Understand that the reason you are being asked a question is that there is a perception that you are the expert. It may be a correct analysis, or it may be one that you must correct. You should view the mere fact that you were asked as flattering. Once asked, your position as the expert will be reinforced or diminished by your answer.

The second point is to *know your subject*. As a rule, you will be more comfortable speaking about a subject you understand. Answer the question that is asked.

Wrong	Right
Q: "What day is it?"	Q: "What day is it?"
A: "Tuesday, January 15, 2006"	A: "Tuesday"

You must listen to the question to formulate your answer. You can use answers that are based on "**talking points**," but you have to make sure that they address the issue, or the reporter will keep asking the question.

Q: "Is it the policy of your department to race through intersections?"

A: "The Blueberry Police Department has developed a rigorous driver training program that teaches our officers the proper techniques to use when driving on our city streets. The safety of the public is our first priority."

Q: "Is it the policy of your department to race through intersections?"

A: (as the public perceives it) "I'm afraid to answer this question because we screwed up and caused a problem."

Understanding the top points you want to make during any interview and always going back to those points will assist you during the interview. Reporters are paid to ask questions, some of them difficult ones. During an interview, our talking points give us a basis of familiarity.

The third important point for interview success is to learn the benefit of **position statements**. Often contained within our talking points, position statements can help frame the context of an answer. These statements are often difficult for the public to disagree with.

"This is an extremely difficult time for the community. By pulling together we will all get though this."

The position statement provides a platform on which to begin your message track. It can become the door opener to your message and hook the interest of not only the reporter, but also the audience.

Q: "Is it the policy of your department to race through intersections?"

A: "The Blueberry Police Department has developed a rigorous driver training program that teaches our officers the proper techniques to use when driving on our city streets. The safety of the public is our first priority." (The position statement) "It is most definitely not our policy to drive unsafely through intersections." (the definitive answer to the question).

ON TARGET "While the public and reporter may not understand the uniform policies of your agency, everyone in your agency will recognize a mistake in your uniform. You are the representative of your organization, and to it, perfection counts."

Finally, *your appearance* for a television interview speaks loudly and clearly about your credibility. Follow your uniform policies and look the part. If you have been on the front line fighting a fire, it is acceptable to look that part. If you haven't, placing some soot on your face to make you look "busy" is misleading the public. This will hurt your credibility with not only the media and public, but also those in your organization.

Looks are as important as what is said during an interview. If you do not wear a uniform, you should wear clothing that would be donned for a job interview. Business casual dress should be worn only when appropriate. An open collar shirt would not portray a good image for an interview about the death of citizens; however, it might be acceptable for an interview about employees gathering for a charitable cause.

Avoid flashy tie clasps, cuff links, or other such jewelry. Think about how any item you wear might reflect the bright lights used during a television interview.

If possible and applicable, shave just before the interview. Wear your glasses if you would normally wear them; however, avoid a lens that turns dark in light, such as sunglasses. If your agency policy allows members to wear some type of head covering, make sure you wear it properly. Know your hat policy!

Interview "To Do" List

Before the Interview

The most important part of an interview is the time spent preparing for it. If you have to sit in your response vehicle for a moment reviewing notes, or hide in the restroom for a few minutes to study your material, do it. These few minutes can make or break the interview.

While reviewing your talking points, you should reflect on the previous experiences with reporters and the news outlet. If you have never been interviewed by this reporter, think about past work you have observed. This may give you an insight to the attitude being brought to the interview.

When you are ready, straighten yourself up. Make sure that your uniform is properly outfitted and that your professional dress is neat and clean. (Always have a clean uniform shirt in your vehicle. You never know when you will be in your beach clothes when an important interview is requested.)

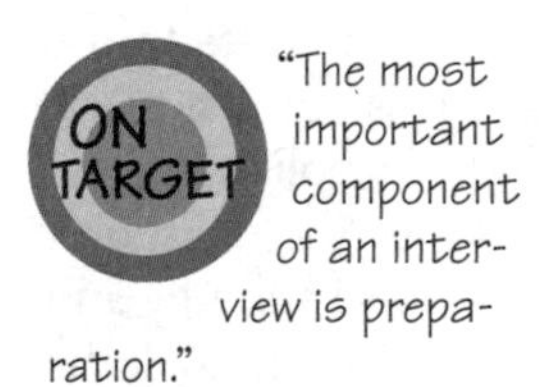

"The most important component of an interview is preparation."

This information is not intended to prepare you to receive a fashion award, but it is important to understand that the wrong appearance may limit the usefulness of an interview. Certain colors can be problematic on television. Bright green is a bad color as it may cause difficulty if you are doing an interview using a **chroma key effect**. Figure 3-1 illustrates this effect. Bright white can also be a problem, although this can be adjusted by the camera. Discuss color choices with your local media; they will appreciate your efforts. If you wear makeup, deep tan is the best color.

Make sure everyone is clear about the topic to be discussed and the format the story will be presented in. The interview may be for background for a much larger story, or the interview may be used as a segment of a story with many aspects. If the story is to be a "**package**," it will generally be a longer story, but it may not all focus on your interview. Television will want additional visuals, the newspapers may schedule a photographic session separate from the interview, and radio may want to do the interview live (as may television.) Regardless, the rules of being interviewed remain the same.

If there are certain items that are off limits, it is important to establish ground rules early. Make sure the reporter understands your limits of authority and expertise. These points may not prevent reporters from asking a question that is "out of bounds," but at least you have informed them up front about what you are going to be able to answer.

When thinking about the upcoming interview, you should always look for potential negative points. Even though you may think the story

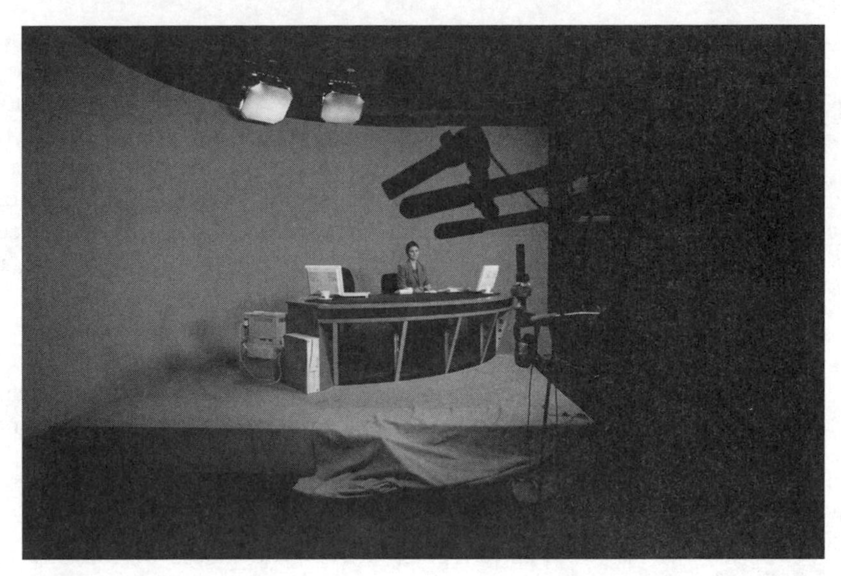

FIGURE 3-1
Chroma Key Effect.

you have pitched to the news outlet is going to be great for your organization, the reporter, some community group, or others within your organization may view the subject in some negative light. Be prepared for the unexpected question.

Verify what material the reporter needs for background; determine the backdrops to be used for photography and the depth of questions to be asked. You may have room for negotiations on the format of the interview. For instance, if the reporter wants to use the dispatch center as a backdrop during the interview, but the dispatchers on duty do not want to be on camera, then suggest an alternate backdrop. This could be a piece of apparatus (e.g., a fire engine, an ambulance, or a police car). You could also attempt to temporarily replace the dispatchers with others for the duration of the interview. The issue of employees refusing to participate in interviews is another subject you may have to deal with. You should never mandate that employees participate, but there should be an educational process that would allow them to understand the value of participation with the media.

Many interview requests a reporter makes of your CEO are not worthy of the CEO's time. However, some circumstances may force the CEO to conduct nearly all interviews in person. These could be a series of interviews on the same subject, or it may simply be the policy of the CEO to be the face and voice of the agency. When presenting a story to the CEO for consideration, the briefing should include information on the reporter doing the story, the news angles typically taken by the media outlet, and the good and bad that might come from the story.

Those who will be interviewed should exercise some common courtesy and watch what they eat and drink prior to meeting with the reporter. There should NEVER be any hint of alcohol on one's breath, and foods such as onions, garlic, or others that might be offensive should be avoided. Use of a breath mint or similar item is encouraged.

If you are supposed to meet a reporter at a certain location, arrive early for the interview. This will not only be appreciated by the reporter, it will give you time to go over the talking points, acquaint yourself with the surroundings, and relax a little.

Being relaxed during an interview is important. A nervous appearance or voice will make the audience suspicious of your work. Physical relaxation exercises, such as deep breathing, can assist with relaxing you. Being prepared is perhaps the best cure for nervousness.

When a Reporter Arrives

When a reporter arrives, you should welcome the interview. It is your job to work with reporters, so you should not look at the visit as an intrusion.

Greet the reporter, and talk with him or her before the interview to get a better understanding of the reporter's needs. Project a positive image. Welcome the reporter and the interview. In addition, you may strike up a casual personal relationship with them. They may be suffering from the same broken lawnmower problem you are. This discussion also may help limit some of the confusion that takes place before an interview. If this is a television interview, there may be lights that need to be positioned. Microphones might need to be placed on you, or you may simply need to find a quiet place to conduct the interview.

You should adopt a philosophy that all microphones are live, all cameras are on, and all newspaper reporters have a photographic memory. YOU ARE NEVER OFF THE RECORD! This includes sending electronic communications (e-mail) and making telephone calls. During the 2005 investigation of the federal response to Hurricane Katrina, the United States House Select Committee reviewed dozens of e-mails from various FEMA officials. Newspaper and broadcast networks ran numerous stories about these e-mails, including one where dinner arrangements were being discussed. When "off the record" comments become on the record, they can quickly become the story of the day, displacing other important messages and challenging the agency's credibility.

Help the reporter get a good story. This will improve your credibility. Additionally, you may be in a unique position to provide the reporter with ideas for **sidebar stories**. These are stories that are in some way related to the main subject.

Main story: "Fire extinguished with help of water from helicopter."

Sidebar story: "Crews received special training on new helicopter just last week."

You should use caution with "**exclusives**," or material that you only give to one news outlet. While certain stories do lend themselves to one medium over another, fair and equal distribution of story ideas tends to make for better overall media relations. The exception might be a story that would enhance a specific series being run by a news outlet.

One of the most important things you can do to help reporters get a story is to respect their deadlines. If faced with a question that requires further research, ask the reporter when the deadline will be, and be honest about the efforts and time needed to get the information asked for. Work with the reporter to make sure that the deadlines can be met. Reporters may want information right away, but will settle for a reasonable deadline if the issues are discussed with them.

If you are not the best person to answer the question, or talk to about a certain subject, then work with the reporter to find the correct person. If that person is someone within your organization, take time to brief that person on what is expected, and cover the basics of interviewing, including dress, the best way to answer questions, and any specific talking points that should be covered during the interview.

During the Interview

During an interview on television, look at the reporter, not the camera. This is important because if you cannot look people in the eye when you talk to them they may question whether you are being truthful. In addition, looking into the camera when you are being interviewed does not play well on television. (See Figure 3-2.) Unless you are at a **remote site** and the anchor in the studio is asking you questions through an earpiece, always look at a reporter. Occasionally, a camera operator will be sent to conduct your interview. You should then look at an imaginary reporter, avoiding looking into the camera. If the reporter is taller or shorter than you are, attempt to look at them at camera level. Looking up or down into a camera can project an image of superiority or inferiority and result in a negative opinion of you.

"Look at the reporter, not the camera."

It is okay to smile during an interview and show your human side. You want to relate to the audience, and the audience relates better to real people. Of course, this assumes the situation is appropriate for smiles. The tone and attitude of your answers are subject to misinterpretation by the audience, either through editing or simply by the way you make your point. If you come across as being angry, people will sense that. If anger is not appropriate, they will become suspicious of your words. While it may seem superficial, studies have shown that your appearance is more important than the message. During an interview, the audience focuses on your face (50%), your voice quality (36%), and then the message (14%).[1]

Make sure you understand the question that is being asked. Listen to the question, and do not be distracted by the surroundings. If you are

FIGURE 3-2
PIO Being Interviewed by News Team.

in a television studio, there will be significant activity going on behind the camera, as floor managers and camera operators prepare for the next shot or segment in the newscast. If you are at a scene, there is always a flurry of activity. These distractions can cause you to misunderstand a question. If there is any doubt, ask the reporter to repeat the question.

Especially for television and radio stories, your answers should be short—20 to 30 seconds in length. Avoid using **industry-specific jargon**, as this will confuse the audience. Speak slowly and distinctly, avoiding terse responses. Chances are the question a reporter is asking is the same one on the mind of someone in the audience. Even if you do not like the reporter asking the question, you certainly do want to insult someone in your service area.

When on camera, do not rock from side to side. Stand still and hold something in your hand so that you are not gesturing wildly. Remember, the camera may only be shooting your body above the shoulders, so gesturing with your hands and arms does no good.

If an answer requires the use of statistics, use care in delivering them. Statistics can be confusing and are often misinterpreted. Be sure they are accurate.

Even though it may seem rude not to address a reporter by name, do not do it. During an interview, simply answer the questions. The reporter may only be there to ask questions, not to put together the whole story.

Using the reporter's name will nearly ensure that your comments will not (cannot) be used. This is not advantageous to your cause.

Interviews are about a subject, rarely about you. An interview is not your personal time to shine. It is not the time to focus on "you."

Emergency scenes and public safety facilities can be noisy locations. Do what you can to diminish background noise. If you are located in a noisy facility, turn down the dispatch scanner or other equipment, if possible. At a scene, be aware of the background noise, and speak at the appropriate volume so that your message is clear, understandable, and heard by the reporters and audience.

Occasionally, you will be faced with what is often called a long-format interview. This will last from 10 minutes to a half hour or more. Approach the long-format interview with no more than three main points to bring to the audience, even though you have a great deal of time. This gives you more opportunity to interact with the host of the program. The longer the interview, the more opportunity you have to use visuals if this is a television interview. These visuals can be supplied to the producer in advance and used to enhance your presentation. When solicited for such interviews, make the producer's job easier by suggesting visuals for the story. When you are seeking time on these long-format shows, investigate the format and mission of the program and of the station to which you are pitching your story. This will allow you to target the story in a way that might be more favorable to the producer.

After the Interview

The time spent with a reporter after an interview can be as valuable as the preparation time you put into the interview. You should always thank the reporter. When time permits and the situation allows, offer a facility tour. Make sure the reporter knows how to get in touch with you in the future. Discuss your information release policy, and if you have one, provide a brochure about your media relations program.

This is also the time to suggest another story to the reporter. Always having a timeless story in your pocket for these occasions can go a long way toward establishing a relationship. This story may be used by the reporter when they have nothing else to report on, yet need something for the evening news or Saturday edition of the newspaper.

"For an interview, the reporter has been a guest in your facility, or you a guest in theirs. Before parting ways, remind them you are always available to help them."

The final step after an interview should actually be a part of your daily activities as a PIO. Monitor the newscast or newspaper where the interview is set to appear. If there is a problem with the facts of the interview, you may need to confer with the reporter. (This will be discussed in greater detail in Chapter Six.)

Challenging Questions

Some people view any interview as a challenge, fearing each question and worrying about the result of their answers. Reporters will ask challenging questions, and you will have to answer them. Above all, never say "No comment." This is simply not acceptable and is as bad as assuming you are "off the record."

The National Highway Traffic Safety Administration (NHTSA) defined a number of challenging questions in the Law Enforcement Public Information program developed more than a decade ago. Box 3-1 provides that agency's definition of these questions, which are still valid today. In this text, we will focus on just the ones you are most likely to be trapped by.

Box 3-1 Challenging Questions (From NHTSA Law Enforcemen Public Information Workshop)

"Closed notebook"—A technique in which a reporter will close a notebook, signifying the end of an interview. Often, as one walks the reporter to a door or an elevator, casual conversation leads to an unintended revelation of a fact or comment.

"Dead air"—A pause during questioning. Dead air is designed to have a PIO continue talking, in the hope that he or she will get off message.

Devil's advocate—A position whereby a reporter takes a stand that appears different from what he or she really believes.

False facts/leading/loaded—Emotionally charged questions designed to elicit an unprofessional response from the PIO. An example is "Is it true that your personnel are poorly trained?"

Feeling or sympathy—Although reporters will tell you that they don't ask "How do you feel" questions, they often do. Emotional responses by a PIO or his or her spokesperson can often be misinterpreted.

Hostile—Questions designed to deliberately elicit emotional responses.

Hypothetical—Dangerous questions often taking the PIO off track. Stick to the facts!

Interrupt—These questions interrupt you before you've finished answering the previous question.

Irrelevant—Questions that have no relationship to the topic at hand.

Multipart—Questions that may confuse both the audience and the PIO. These questions contain other questions within them.

Needling or persistent—Similar to a "repeat" question, this style attempts to get the PIO to change an answer.

Negative—Questions phrased negatively—for example, "I assume you do not agree that. . . ."

Puffball—Simplistic questions such as "How many stations do you have?" The question often has nothing to do with the topic and may be posed by a less experienced reporter.

Remedial—Questions seeking a resolution to a problem.

Repeat—A method used by reporters to get a PIO to say what the reporters want them to say.

Yes/No factual—Closed questions that do not allow the key message to be delivered.

Interview Formats[2]

Radio Telephone Interview

No one can see anyone, but while the interviewer is in his or her studio, you could be in your kitchen.

Being "Door Stopped" or Ambushed

When a reporter attempts to talk to you through a mail opening in your door or by pursuing you down the street the situation is often called being "door stopped." (See Figure 3-3.) It is not uncommon for reporters to stay outside of a person's office or residence in an attempt to get an interview.

TV and Radio Phone-Ins

These are usually more relaxed and informal chats, but occasionally unplanned and difficult questions will be thrown in when you are off guard.

The charts that follow show the amount of time each of the three 24-hour cable news networks devoted to three formats of interview in its primetime programming (Jan. 21, 2002–Jan. 25, 2002) in both interview-format programs and newscasts. CNN had a total of 565 minutes of interviews; MSNBC 370 minutes; FNC 470 minutes.[3]

FIGURE 3-3
Ambush Interview.

FIGURE 3-4
In-Studio Interview.

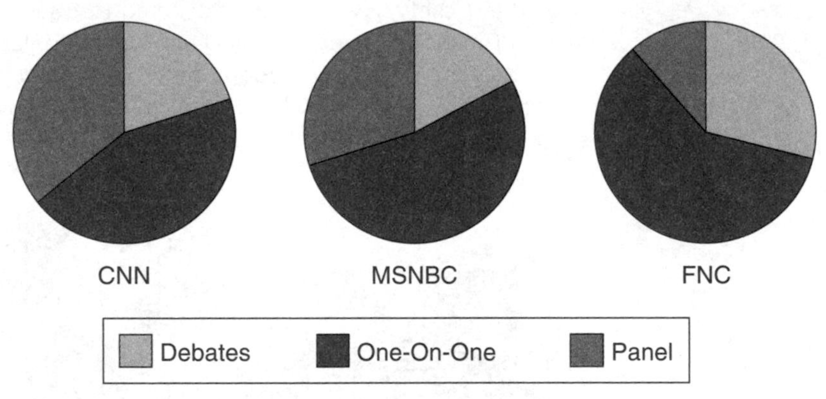

FIGURE 3-5
Types of Interviews Used by Networks.

Press Conference

ON TARGET "Press conferences are controlled by the PIO, not the media."

Of all the types of interviews, the **press conference** (news conference/media event) is the interview over which you will have the most control. Usually, you invite the media to this event. The press conference will be more on your terms, and you will have prepared your message well beforehand. Of course, since press conferences are under your control, the media do not like them. Press conferences are often looked upon as unavoidable, and they serve as a launching point for other stories.

FIGURE 3-6
News Conference.

Reasons for Press Conferences

There are a number of reasons to call for a news conference (see Figure 3-6), the least of which is to explain a complex or sensitive issue. Press conferences are also used to introduce specific people in the agency, such as a new chief executive. When many media outlets must hear information, such as during a disaster or a hazardous material emergency or search, or when there is an event that has community-wide impact, a press conference can be the best way of getting information out. This could help avoid favoritism and message confusion.

A press conference can also be used to avoid numerous media interviews on the same subject. However, this rarely works, because each news outlet wants its own question answered and will seek an interview after the press conference. This may not be all bad, as it gives more media outlets the ability to cover the event, each taking its own direction on your spin.

A press conference can promote good relations with the media, if for no other reason than the inference that you are not playing favorites.

When a number of agencies are working on an incident, a **joint information center** can be established and press conferences scheduled so that all parties can get their message out in a unified approach. In such instances, the various media hear the *same message* at the *same time.*

Determining whether a press conference is the best way of providing information to the media is a very important decision. Some agencies use press conferences as the only way of putting out stories. This is not the best way to develop a media relations plan, and it is often an unsuccessful tactic. Press conferences should be used under very specific circumstances, as discussed earlier. You should ask yourself the following questions when determining if a press conference is necessary:

- Is the news timely and of significance?
- Would a **news release** do?
- Would reporters appreciate asking questions?
- Would this issue take up a lot of agency staff time if the CEOs, commanders, officers, and other principals had to do separate interviews?
- Are there competing events that would limit turnout?

Location and Staging

Once you have determined that a press conference is necessary, setting one up at the correct location is the next step. Perhaps the most important item on your to-do list is to remember that the press conference is *yours*, not the news media's. You control the event. You control your environment.

The venue is important. Make sure that it is large enough to accommodate the expected media members and all of their equipment. Ensure that the media have the ability to run cables and get signals to the outside of the building. Make sure that there is a good backdrop and that there is a way for those speaking at the press conference to exit. If things start to go badly, you will be able to close the press conference and get everyone else out.

If you hold your press conference outside, attempt to minimize distractions. You need to be able to deliver your message without the backdrop taking front stage.

The press conference "staging" is no small consideration. You must consider the props to be used, the number of people speaking, whether a public address system is necessary, and whether there is a potential for controversial questions or perhaps even protests. Camera and microphone settings must also be considered. If the press conference is designed to be a panel-style conference, microphones must be able to pick up the voices of all participants. This may be accomplished by using a "**mult" box**. This devise allows multiple microphones to be fed to multiple news outlets. If a podium is to be used, school those participating in the press conference in how to use the microphone, adjust its height, and work with the voice pickup.

"Always allow for an open and easy route of exit for the speakers. If the news conference takes a negative turn, you can close it off and make a quick exit."

You should not allow cameras to be behind the speakers. Cameras should be set at the same level as the speakers. When a camera is shooting down, the speaker and the message are diminished; if the camera is from an upwards vantage point, the image places the speaker in a position of greater authority—which is not recommended.

To summarize, for a PIO to pull off a good press conference advance planning is required. You should first determine whether the press conference is necessary. Then, if so, identify the purpose and limits of the press conference and how it should be conducted—whether a simple statement will be read or whether various people will be answering questions. Does it need to be a joint news conference, bringing together others involved in the incident or event? Many press conferences are designed around a combination of statements and question-and-answer sessions.

"The day and time of a press conference are important considerations."

Scheduling

Proper scheduling of the press conference is critical to its success. If you are an active PIO, at some point in your career you will call a press conference, and no one will come. Holding a press conference about a new piece of equipment on a day that a major news event occurs could doom that press conference to failure. The time of a press conference is sometimes dictated by circumstances, but is best be dictated by newsroom schedules and deadlines. A noon news conference does not guarantee coverage on a noon news program. You should get to know your local newsrooms' schedules and discuss the timing of news conferences with their staff to make sure you are accommodating as many media members as you can. Many PIOs believe that 10:00 A.M. and 2:00 P.M. are the best times for press conferences because they give reporters time to attend the press conference and then time to write and research their story so that it fits into the next newscast. The day of the week is also critical. Tuesdays or Wednesdays are seen as the best days.

News conferences should generally not last more than 30 minutes. Press conferences are frequently promoted by using a **media advisory**. (More information on this topic can be found in Chapter Four.) A PIO should announce a press conference early enough so that the media have time to plan for coverage of your event. You should produce a media kit to hand out at the event. This kit should contain a more in-depth press release, as well as supporting documents. You may include digital images, biographies of those being highlighted, and a brief history of your organization. You should always include your contact information.

Prior to the Press Conference

Contacting the media may be the most difficult part of preparing for a press conference, because you may be contacting members of news

"Web sites are great for getting information out to the public and the media."

organizations with whom you are not accustomed to working. If you are bringing in media from outside the area, you should provide directions to the venue. Many press clubs or organizations, such as "Women in Communications" or the local Chamber of Commerce, will publish local media guides. Media contacts across the country are available through commercial services such as Vocus.[4] This service allows you to send news releases and media advisories, as well as keep track of media inquiries.

If your press conference is in conjunction with a national event, such National Fire Prevention Week or National Emergency Medical Services Week, you may be able to get complete press kits from the sponsoring organizations. These kits might also include graphics that can be used when designing posters about the event, or may be used on the agency Web site.

In addition to the media advisory and press kits, you should have pre- and post-event information posted on your agency's Web site. Members of all segments of your constituencies will access your Web site for information at one time or another, and while they may have missed the actual press conference, they will have access to the information you wanted them to have.

Leaking information about the news conference may or may not be advantageous. For instance, if you want to make an announcement such as "Central City Police Department to name new Police Chief on Tuesday" or "New Evacuation Routes to be outlined on Wednesday," these advances can enhance the content of a press conference. Pre-conference press releases can outline why things are changing, while the press conference will outline the specifics of the change. This is also a method of making the story last longer than one news cycle.

Certain media events may include invited guests or members of the public. You should determine in advance whether these groups would be allowed, where they will be seated, whether they will be allowed to speak, and whether they will be able ask questions. Nonmedia attendees can be disruptive, but can also enhance the event. Announcing a heroic deed by a police officer is an important event, but having family members there to show their pride makes it more relatable to a larger audience.

As part of your event planning, assign a photographer from your agency. This person can take photos that can be used on your agency Web site and newsletter, for future presentations about your organization, or simply to chronicle your agency's history. You should also plan to record the remarks made during the event. This can help if issues arise about how the event is reported, or for use in preparing Web site, newsletter or historical documents.

Prior to the event, review the logistics of the event. Go through every aspect of the press conference prior to anyone arriving, so you can make changes then, instead of disrupting the flow of the event.

"Make contact with the media before the event."

Several days before the event, make follow-up calls to the media. This will help you get a better feel for who will be attending, what they might expect, and which reporters you might encounter. You may also consider developing a seating chart for the event. This might be the time to discuss issuing temporary press passes for admittance to the event.

Reviews of your agenda and media kit are very important. Make sure that each kit has the most up-to-date information and that the agenda accurately reflects the order of those speaking.

The Day of the Event

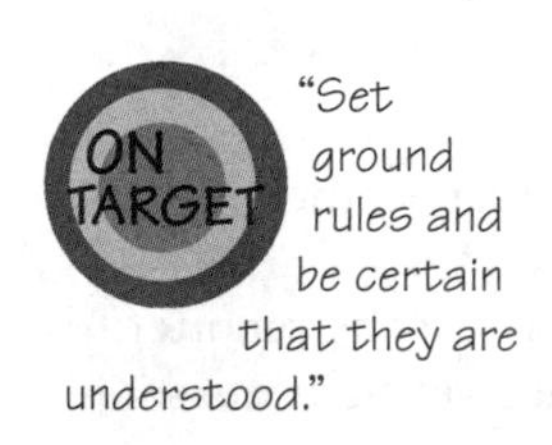

"Set ground rules and be certain that they are understood."

The day of the news conference, make sure everyone knows where they are to sit. Using name tents (cards) is a good way of assuring that guests are in the proper location. If possible, assign a "floor supervisor" to assist you with guiding the media to their designated areas, including their camera and microphone locations.

Identify a place for news releases and media kits. They are often located at a table near the entrance to the venue. Attendees may be asked to register (which is a good way to obtain accurate contact information). During registration is a good time to distribute the media kit.

Make sure the ground rules are clearly understood. Allow for additional microphones and additional cameras no more than five minutes prior to the event. Discuss with the media how individual photo opportunities and interviews will be handled and what the structure of the event will be.

Start the press conference on time. You should begin the event by outlining the ground rules, if any, reviewing the timetable and media kit, going over the purpose of the press conference, and, finally, introducing those who will be speaking.

The actual press conference presentation should be short and to the point. Limit individual speakers to presentations of about five minutes. You may consider reading the press release, but this is often a waste of time, since the reporters have it in their media kits. Speakers should speak extemporaneously, avoiding a canned statement unless it is absolutely necessary because of specific wording approved by legal council.

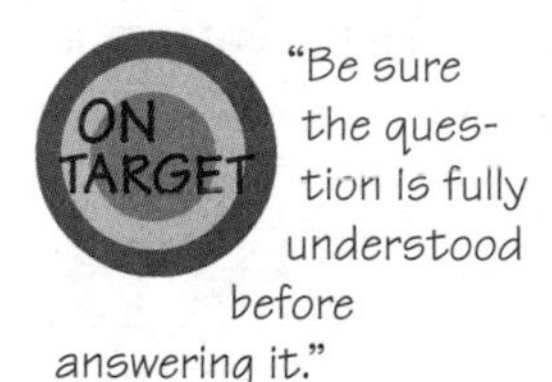

"Be sure the question is fully understood before answering it."

If using visuals or charts, make sure they are in camera range and visible to those in attendance. While these can enhance the press conference, they can also make it very confusing and appear unprofessional if they are not well designed. The size, color, and positioning of these visuals are important considerations.

If the plan is to allow for questions, end that segment at an appropriate time, when the questions stop coming from the media, or when they turn in a direction that you do not want to go. Speakers should be briefed on response techniques, including how to handle challenging questions. You may want to assign a moderator to direct the questions to the most appropriate panelist.

Simultaneous Questions

From the left side of the room:	From the right side of the room:
"Is it your policy to kill innocent people?"	"Are the officers involved receiving counseling?"

THE ANSWER TO THE QUESTION YOU HEARD FROM THE LEFT SIDE OF THE ROOM

"We would never consider such a thing!"

When answering questions, the speaker should repeat the question. This will avoid a misunderstanding about the answer.

"Reasons to end a news conference early:

- Questions begin to get off the issue,
- Questions address off-limit topics,
- Same questions rephrased,
- Pauses occur between questions,
- Something of greater importance has occurred."

If a speaker does not understand the question, ask the reporter to clarify it before answering the question. When answering a question, make sure you fully understand it.

Speakers should respond to all media present and avoid using the reporter's name with sound bites. This allows more news outlets to use the quotes.

Once the question has been clarified, start with the essence of the question when delivering your answer. Vary your eye concentration on different sections of the room. This also applies to selecting questions. They too should come from all sections of the room.

Prior to a question-and-answer session, determine whether activists may ask questions. Use care in preparing speakers for these questions, and make sure they are on topic. Do not allow questioners to give speeches.

The PIO should take notes during the press conference and, after the event, deal with problems and answers to questions that could not be answered during the event.

Conclude the event by thanking those who attended and the staff that helped you put it together. Make any closing announcements about follow-up information, procedures for leaving the facility, or additional activities available, such as tours.

If things have turned negative, the only concluding statement might be to say "thank you" then get everyone out of the room.

Other Considerations

An additional consideration for a press conference might be to escort the speakers into the room, or call them to the podium at specific times. If presenting them with something like a plaque, determine when and how photos of the presentation will occur. These are often done in a separate

"The only thing better than practice is more practice."

part of the room, so all pictures look similar; it is easier to control the picture-taking segment without taking up time during the event.

PIOs could gain valuable experience by planning press conferences as part of emergency exercises. The press conference could be about the exercise, or be simulated as if the exercise were a real event. The only thing better then practice is more practice.

"Taking time out to practice your craft with journalism students can be a valuable learning experience for both you and them."

Aside from setting up press conferences for practice, PIOs should seek out local journalism schools and encourage student reporters to practice their craft with them. These interviews can teach you a lot about your style and help you improve your presentation. They often take more time than seasoned field reporters do, and their production teams take more time to set up, but the extra time will be worth your while. These young reporters might be on the front line someday. They will remember the experience you provided for them.

Summary

The interview is one of the most important moments in a PIO's day, yet can be one of the most frightening. Being prepared for an interview can limit anxiety, ensure a good performance, and allow the PIO to bring forth the key messages determined by the agency as responses to the interviewer's questions.

REVIEW QUESTIONS

1. Before an interview, a PIO should do all of the following except
   a. Be early
   b. Mentally prepare for the interview
   c. Eat something spicy and have an adult beverage; this will calm your nerves
   d. Talk with reporter
2. During the interview, a PIO should do all of the following except
   a. Use the reporter's name during the interview
   b. Not look into the camera lens
   c. Be cautious of background noise
   d. Watch his or her posture
3. A dead air question is
   a. One that is caused by a technical malfunction
   b. Designed to keep you talking even though you have completed your thought.

c. Inevitable with the complexities of live broadcasts
d. Your chance to make your point more completely

4. When doing a live "TV Remote Booth" interview
a. Look into the camera, just as if the person was standing in front of you.
b. Look to the left
c. Look to the right
d. Prepare for the interview to be conducted inside a small booth.

ENDNOTES

1. Mehrabian, A. (1972). *Nonverbal communication.* Chicago: Aldine-Atherton.
2. http://www.impactfactory.com
3. http://www.pbs.org/newshour/media/cablenews/pu_4.html
4. http://www.vocus.com

CHAPTER 4

Writing News Releases

Objectives

- Identify the components of a sentence
- List several reasons for writing press releases
- Describe the style used when writing press releases

A police chase results in the death of a civilian. A PIO for the city police department issues the following press release:

The Police Chief says everything is fine within his department, but that the Sheriff caused great harm by having his men start a chase and bring it into the City.

Donald Badge says that his men were protecting the citizens when they chased the vehicle and that they never knew the girl was in the intersection when they went through it. He says that parents should pay attention to their children when near a street and that the perpetrator is the car driver.

Badge reports he will not return from his vacation in Florida since his men won't be disciplined. "The sheriff should be ashamed of himself," he said.

Case Study Review Questions

1. This press release represents an accurate review of the fatal incident.
   a. True
   b. False
   c. Unable to determine

2. In the introductory sentence to the case study, the noun is
   a. chase
   b. a
   c. results
   d. none of the above
3. A press release should be written in a format called
   a. Aggressive and accurate
   b. Objective and benign
   c. Inverted pyramid
   d. Technical writing

Introduction

Many PIOs begin their careers as paramedics, police officers, or firefighters. For people in these positions, writing is much more technical: *"At 0800 (zero-eight hundred) hours, on 27-July-2005, unit 2237 was dispatched to a 10–37 crime in progress. . . ."* While this type of report writing may be accepted as standard practice in the public safety discipline, it does not conform to normal English rules of grammar.

These reports rarely meet the standards of media writing as outlined by the Associated Press Style Guide or other guides, such as the one used by those with the U.S. Department of Homeland Security's Federal Emergency Management Agency (FEMA). As the preceding press release illustrates, all those assigned to the position of PIO will be forced to go back to the basics as they begin writing **news releases**, Web site content, and promotional material for their agencies.

This chapter will review the basics of English grammar and discuss standard techniques used in writing news releases.

KEY TERMS

Adjectives, p. 65
Adverbs, p. 65
Body, p. 71
Close, p. 71
Embargo, p. 67
Fact sheets, p. 64
"Five W's and an H", p. 70
Inverted pyramid, p. 72
Lead, p. 72
Media advisory, p. 61
News releases, p. 60
Noun, p. 65
Predicate, p. 65
Prepositions, p. 65
Pronouns, p. 65
Slug line, p. 68
Talking points, p. 64
Tense, p. 69
Verb, p. 65

The Purpose of News Releases

Writing news releases can take up much of the PIO's time. News releases have many purposes including simultaneously informing the media. A modification of a standard news release, called a **media advisory**, is often written and distributed to the media announcing a news conference or an event for the media to attend or perhaps promoting a new agency policy. On the other hand, when it comes to stating an agency's official position on an issue, a news release might be the best solution. When reporters make mistakes, or information released by the PIO is in error, a written new release can help clarify the situation while at the same time making corrections. Sometimes a news release is an excuse, written to explain an action of an individual or agency.

When the agency has specific programs it needs to promote, a news release can be a viable option, allowing for a more detailed explanation of the project, the benefits to the community, and an outline of how the programs will work.

People are an important component of any agency; therefore, announcing significant staff changes can bring welcome recognition to an employee for a job well done. These announcements are often made using news releases, or a combination of media advisories and more formal new releases that will be issued at the event. These releases can provide specific details about the person being promoted or honored.

News releases are written to get a message across to the PIO's constituents. News releases are not written to fill the pages of a newspaper, to put on Web sites, or for news broadcasts. However, many news releases

Box 4-1 Sample Media Advisory

American County Office of Emergency Management

FOR IMMEDIATE RELEASE

CONTACT: Your Name
Public Information Officer
315-555-1212

MEDIA ADVISORY

WHO: Emergency Management
WHAT: Emergency Road Closures
WHEN: Immediately until further notice, 7:28 P.M.
WHERE: I-111 North and South between Brighton and Court, and Adams St between Crouse and Townsend
WHY: Tank Truck Rollover

are cited exactly the way they are turned in to the media outlet. A good writing technique using proper grammar and proper style will improve the chance that your story is picked up by the media.

Proactive media relations are a must for a PIO. News releases can keep the media informed about your agency's activities. This information may move the press toward using your agency as an expert source for other stories.

ON TARGET "The content of a news release is as important as proper writing style. Better content coupled with proper style will make your news release more interesting to an assignment editor."

Because press releases can be rapidly distributed to many newsrooms nearly simultaneously, a PIO is able to get the message to a wide audience, allowing better contact with various constituencies.

Determining what subject warrants a news release is a challenge faced by public relations professionals daily. Those who look at a public safety agency from the outside may see interesting happenings that those inside the agency do not believe are interesting. The PIO must act like an outside reviewer, as well as encouraging others within the agency to think about unique topics that would make good news releases.

An EMS agency might take delivery of new spine boards for use on its ambulances. The PIO should ask, "What is different about these boards?" Perhaps there is a unique color aimed at calming patients, a specific scientific approach for using the boards, or a special grant used to purchase much needed equipment. A standard backboard purchase now becomes a newsworthy event.

Pros and Cons of News Releases

As popular as news releases are with some PIOs, others will tell you that they do not like to use them. Reasons vary, but often boil down to a lack of understanding of proper writing style. Another reason news releases get bad reviews is that some news media outlets do not like them.

Releases are often too structured. Some organizations use new releases as the only method of communicating with the press. These organizations frustrate the media by limiting opportunities for clarification of the information in the release.

Traditional news releases have no visual appeal, since they are simply words on paper. Today's media crave visuals to enhance stories. Videos and high-resolution photographs can be offered along with news releases. Often, in a Joint Information Center established after a disaster, a broadcast operations division will develop video, audio, and still photography for release to the media.

News releases can promote events that are visual in nature. New equipment, families saved by rescuers, or structures that withstood a natural disaster are examples of subjects for which events could be staged.

While news releases are disliked because they are often rigid, the fact that they are rigid brings uniformity and clarity to a statement. The uniformity also allows a PIO to provide information to the media in a fair, simultaneous manner and maintain greater control over the information being released.

Throughout this text, the PIO is encouraged to be proactive in working with the media. News releases are a simple way to maintain proactivity, while allowing a PIO to target distribution of the information to specific audiences.

Finally, a news release provides the PIO with a hard-copy record of statements issued to the media. This may be needed during court cases or when reviewing incident responses, while managers determine the timeliness and accuracy of emergency public information.

Alternatives to News Releases

The PIO has alternatives and enhancements that he or she can make to a standard news release. Provided that the PIO has access to the proper equipment, recording news releases or components attached to news releases can provide a PIO with the edge necessary for a media outlet to pick up the story idea. These recordings can take the shape of video, audio, or telephone releases.

Modern computers allow the PIO to create video and audio segments that can make up the entire release, or parts of the release, thus enhancing certain aspects of the written release. These computer programs require moderate skills, and a PIO might benefit from courses on these programs offered through local colleges or technical schools.

Perhaps one of the easiest ways to use recorded material is on your agency's telephone system. This system may allow you to record new releases for use when customers are "on hold." The system may be used to place certain emergency public information messages on your phone recording. Reporters who call looking for information can retrieve these messages. It is a fast way to disseminate emergency public information when the demands and requests from the media overwhelm your ability to answer individual questions.

While a PIO will write many news releases, there will also be occasions when the PIO will need to write speeches or testimony to be given before legislative bodies; the agency CEO may be the person giving the speech or testimony. This style of writing is very different from that of writing news releases, and this text will not focus on that style. A PIO can obtain education related to writing in these genres through local colleges.

The speech or testimony text is often released to the media at the same time it is being given to the designated audience, or shortly before.

If the material is released before the live presentation, the PIO must know the terms of the presentation, as some venues do not allow for the pre-release of material. If material pre-release is approved, then the PIO should prepare **fact sheets** about the document. Fact sheets are bullet point documents outlining main points of discussion on a specific topic.

If the CEO of your agency is testifying before a state legislative body promoting an increase in funding for a project, the speech may be long. It may include statistics, citations of studies, experiential anecdotes, and even a history of the agency. While this document may be released to the news media, the media will have several questions relating to it. A fact sheet can be included with the large document, highlighting the previous use of government funding for similar projects and the positive results of those projects. **Talking points**, on the other hand, are statements for use by personnel assigned to answer media questions. These talking points emphasize the key messages in the speech such as "The agency has derived significant benefits from this funding, and more importantly, the citizens have benefited in receiving more effective service from our agency."

ON TARGET "When speeches are released to the media, fact sheets should accompany the release and talking points should be provided to agency media spokespersons."

Another alternative to using news releases is to utilize documents containing specific information and data sheets. These are sometimes developed in the form of brochures for distribution to a wide audience or as one page handouts included in media packets. Caution should be taken when presenting statistics. The PIO should be sure that there is a solid explanation of the statistics to avoid misinterpretation, or more correctly stated, reinterpretation of those statistics.

To avoid writing news releases, a PIO may use phone or in-person contact with the media to promote story ideas. It is a good idea to follow up news releases with phone calls. Interviews often result from the distribution of news releases, but many PIOs are best at selling stories with personal contacts. These personal contacts are more time consuming and may not result in any more interviews. This book tackles interview techniques in Chapter Three.

News Release Topics

News release topics are limited only by your imagination. Topics will vary, depending on the audience you are attempting to reach. A story about business continuity planning may sell well to a business newspaper, while a story about a new piece of public safety equipment may best sell to the mainstream media.

Typical topics addressed by PIOs include traffic crashes, criminal activity, fires, multivictim incidents, a crisis, emergency public information, prevention programs, and community relations programs.

Whatever the topic, there should be some "hook" that makes it stand out. Just because a topic is interesting to you as the PIO doesn't mean it is interesting to a news audience. However, the contrary is also true. Something that seems mundane to a PIO may be interesting to a news audience.

Regardless of the topic, the PIO must obtain all the facts prior to writing the release. Releases should be proofed for style and accuracy and should be approved by the proper authorities prior to their release to the media.

Basics of Writing English for the PIO

Contributing author Jerry Payne, Deputy Chief, Liverpool Volunteer Fire Department, Liverpool, NY

The English language is one of the most difficult languages to learn, mainly due to the numerous "exceptions to the rule." In fact, people just learning to read, write, or speak the language may believe there really are no rules because there are so many exceptions to them. In addition, with advanced technology, many slang or abbreviated words and phrases are used so frequently that the true meaning of the word is lost.

When writing official documents, it is important to utilize proper grammar, spelling, and punctuation. Computer software that checks for all of these properties cannot always be relied on to accurately portray your message. An example is the last sentence:

Computer software that checks for all of these properties cannot always be relied on to accurately portray your message.

The software program sees that there is an "s" on the word "checks" and assumes that the noun "computer software" is singular and therefore suggests to the writer that "portray" should be "portrays." This is what the software suggests:

Computer software that checks for all of these properties cannot always be relied on to accurately ***portrays*** *your message.*

Computer software will only check for words. It would find no mistakes with the sentence, *"Computer software cheeks four spilling errors."*

Therefore, it is important to have a basic understanding of proper English and how to write it.

A proper sentence must consist of at least a **noun** and a **predicate**. The noun is a person, place, thing, or idea, which may or may not be specifically referenced in the sentence, and a predicate is the action word or phrase that tells the rest of the story about the noun. It can be as simple as a **verb**, or it may be much more complex.

Other important parts of sentences include **adjectives**, **adverbs**, **prepositions**, **pronouns**, and verbs. Although you do not need to be an English major to write complete sentences and paragraphs, it is important to understand how and why each of these is used.

Adjectives are descriptive words. They help give the reader a better understanding of the noun. An adjective may be as simple as the word "a," "an," or "the" or more elaborate, such as "blue", "rotten", or "beautiful."

Adverbs generally answer the question, "How?" They modify the action word to give a bit more description. For example, a sentence could be written that says, "The firefighters extinguished the blaze." This sentence certainly gets the message across, but by adding an adverb, the reader finds out a bit more about the action. "The firefighters quickly extinguished the blaze." "Quickly" is the adverb that modifies "extinguished." Many times, adverbs will end in "-ly."

A preposition describes a relationship between two words or phrases in a sentence. Many times, the preposition will not have much meaning without the other words to compare it with. Consider, for example, the sentence "There was a struggle between the police and the bank robber." The preposition "between" gives the reader an understanding of the relationship between the two nouns, the *bank robber* and the *police*. Many words can be used as prepositions, but there are 44 common such words, as shown in Box 4-2.

The most important thing to remember about prepositions is not to have one at the end of a sentence. An example of what not to do: "It was a hot dog of which they were fighting about." Generally, if you take the time to read or listen to what is written, a sentence that ends with a preposition sounds confusing and does not always make sense.

Pronouns are replacements or substitutes for nouns. It is important to make a correlation between the noun and pronoun when writing, so that the reader has the proper understanding of the meaning of the sentence. Examples of pronouns are "he," "they," and "we." If the pronoun is not clearly defined in the sentence or previous sentences, the sentence may not make sense, and the reader may become confused.

Box 4-2 Common Words Used as Prepositions

about	below	except	off	to
above	beneath	for	on	toward
across	beside	from	out	under
after	besides	in	outside	until
against	between	inside	over	up
around	beyond	into	since	upon
at	by	like	through	with
before	down	near	throughout	without
behind	during	of	till	

In the sentence "They say that too much rain will cause widespread flooding," the word "they" is the pronoun. However, nowhere is the word "they" clearly defined, so the reader may wonder who says that too much rain will cause flooding. Is it someone with expertise and authority, is it the local citizens who have experienced too much rain before, or is the author just giving an opinion and hiding it behind a pronoun?

Writing can be an extremely challenging job. There are numerous rules to follow and many more exceptions to the rules. Keeping the wording simple and following some of the basic principles of sentences will help create easy-to-read, concise, and accurate documents every time.

Writing the News Release

When a police officer, emergency medical technician, or firefighter completes a report, there is a specific format to follow. The format could be a fill-in-the-blank style form, or it might be a narrative following certain guidelines prescribed by agency policy, law, and tradition. Likewise, news releases follow specific formats.

Distribute all news releases on official agency stationary or a form recognizable as an official document from the agency. When issuing news releases on disasters, FEMA typically places both the FEMA seal and the seal of the state in which the disaster has occurred as a method of identifying an official document.

The format style should have equal margins, generally at least one-half inch, on all sides. If the document is to be faxed, this is particularly important, as some fax machines cannot interpret information outside of certain margins. Prepare releases using both upper and lowercase letters in a standard type style such as Times New Roman 12 point. Smaller type can be used if necessary, but should not go below 10 point, as this may be difficult to read on a faxed copy.

At the top of the release, you should place information about the timing of the release. This might be worded "for immediate release," "**embargo**" until 5:00 P.M.," or "for distribution at news conference." The term embargo tells the news editors receiving your release that it can't be used until a certain time. You should use this sparingly and only if you want to give the media time to prepare stories about this release, prior to official publication. Frequently, medical organizations use this technique when announcing the results of studies. Embargoed releases also can herald a major personnel change, such as appointment of a new fire chief or other leadership figure.

Releases should contain at least one contact person, along with a phone number where the contact person can be reached at any time.

This is usually the main phone number of the PIO. Other contact numbers may be used as well; however, the PIO is responsible for alerting and receiving approval for use by those listed.

Each release will include a working title, often called a **slug line**. This will alert the reader to the topic being presented. It is rarely used as the headline by the news agency picking up the story; rather, it serves to alert them to the content.

These simple news release components start the process for a PIO's news release to be recognized by a media outlet. The editor assigned to review incoming releases will first note that the release is from an official agency, then decide whether the subject is of interest for that news day, and, finally, allow for a phone call to set up an interview. The remaining content of the release provides additional background for the editor or reporter assigned the story.

Releases should be kept to one page if possible. When a release is longer than one page, print the word MORE in capital letters at the bottom of the page. The top of the second page should contain the slug line and page number in a format such as "2-2-2-2-2." Pages should be broken at paragraphs.

Writing Style

For some, the news release writing style is a difficult one to master. There are some basics to observe, including keeping the sentences short with only one thought or piece of information per paragraph. Short sentences are simple to write and easy to understand. Using more periods than commas prevents the reader from becoming confused about the thoughts being presented. (See Box 4-3.)

Box 4-3 Sample News Release

Disaster News

September 1, 2006
DR-OMNI-1-004
Hurricane Recovery News Desk
518-337-4107

Four shelters damaged by storm, others open;
Some roads beginning to be cleared;
State of Emergency remains in effect

Town of Americaville—Town of Americaville Supervisor Belltone reminds residents that a State of Emergency exists and only emergency travel is permitted. There is also a dawn-to-dusk curfew in effect.

Shelters in Village Lakes, the Edmund W. Miles Middle School at 501 Rte. 110 & North Drive, and Northeast Elementary, 420 Albany Avenue, were damaged during the storm, with people inside. Urban Search and Rescue Teams (USARs) are on scene assessing the situation and performing search and rescue.

The Shelters at William Rall Elementary School, 761 North Welwood Avenue, in Watervilla, and Woods Road Elementary at 110 Woods Road in North Americaville, NY, were both damaged and cannot be used.

Other shelters are open with limited food and water, and are located at the following addresses:

SHELTER NAME	ADDRESS
Belmont Elementary School	108 Barnum Street
Deer Park High School	30 Rockaway Avenue
Forest Avenue School	200 Forest Avenue
John F. Kennedy Elementary School	101 Lake Avenue
John Quincy Adams Primary School	172 Old Country Road
Lincoln School	300 Park Ave
Marion G. Vedder Elementary School	794 Deer Park Avenue
Martin Luther King Junior Elementary School	792 Mount Avenue
May Moore Primary School	239 Central Avenue
Milton L. Olive Middle School	140 Garden City Avenue
North Babylon High School	1 Phelps Lane
Parliament Place Elementary School	89–90 Parliament Place
Robert Frost Middle School	450 Half Hollow Road
Robert Moses Middle School	234 Phelps Lane
Santapoguc School	1130 Herzel Boulevard
Tooker Avenue School	855 Tooker Avenue
William E. DeLuca, Jr. Elementary School	223 Phelps Lane
Wyandanch Memorial High School	54 South 32nd Street

MORE MORE MORE MORE MORE

SHELTERS PAGE 2-2-2-2-2-2-2-2

Several roads are currently listed as open and passable:
Sunrise, open east–west; one lane open.
Southern State Highway east–west; one lane open.
County Routes 109 and 110 North–South; one lane open.

Most often, the **tense** of the news release is past, unless it is promoting an upcoming event. Examples include "The fire was extinguished" and "The agency will announce . . . ."

Although this has been stated before in this book, it is important for to you remember to avoid industry terminology and jargon. Times should be illustrated using standard civilian time. Instead of saying "2230 hrs", say 10:30 P.M. Likewise, dates should be written out in a standard month–day–year format, such as "January 13, 2007", and not abbreviated.

The main approach to writing a news release is commonly called the **inverted pyramid** style. (See Figure 4-1.) It focuses the most important information at the top of the release, with the less important information toward the bottom. Newspaper stories are written in this style, and you are encouraged to look at newspaper articles to learn more about that style of writing. You should be able to fully understand the important aspects of the story from the first few paragraphs, while realizing the last paragraphs could be left out of a story and not significantly affect the true meaning.

The first paragraph in an inverted pyramid is the **lead**. After editors reads the slug line, the editor proceeds to the lead; the lead should continue to attract the reader's attention.

The lead is generally 30 words or less and includes what journalists refer to as the **"five W's and an H"**: "who," "what," "when," "where," "why," and "how." "Who" refers to either who is making the announcement or who is the subject of the release. "What" describes what happened.

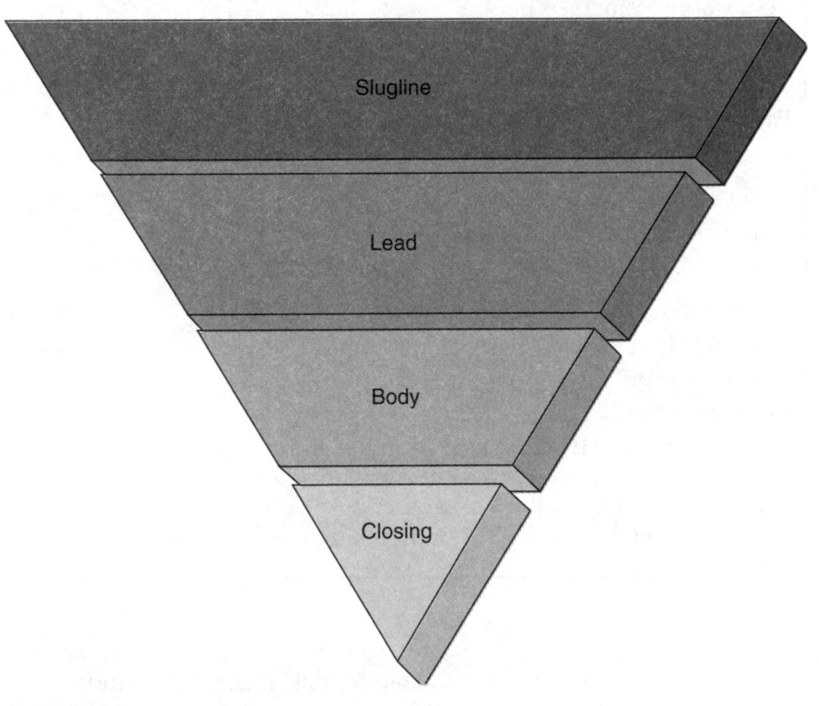

FIGURE 4-1
"Inverted Pyramid"

"When" refers to the time of the event and where the location. "Why" could be why the event is being scheduled or why the event happened in the first place. "How" provides more in-depth information about the incident.

There are several types of leads which PIOs can use when writing releases. Your writing style should include all these, realizing some are more appropriate for certain releases than others. The types of leads include:

- the question lead,—"Did you ever wonder why bottled water is part of an emergency kit?"
- the direct quotation lead,—"Emergency Manager John Doe says 'storm damage could exceed 100 millon dollars.'"
- the comparison lead—"Unlike last winter, this year's heavy snow has Emergency Management personnel concerned about serious flooding."
- the descriptive, or picture, lead—"As the wind blew apart their homes, many area residents were well prepared for this week's devastating wind storm."
- the direct-address lead—"Twelve people are homeless today after a predawn fire in a multistory apartment complex."
- the declarative lead—"Three people died when their car collided with a bridge abutment."

Knowing when to use a certain type of lead will improve the PIO's chances for positive stories to be written. The declarative lead would be more suited to your release than a question lead if it was about a crash or other disaster; for example, "Can you guess who died in a crash today?" should be stated as a sentence rather than as a question.

The **body** of a news release will contain the bulk of information. This information will include any of the "5 W's and the H" not already covered in the lead.

PIOs are cautioned to avoid placing any material in releases not authorized for publication.

End the release with the **close**. This might include additional quotes, but most often is a standard statement used by an agency, such as "The Liberty County Office of Emergency Management leads programs and has developed policies governing disaster response and recovery activities in Liberty County and associated towns and villages."

There should be a "-30-", "###" or "END" to indicate the end of the release. The "-30-" is a symbol recognized by the old teletype machines as an end point of a news story.

Tips for Writing Releases

Write as if you are telling someone the story. Use a tape recorder or voice recognition software contained in modern word-processing programs to record your thoughts.

Before you begin writing the release, ask yourself, "Who cares about this and why?" This will allow you to concentrate on the message in the most effective direction. Finally, distribute the release to the media outlets most appropriate for the audience.

There is no substitute for being prepared to write your release. Learn the subject by researching it. Read past press releases, newspaper stories, and trade journals. Ask questions of those in the agency and the industry who are well suited to answering questions about the issue.

Once the research is completed, start writing. Many find it best to begin writing and continue as ideas flow. You can correct and reorganize ideas later. When you think you've placed your thoughts in the correct inverted pyramid order, print a rough draft. This should be double-spaced with wide margins so that corrections and notes can be easily placed.

Be completely brutal with your first draft; nothing should satisfy you. You can delete, substitute, rearrange, and insert new material. Check the release for the use of jargon. Make sure that your grammar is proper and that the spelling is correct. Have the release proofed by a trusted friend or colleague. One way to determine whether the release makes sense is to read it aloud. You can hear things more easily than you can see them.

Before you begin rewriting the release, put it aside for a while. When you get back to writing, you will have a fresh perspective. Play the "devil's advocate" and look at the release from an opposing view. This will help you determine whether there is anything open for misinterpretation or that can be misrepresented by the release.

Check for any final errors. Make sure that the phone numbers are correct—call them. Make sure that all of the Internet addresses work and that e-mail addresses are accurate. Verify street addresses and the spelling of names and titles for accuracy. Reread the release just prior to its dissemination, and evaluate it for any last-minute changes.

Distributing News Releases

Several methods, including regular mail, e-mail, and fax, can be used to distribute news releases. Some releases are hand delivered to newsrooms or reporters at a scene or at news conferences.

During major emergencies and disasters, news releases are posted on situation boards or at the Joint Information Center for all to see.

Many times, news releases are uploaded to Web sites for Internet viewing. Commercial distribution services can also be used for news release distribution.

Summary

This chapter has taken you through the aspects of news release writing, including a review of the basics of writing English. We have identified the components of a sentence, reviewed several reasons for writing press releases, and described the style used when writing releases.

The news release is an important tool in the PIO's repertoire. He or she must master the skill of writing releases that can play a vital role in successfully delivering key messages to the intended audience.

REVIEW QUESTIONS

1. Sentences are composed of two parts.
   - **a.** Predicate and antecate
   - **b.** Noun and verb
   - **c.** Noun and predicate
   - **d.** Purpose and action
2. The inverted pyramid style of writing places the most important information last and leads up to it with minor details.
   - **a.** This entices the reader to go deeper into the release to find the true meaning
   - **b.** This is an incorrect statement
   - **c.** This style is preferred by news departments because editors will have to read the entire news release in order to get the meaning of it.
   - **d.** Both A and C
3. A media advisory is a form of a news release
   - **a.** that provides only basic information
   - **b.** that is often used to announce a media event
   - **c.** that is written in a format of who, what, when, where, why, and how
   - **d.** all of the above

ENDNOTES

1. http://www.apstylebook.com/

CHAPTER 5

Critical Incident Stress and The Public Information Officer

By Dr. Marley Barduhn

Objectives

- Describe the human stress response
- Understand critical incident stress as it relates to the field of the public information officer
- Compare post-traumatic stress incidence in samples of traumatized individuals
- Identify the standard of care for those involved in critical incidents
- Know the components of comprehensive critical incident stress management
- Describe the seven phases of critical incident stress debriefing
- Understand the controversy surrounding critical incident stress debriefing, including a review of evidence and best practices
- List major signs/symptoms of post-traumatic stress disorder
- Explain health promotion strategies for the public information officer

CASE Study

Derek Smith is working as a PIO for a fast-paced commercial ambulance company in a medium-size city. One of his company's ambulances has just been involved in a collision with a pedestrian as it was responding to an emergency call. The pedestrian was a 6-year-old girl, who darted out between two parked cars. He quickly responds to the chaotic emergency scene, witnesses the lifeless child's body being draped with a white sheet, and hears the anguished cry of a mother crying out for her child. He sees the angry and shocked crowd that has gathered. The police have cordoned off the perimeter, and the distraught paramedics are packing up their equipment after pronouncing the child dead. Reporters and photographers strain to get a picture of this scene for the evening news. The ambulance crew returns to quarters, and Derek is flooded with calls for information about the accident, the status of the child, and the involved crew as he begins to write his press release.

Case Study Questions:

1. Would this situation qualify as a "critical incident"? Why/why not?
2. What factors should be taken into consideration when Derek writes his press release?
3. What would be the general standard of care for the ambulance crew?
4. What signs/symptoms of critical incident stress are evident in the case study?
5. What critical-incident stress management services should be available to the PIO, if any?

Introduction

The frontline work of the PIO makes stress a daily part of the job, as PIOs rush to meet media deadlines and provide up-to-the-minute press releases. But beyond the routine aspects of the daily job lies a potentially career-stopping phenomenon: critical incident stress. Recognizing unusual events as being critical incidents and knowing how to effectively manage them is a key component of career longevity as a PIO.

The purpose of this chapter is to describe the normal human response to stress, including both the physical and emotional components.

Critical incidents, as they relate to the field of the PIO, will be defined. A management plan for critical incidents will be explained, including **critical incident stress debriefing (CISD)** as well as the general **standard of care** for the industry. Current controversy surrounding CISD will be described along with a summary of best practices. Finally, **health promotion** practices to assist PIOs in staying fit and healthy on and off the job will be provided.

KEY TERMS

Adrenalin, p. 69
Comprehensive critical incident stress management, p. 75
Confidentiality, p. 78
Conflicting research, p. 80
Cortisol, p. 69
Critical incidents, p. 69
Critical incident stress debriefing (CISD), p. 69
DART Center for Journalism and Trauma, p. 78
Distress, p. 69
Diuretic, p. 82
Eustress, p. 69
Health promotion, p. 69
Human stress response, p. 69
International Critical Incident Stress Foundation (ICISF), p. 75
Post-traumatic stress, p. 73
Standard of care, p. 69
Stressors, p. 69

Human Stress Response

All of us experience stress in daily living. The **human stress response** was first recognized by Dr. Hans Selye, a Hungarian-born Canadian physician who is generally thought of as the "father of stress" for having described a predictable physical sequence of events to various threats, or **stressors**. Stressors may be people, events, or objects that initiate the human stress response. They may be viewed as positive (termed **eustress**), such as getting married, or negatively, such as encountering a growling bear (termed **distress**). For example, fear of public speaking is a stressor for many people, and just the thought of it can initiate the stress response for some.

ON TARGET

"Regardless of what initiates the human stress response and whether it is perceived as positive or negative, the sequence of three-stage reactions is the same in all humans."

The first stage of the stress response is fairly recognizable to most people: sweaty palms, a racing heart, and increased breathing. Selye described this stage as the "alarm stage," whereby certain hormones, such as **adrenalin** and **cortisol**, are poured into the general blood circulation, preparing the person to "fight or flight." Some people experience a mild "rush" as these hormones are internally released into the blood.

The purpose of this alarm is to alert the person to imminent danger and assist the person in saving his or her life, if need be. Blood is shunted away from the trunk of the body to the arms and legs, to assist in running away from the stressor. Water is released through perspiration and increased urination. Stored energy is released from the liver. In earlier times, the physical threat of danger predominated, while today more stressors are emotional in nature. The alarm stage can be as little as a few seconds of time or extend for hours or days if the stressor is prolonged.

In the second stage, sometimes called the resistance or the adaptation stage, the body mobilizes its resources to assist in normalizing or adapting as part of the stress response. Vitamins (particularly water-soluble vitamins such as Vitamin B complex and Vitamin C), minerals, and other hormones are released, and every attempt is made to restore balance to the person. Adaptation can take as little as several minutes, or several hours or days, depending on the severity and intensity of the stressor.

The last stage of the human stress response is the resolution stage, whereby the stress response is reduced as the body returns to its pre-stress levels. Energy is once again stored back in the liver; vitamin, mineral, and hormone levels are replenished; and internal balance is restored. Once the stress response has been initiated, it may minimally take up to 48 hours for normal levels of these body chemicals to be restored. If, however, the stressor continues and is severe, this third stage may be termed the exhaustion stage. Eventually the person can suffer serious physical impairment or even die from prolonged stress because the affected organ or body would be unable to recover. Selye was the first person to make the connection between stress and disease.

What Selye described has huge implications for working in the emotionally charged atmosphere of the PIO. It may be difficult to interview traumatized individuals following a critical incident. Some people may be so horrified by the events they have witnessed that they simply cannot speak. Others may have difficulty recalling or remembering certain aspects of the event. Some may be so enraged they are incoherent. They may be physically incapable of being interviewed, particularly if they are in the early portion of the adaptation stage. Figure 5-1 lists the wide range of human stress responses that may be seen with interviewees.

If PIOs have been directly exposed to a stressful situation, it may be difficult for them to concentrate and focus on details while their body is still reacting to particular stressors. Sometimes, even secondary exposure, such as reading and writing about a critical incident can initiate the stress response. A good example of this is emergency dispatchers, who are not at the emergency scene, but who experience it vicariously through radio communications. Photo or video journalists are sometimes

Clinical Sign	Physical Effects/Symptoms Reported
Pulse and blood pressure increase	Heart felt like it was racing; felt like my heart was in my throat.
Breathing rate increases	Couldn't catch my breath.
Circulation shunted away from trunk	Felt nauseated (occasionally vomit).
Pupils dilate	Widened pupils to increase vision and take it all in.
Adrenalin (epinephrine) released	Started shaking; felt myself break out in a cold sweat. Heightened senses: sound, smell, vision, touch.
Enlargement of adrenal glands	Muscle tension in back, neck, felt achy.
Cortisol released	Increased craving for carbohydrate.
Carbohydrate craving	Depletes vitamin stores. Sugar uses B complex vitamins to metabolize the carbohydrate.
Atrophy of lymph glands	White blood cells measurably decrease; reduced function of the lymphatic system, increasing susceptibility to disease. Decreased immune function causes decreased function of B-complex vitamins, which assist the brain. Body demands more Vitamin C. Usual recommended daily dose is 60 mg; Under stress, 200 mg is needed.
Stored energy is released from liver	Dramatic rise in blood sugar. Repeated fluctuations of blood sugar leads to pronounced fatigue, headaches, and general irritability.
Vitamin depletion	Leads to increased fatigue, anxiety, and irritability.
Mineral depletion	Minerals such as zinc, copper, iron, magnesium, and chromium become depleted; they help the immune system function.

FIGURE 5-1
Human Stress Response Chart

affected by the pictures they take of an incident; just because they are behind the camera doesn't make them immune from the effects of the situation.

There is no life without stress, and eustress, or "good stress," may be a motivator for us to encounter new and more challenging aspects of life. It may serve a function to prepare us to deal with the more negative stress, called "distress". Prolonged distress, however, may have serious health implications for people who experience repeated and chronic exposure and may lead to compromised health or, in extreme cases, death.

Critical Incident Stress

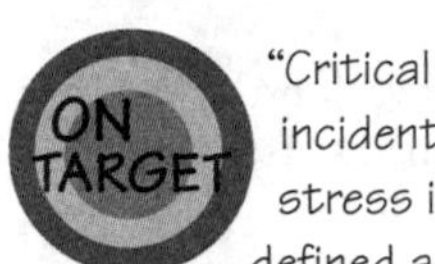

"Critical incident stress is defined as 'the type of stress associated with direct exposure to a severe situational crisis . . . and is a normal response of healthy, normal people to an abnormal event.'"[1]

Critical incident stress is the "strain on the human body resulting from a specific event which shocks, stuns and horrifies"[2]. Critical incident stress includes cognitive, physical, emotional, and behavioral effects of the normal human stress response. Critical incidents are unusual in the sense they are rare, out-of-the-ordinary events or situations.

Coined by Mitchell and Everly, the term "critical incident"[3] was first used with emergency medical services and firefighters and included events such as the death or serious injury of a child; death or serious injury of a coworker; events with unusual media exposure, mass casualty incidents; situations in which prolonged rescue attempts have failed; workplace violence; perceived threats to the emergency worker's life, such as contact with life-threatening illness; and events in which the victims are known to the emergency worker or resemble loved ones. As this term has evolved since the 1980s, its definition has expanded to include involvement with virtually any traumatic situation, such as a sexual assault or a motor vehicle accident. The term "critical incident" now includes a community focus as well, such as natural and human-made disasters (e.g., tsunamis, floods, tornados, and terrorist attacks).

The precursor to the term "critical incident stress" was the term "shell shock," which was noted as early as World War I, describing psychological casualties in military responses to war zones. Lindeman's seminal work on the famous Coconut Grove fire, in which over 400 people in a nightclub died when it caught on fire, focused on severe loss and grief reactions in survivors.[4]

Many times, particularly in the disaster situation where the emergency effort spans days and weeks, the signs of critical incident stress do not immediately appear. Studies reported by Mitchell indicate that while emergency workers are on duty, they maintain an intense focus on the job, and it's only when they are not in their professional role any longer that their bodies go off "auto pilot" and the symptoms first appear.[5]

Most people who experience critical incident stress, while deeply disturbed at the time of the incident, progress with varying degrees of recovery without treatment to a sense of normalcy within a month or so. Some percentage, however, will go on to develop more serious disorders, depending on the amount and severity of trauma exposure, crisis intervention services rendered, and their own predisposition. Early intervention with critical incident stress may be able to prevent or mitigate

Table 5-1 Signs and Symptoms of Critical Incident Stress

COGNITIVE	Difficulty concentrating and making decisions; impaired thinking; inability to process complex thought; confusion; obsessional review of the incident; inability to stop thinking about the event; self-blame; easily startled; decreased self-confidence and self-esteem; preoccupation with the event.
EMOTIONAL	Irritability; shortness of temper; anger; fear of repetition of the event; anxiety and apprehension; rage; feelings of resentment, guilt and/or shame; depression and withdrawal; feelings of hopelessness, sadness, helplessness or isolation; feeling overwhelmed; lack of direction; emotional callousness or apathy; feeling "numb" or detached from life.
PHYSICAL	Feeling nauseous; trembling or shaking; heart palpitations; diarrhea; profuse sweating; loss of appetite, heartburn; feelings of exhaustion and fatigue, often not relieved by sleeping; nightmares and other sleep disturbances.
BEHAVIORAL	Inability to relax and needing to be physically active, e.g, pacing, restlessness. Fast speech; crying; increases in smoking and/or drinking; fatigue (sometimes extreme fatigue); appetite disturbances; loss of energy; social withdrawal or isolation; increased use of alcohol or other mind-altering substances; changes in typical behavior.

the development of more serious mental health issues such as **post-traumatic stress**.

Every time a PIO responds to a call or assignment, the potential exists for critical incident stress. Longevity on the job doesn't confer immunity, and some PIOs have carried the memories of such calls with them for a long time and endured much pain. Knowing about critical incident stress enables the PIO to recognize it when it occurs (see Table 5-1 for signs and symptoms of critical incident stress) and combat it with resources and assistance to minimize its effects on his/her professional life.

Knowing the critical incident stress response also enables the PIO to suspend judgment on those people being interviewed following traumatic incidents. The wide variation in individual response to a critical incident means that expectations of people behaving in "appropriate" ways may be faulty. Just because someone is not displaying a "usual" emotional reaction, does not mean they are not feeling significant pain and grief.

"It is important to keep in mind that discussing a traumatic event soon after exposure may have a detrimental effect on some traumatized individuals"[6] The timing of the interview, and the decision of whether or not to interview should be balanced against the potential for harm.

Post-Traumatic Stress Disorder

Post-traumatic stress disorder (PTSD) is a complex stress-related reaction to a critical incident whose signs/symptoms of stress continue beyond 4 to 6 weeks, and varies depending on the nature of the original trauma. Again, this was noted in World War I victims as "shell shock," and it is now widely recognized that PTSD can occur in virtually any traumatic situation, including sexual assault, rape, natural disasters—such as floods, hurricanes, tornados, tsunamis—as well as human-made disasters such as terrorist attacks and mass shootings. The incidence of PTSD in the general population is between 1 to 2%. With exposure to traumatic situations, that percentage significantly increases. However, research from mental health professionals indicates higher percentages when people have experienced a critical incident. Figure 5-2 depicts the percentage of various study samples of people with PTSD symptoms following exposure to critical incidents.

There is wide variation in the types of occupations affected by PTSD related to critical incident stress, along with a variation of less than 10% to greater than 50% of workers who are affected by PTSD.

There are three major groups of stress symptoms evident in PTSD:

- Intrusive thoughts/memories and recollections of the event in the form of persistent dreams/nightmares or flashbacks (daytime intrusive thoughts or memories of the event).

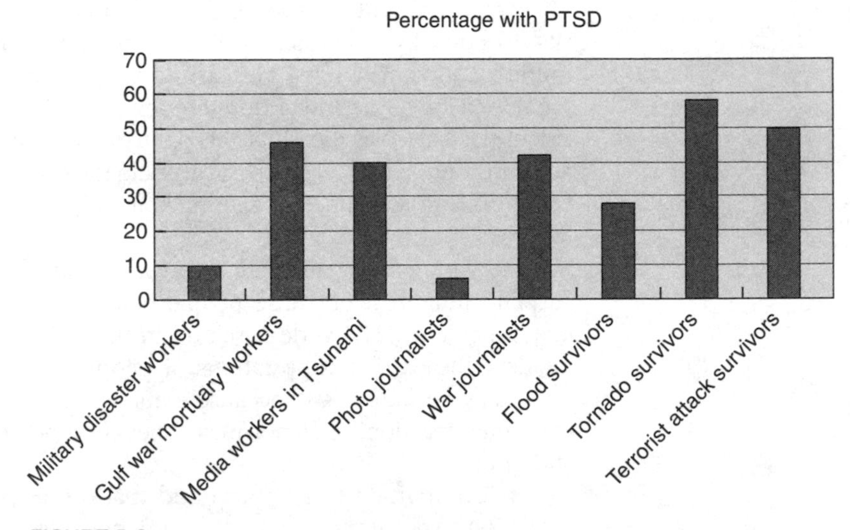

FIGURE 5-2
Percentage of PTSD in Various Samples of Individuals Associated with Critical Incidents

- Avoidance of, and withdrawal from, people, places, or things associated with the event, including depression and sadness.
- Nervous system arousal, such as being startled easily, sleep disturbances, irritability, and angry outbursts.

ON TARGET "Together with rescue workers, the media are often one of the earliest responders at any disaster site . . . they are not shielded from the sights, smells, and overwhelming emotions that surround them.[8] They are at risk of developing PTSD as an occupational hazard."

Research on the effects of critical incidents on the media is just beginning to emerge. A pilot study of the impact of the Asian tsunami on a group of Singaporean media workers in December, 2005 indicated that 40% of them reported PTSD symptoms.[7] Although their symptoms began during that disaster, many experienced long-term effects such as intrusive mental images of the sights, sounds, and smells of the disaster site, including the horror and grief of being exposed to large numbers of corpses and devastated grieving families. Many experienced the guilt and frustration of not being able to do more for the victims and felt overwhelmed at the extent of the devastation.

Mental health treatment for PTSD, such as psychotherapy, is generally effective in restoring balance to people's lives, yet is costly and time consuming; once PTSD is present, it is more difficult to resolve than if the symptoms were treated at an earlier time. The key is prevention and intervention in an earlier stage before symptoms become persistent and chronic. Workers with PTSD may become disabled and unable to function in their jobs. Workplace incidents, if inadequately addressed, may result in excessive employee turnover and attrition.

Comprehensive Critical Incident Stress Management

Comprehensive critical incident stress management is an integrated form of crisis intervention that includes a range of services and techniques provided to prevent or minimize the effects of critical incident stress. Workplaces which have written CISM plans in place usually have policies and protocols to follow in the event of a critical incident.

"CISM is a package of crisis intervention techniques that have been bundled together to achieve a maximal effect of reducing stress reactions and identifying people who need help and assisting those people in recovering from exposure to a traumatic event."[9]

Official standards and criteria for training in the field of critical incident stress management have been created by the non-profit **International Critical Incident Stress Foundation (ICISF)**, headquartered in Ellicott City, Maryland. Training for basic and advanced CISM, pastoral care, corporate crisis response, mass disasters/terrorism, and mental health clinicians' treatment for complex PTSD is organized through an international network of CISM courses. Founded in 1989,

Table 5-2 Key Components of Comprehensive Critical Incident Stress Management

Pre-incident Education	Orientation to critical incident stress, conducted primarily as part of general employee orientation in organizations where there are established policies and protocols for CISM. The goal is to introduce stress recognition and management concepts to plan ahead for critical incidents.
Defusing:	Brief intervention following a critical incident designed to quickly assess for presence/severity of symptoms to determine safety considerations for continuation with work and whether further intervention is necessary.
On-Scene Support Services:	On-scene assessment and intervention for individuals or groups involved with a critical incident. The focus is on presenting symptoms directly related to the unfolding incident.
Debriefing:	Planned intervention, usually occurring 24–72 hours following an incident. Conducted by trained peer support and mental health professionals for those involved with the critical incident.
Demobilization:	Brief form of crisis intervention provided at the time of shift disengagement, often with large-scale (e.g., multiple-casualty) incidents. The goal is to prepare personnel for the next 24 hours and to provide stress management education.
Individual one-to-one support:	Individual consultation and services with the goal of returning to normal function or referral for further services as needed.
Family and significant other CISM:	Crisis intervention services provided to families and significant others affected by their loved ones' critical incident. The focus is on education and support, as well as on emotional processing of the event.
Crisis Management Briefing:	Provided to corporations, businesses, schools, and community agencies following a critical incident. The focus is on consultation with management and planning for interventions at the worksite and appropriate follow-up.
Pastoral Support:	Provided by a clergy member and focused on providing spiritual support.
Follow-up/Referral:	Individual follow-up with affected individuals after crisis intervention. Individuals are referred to appropriate sources as needed if issues are not resolved.

ICISF has over 600 CISM teams worldwide and trains thousands of people annually. Mitchell states, "The primary focus of CISM is to support staff members of organizations or members of communities which have experienced a traumatic event."[10]

Critical incident stress management represents an entire range of services which can be tailored to individual worksite or community needs, depending on the type of critical incident at hand. As such, this represents state-of-the-art care for those groups at risk of developing the devastating effects of critical incidents (See Table 5-2 for a full listing of CISM services).

Critical Incident Stress Debriefing

ON TARGET "Critical incident stress management is an integrated system of crisis intervention for managing traumatic incidents and has been adopted by national and international disaster relief agencies, emergency medical services organizations, law enforcement, fire services and various branches of military service and other agencies throughout the world."

Critical incident stress debriefing (CISD) is a form of crisis intervention involving group sessions conducted by trained mental health professionals and peer debriefers. First introduced in 1974 by Mitchell and Everly, and named the "Mitchell Model," CISD was used primarily with homogenous groups of emergency services personnel such as paramedics, firefighters, and police officers who were involved with the same critical incident in their line of duty. (See Figure 5-3 depicting a CISD in progress.) Since then, CISDs have been used in many different settings with traumatized people, such as community disasters; hospitals;

FIGURE 5-3
Of CISD in Progress

banks; late-night convenience stores and pharmacies following robberies; psychiatric facilities following assault by patients; military installations; corporations following downsizing; and schools and colleges following mass shootings. A debriefing offers the opportunity to process and integrate the critical incident experience into their lives, putting the event into perspective. Debriefings are generally offered between 2 and 7 days after a critical incident.

Debriefings are not considered psychotherapy, but are a component of CISM and crisis intervention that allows for emotional ventilation and reconstructing the event with others who were part of the critical incident. No notes are taken and the proceedings are confidential. **Confidentiality** means that the group proceedings are not revealed outside the group. Confidentiality is essential for traumatized people to feel safe in the group environment and to ensure that individual statements will not be repeated outside the group setting. Ideally, trained peer debriefers are members of a group similar to the one being debriefed and, therefore, have credibility for understanding the nature of the work or occupation. Mental health professionals assist with the debriefing process and can identify individuals who might be at risk for development of PTSD or other mental health conditions.

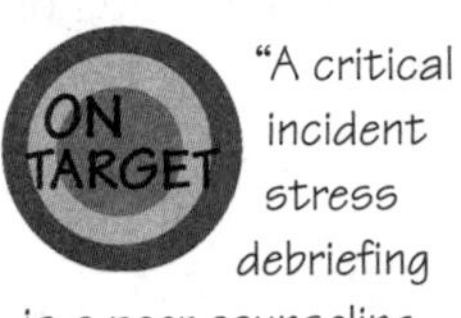

"A critical incident stress debriefing is a peer counseling group intervention with psychoeducational components designed for people who experienced the same event, or critical incident."

Standard of Care

With the proliferation of CISD teams, along with occupational policies and procedures for the provision of debriefings, a standard of care for the management of critical incidents has emerged. A standard of care represents the expected norm for routine services provided in the wake of a critical incident. Table 5-3 lists the seven steps or phases of a typical debriefing using the ICISF standards. The increase in the number of CISM teams and in the expectation of services has led to the elevation of CISM as the standard of care following traumatic incidents. Failing to provide such services will undoubtedly be viewed negatively by both the workers and the public at large and can be interpreted by employees as an uncaring act by their employers.

"CISD is a highly valued people management tool in organizations. . . . it is appreciated by both the traumatized and their managers. Doing nothing in response to a traumatic event is not an option for managers where expectations of appropriate post-trauma care are part of the implicit bargain between employers and employees . . ."[11].

Industry spends a great deal of effort to educate its workforce about physical dangers inherent in the job, yet relatively little time is spent on potential emotional dangers. Within the media industry, few organizations have standardized procedures for dealing with the aftermath of a traumatic incident. The **Dart Center for Journalism and Trauma**

Table 5-3 Phases of a Critical Incident Stress Debriefing

Phase	General process
Introduction	Ground rules are reviewed, such as speaking for oneself; not interrupting others, turning off electronic devices. Confidentiality of proceedings is emphasized. Participants are informed that this is not psychotherapy. Goals of the process are introduced.
Fact	Participants are asked to introduce themselves by first name and briefly describe their role in the incident. Descriptions of the event and the associated sights, sounds, and smells are encouraged. The factual base of events and the time sequence are established.
Thought	Participants are asked to describe their first thoughts of the event.
Reaction	Participants are asked about their own emotional reactions to the event, and their reaction, both at the time of the event and now.
Symptoms	Participants are asked about their symptoms. Expression of common reactions of others is encouraged and leads to a shared experience among the group. Leads to a transition back to a more cognitive level.
Teaching	The CISD team uses the information presented during the course of the debriefing to explain why these symptoms occur and what can be done to address a person's concerns. Normal reactions to abnormal events are emphasized, along with resiliency and coping methods.
Reentry	Brings the debriefing to a close and summarizes results, reminding participants about confidentiality. Closing statements from participants and the CISD team are elicited. Reassurance and hope are provided, and information about available resources is described.

(2003) surveyed photographers and found that only 11% had been warned by employers about the emotional effects of the job, while 34% had been warned of physical dangers and only 25% of the employers provided counseling to employees. Critical incident stress management should be the standard of care for media organizations.

Al Tompkins of the Poynter Center for Media Studies wrote the following for poynter.org on September 14, 2001:[12]

> *Reporters, photojournalists, engineers, soundmen, and field producers often work elbow to elbow with emergency workers. Journalists' symptoms of traumatic stress are remarkably similar to those of police officers and firefighters who work in the immediate aftermath of tragedy,*

"All organizations that have personnel, including the media, need to be aware of critical incident stress and its effect on employees, and need to both prepare them well for this aspect of their job and provide an industry standard of care in the aftermath of a critical incident."

yet journalists typically receive little support after they file their stories. While public safety workers are offered debriefings and counseling after a trauma, journalists are merely assigned another story.[13]

Clearly, then, media organizations can no longer afford to ignore this important aspect of employee health following traumatic incidents. In addition, corporations that employ PIOs should include them as part of a debriefing when they are involved with critical incidents. Sometimes, however, PIOs are "on duty" writing press releases or speaking with the media while defusings and other crisis intervention services are being conducted. If that is the case, then one-on-one services should be offered.

Controversies Surrounding Critical Incident Stress Debriefing

Critical incident stress debriefing has come under criticism in recent years. What follows is a summary of the major **conflicting research**, as well as the best practices in the field.

Critics of CISD have sometimes confused this seven-step, small-group traumatic stress processing technique with the more comprehensive CISM. CISD is but one of many crisis intervention tools employed under the larger CISM umbrella. Some critics have incorrectly studied the individual debriefing model (the Mitchell Model) and declared it ineffective. But that model is based on group support and intervention with CISD and was not intended for use with individuals. Timing appears to be a growing area of concern among researchers, since the timing of data gathering has not been systematically controlled in conducting these studies. Debriefing is also a general term, one never intended for use with individuals. The Mitchell Model is used in this chapter as the clinical standard group crisis intervention technique, but several other forms of debriefings have also been evaluated. Critics also contend that CISD is harmful, yet the evidence for this claim is weak and likely based on nonequivalent groups under investigation or inappropriate interventions or outcome measures.[14] One of the outspoken critics of CISM is Dr. Bryan Bledsoe, who has frequently written articles condemning CISM in the *Journal of Emergency Medical Services* (http://www.jems.com/newsandarticles/columns/Bledsoe/KillingVampires.htm). However, studies cited by Dr. Bledsoe that have found CISM harmful have not employed standardized CISM training and implementation protocols. A full review of the debate may be found at http://www.icisf.org/articles. Dr. Jeffrey Mitchell's article "Crisis Intervention and Critical Incident Stress Management: A Defense of the Field" documents a thorough review of CISM critics' studies, as well as the abundance of support for comprehensive CISM strategies. Dr.

Mitchell states, "There has never been a study that indicates that harm has been done by any CISM service if the following two conditions are present:

- Personnel have been properly trained in CISM, and
- Providers are adhering to well publicized and internationally accepted standards of CISM practice." (p. 43)

With the evolution of CISM over the past three decades, it is inevitable that controversy and calls for clinical validation have occurred. Increasing numbers of studies have found beneficial effects of CISD[15] in reducing symptoms of critical incident stress. The effectiveness of CISD and its value to participants are well documented. Best practices for the field recommend the use of comprehensive CISM as a total package of crisis intervention services aimed at mitigating the effects of critical incident stress if used with the criteria, training, and standards of the ICISF. However, caution must exercised, because CISM is not intended to replace psychotherapy and it has not been solidly determined to prevent PTSD. Even with the full range of CISM services, there are likely to be individuals who will require a higher level of mental health care to fully recover from the effects of critical incident stress.

Health Promotion for the PIO

Staying healthy is a key part of having a happy and productive work life. Health promotion includes all those activities or strategies that are designed to maintain or improve one's health:

- Maintain optimal weight
- Eat a healthy diet
- Engage in regular aerobic and strength exercise
- Refrain from smoking or using tobacco products
- Limit alcohol and caffeine consumption
- Create a balance between work and the rest of your life
- Get sufficient sleep
- Limit the effects of stress

"Health promotion provides the strategies to achieve optimal health and wellness."

As a nation, we are healthier now and have achieved the longest life span of any generation in history, yet the very modern world we live in endangers our health in many ways through sedentary lifestyle, poor diet, and the effects of stress. It now takes committed personal action to create and sustain a healthy lifestyle in the face of everyday time constraints.

Stress and Health

When faced with stressful events, the human stress response, which was previously discussed in this chapter, is activated. As the stress hormones of adrenalin and cortisol are released into the body, there are predictable physiological effects. To help your body deal with the effects of stress,

- Drink fluids without caffeine. [Caffeine is a **diuretic** that pulls water (and, with it, Vitamin C and B-complex) out of the body.]
- Eat lightly, but well, and avoid large amounts of sugar and fat, since these may leave you feeling thirsty, nauseated, and uncomfortable.
- If you are a smoker, limit smoking. (Smoking during stress is particularly harmful to the body, since nicotine is also a diuretic. Many smokers are unaware that smoking uses up about 50% of the body's Vitamin C, in daily nonstressful activities. The recommended daily allowance of Vitamin C for nonsmokers is 60 mg; in stressful situations, it approaches 200 mg per day. Pair smoking with increased stress, and the levels of Vitamin C may become seriously depleted. It is important to restore vitamin and mineral levels used during the stress response with adequate nutrition or supplements.
- Regular aerobic exercise helps stress hormones to return to normal levels and assists in becoming naturally tired and promoting sleep. Exercising muscles removes lactic acid which builds up during periods of inactivity. High levels of lactic acid make you feel tired and lethargic.
- Limit soda consumption. Soda contains phosphoric acid. Your calcium level should be in balance with the phosphorus, and Vitamin D is necessary for calcium absorption. If soda contains caffeine, a diuretic, more water and water-soluble vitamins (C and B-complex) will be lost.

It may be difficult to sleep when you've experienced high levels of stress. Lying awake at night, the mind can play the "what if" game. (What if I had done this differently? What if this hadn't happened?) Or it can keep reviewing the day's events, almost like an endless loop video replay (sometimes called an "obsessional review"). It's important to break that cycle and get the rest and sleep that are so needed.

- Progressive muscle relaxation can promote sleep by gently exercising each muscle group. Starting with the toes, flex and point them toward your head and hold for a slow count of 15. Then extend them by pointing them away from your body and hold for a count of 15. Move on to your calf muscles, then your thigh muscles, and so on, progressing from toes to head. As you relax each muscle group, you should feel a tiredness that will help you to sleep. This technique requires repetition and practice to train the body to relax.

- Visual imagery of relaxing environments—for example, a sun-filled beach with gentle ocean waves rolling in—and deep breathing also interrupt the constant review of the critical incident.

The PIO needs to keep these health promotion principles in mind. To eat healthfully and stay physically fit enables you to live your life well, and when those peak stressful moments come, you will be in better overall shape to confront and manage them well.

Summary

In the past, PIOs were often overlooked when it came to critical incident stress management. This chapter outlines important information for PIOs to have in order to be able to recognize a normal stress reaction to a critical incident and describes CISM as the standard of care for the field. The significance of stress awareness and appropriate crisis intervention is very important in promoting health and wellness for PIOs. Understanding the human stress response enables a PIO to function more effectively with the public and with other media workers and emergency responders in the highly charged atmosphere of the media. Every day, media workers risk their lives to keep Americans informed of the latest events in their communities and around the world. They both deserve and are entitled to the best of post-incident care to maintain their health and protect their careers.

REVIEW QUESTIONS

1. What are the components of critical incident stress management?
2. What are the seven phases of CISD?
3. Name the three stages of the human stress response.
4. Identify at least seven types of critical incidents.
5. What is the definition of a critical incident?

6. Define the terms "eustress" and "distress," and give examples of each.

7. Describe the signs and symptoms a PIO may experience on assignment.

8. What are the recognized best practices for using CISM?

9. Describe the controversy surrounding CISM.

REFERENCES

Antai-Otong, D. (2001) Critical incident stress debriefing: a health promotion model for workplace violence. *Perspectives in Psychiatric Care*, 37(4), 125–139.

Dart Center for Journalism and Trauma (2003, January 28). Study: Photographers and Trauma. Retrieved July 29, 2006 from http://dartcenter.org/articles/headlines/2003/2003_01_28.html.

Jenkins, SR (1996) Social support and debriefing efficacy among emergency medical workers after a mass shooting incident. *Journal of Social Behavior and Personality*, 11(3), 477–492.

Everly, GS, Jr., & S. Boyle (1999) Critical incident stress debriefing (CISD): A meta-analysis. *International Journal of Mental Health*, 1, 165–168.

Everly, GS, Jr., Flannery, RB, & V. Eyler (2002) Critical incident stress management: a statistical review of the literature. *Psychiatric Quarterly*, 73, 171–182.

Lindemann, E (1944) Symptomatology and management of acute grief. *American Journal of Psychiatry*, 101, 141–148.

Mitchell, JT "Crisis Intervention and Critical Incident Stress Management: A defense of the field"; found at http://www.icisf.org/articles.

Mitchell, JT (1983) When disaster strikes . . . The critical incident stress debriefing process. *Journal of Emergency Medical Services*, 9, 36–39.

Mitchell, JT (2003) Major misconceptions in crisis intervention. *The Lancet*, (5)4, 185–197.

Richards, D. (2001) A field study of critical incident stress debriefing versus critical incident stress management. *Journal of Mental Health* 10(3), 351–362.

Selye, H. (1956) *The stress of life*.

Sin, SS, Huak, CY & A. Chan (2005) A pilot study of the impact of the Asian tsunami on a group of Asian media workers. *International Journal of Emergency Mental Health* 7(4), 299–306.[16]

ENDNOTES

1. Mitchell, 2003
2. DART Center, 2001
3. Mitchell and Everly 1983
4. Lindeman 1944
5. Mitchell 1983
6. DART Center, 2001
7. Sin, Huak & Chan, 2005
8. Sin, Huak & Chan, 2005
9. Mitchell, 2003, p. 187
10. Mitchell at http://www.icisf.org/articles, "Crisis Intervention and Critical Incident Stress Management: A Defense of the field," p. 5
11. Richards, 2001, p. 360
12. http://www.poynter.org/content/content_view.asp?id=5837
13. DART Center, 2003
14. Mitchell, 2003
15. Jenkins, 1996; Everly & Boyle, 1999; Everly, Flannery & Eyler, 2003; Mitchell, 2003

CHAPTER 6

Crisis Communications and Emergency Public Information

Objectives

- List the circumstances within an agency that might cause a crisis
- Define plans to effectively deliver emergency public information
- Demonstrate the ability to manage situations caused by an Incorrect news story

CASE Study

As people woke on the morning of January 4, 2006, the news on the radio was tragic: twelve miners dead after an explosion in a West Virginia coal mine. Shaking their heads in disbelief after hearing the heart-wrenching news, they stroll to the driveway, only to find the newspaper headline announcing what would be considered to be a miracle: "miners found alive!" What? Who's right? How could this be?

Company executives later explained the mistake as "a great tragedy," noting initial reports to the command post caused cell phone calls to be placed with the optimistic news; news initially delivered just before most newspapers went to press. Three hours later, the correct information was reported — twelve miners had died.[1]

Case Study Questions

1. How can a PIO control information flow within a command post?
2. What harm can be done to regain the public trust when incorrect information is reported?
3. How do media deadlines influence information release?

Introduction

A public information officer's role is often mundane. Some have described it as "days of boredom interrupted by hours of sheer terror." The terror comes when a crisis arises. The crisis may be centered at the agency the PIO is assigned to, in the community being served, or with an individual or family. According to *Webster's Dictionary,* crisis is defined as the turning point in a disease; the decisive moment in a tragedy; a time of danger or suspense. Of course, every individual, and in fact some agencies, may interpret these definitions slightly differently. In a small community, a child struck by a car while riding on a bicycle may be considered a crisis because it is a rare occurrence. In a larger city, the same event may be routine, and evoke fewer emotions. A PIO will need to develop an understanding about what constitutes a crisis and determine what action is appropriate. In his book titled *The Mass Media, Disasters and Risk: Entwining Communication and Culture,* Lee Wilkins notes "the media's ability to function as a warning mechanism is much more problematic for slow-onset hazards. If news is assumed to be a report of an event, then reporting about an event, which might or could happen, falls outside this definition and, hence, remains unreported."[2] If this is the case in the public information officer's market, the PIO will have to work to change media attitudes by educating them. This will allow the media to become a partner in **emergency public information** and crisis communications. Developing a realistic appreciation for a crisis in a community might be the most difficult task an information officer encounters.

KEY TERMS

Broadcast Operations, p. 123

"B-roll", p. 123

"Citizen Journalist", p. 98

Control of Electronic Radiation System (CONELRAD), p. 114

Disaster Recovery Centers (DRCs), p. 125

Editorial Production, p. 125

Emergency Alert System (EAS), p. 90

Emergency Broadcast System (EBS), p. 114

- Emergency Declarations, p. 115
- Emergency Operations Plan (EOP), p. 90
- Emergency Public Information, p 111
- Emergency Public Information Annex, p. 90
- External Affairs, p. 116
- Field Operations, p. 122
- Go Kit, p. 100
- ICS-209 Incident Summary, p. 101
- ICS-214 Unit Log, p. 104
- ICS-221 Demobilization Checklist, p. 104
- Incident Action Plan (IAP), p. 101
- Incident Command, p. 93
- Joint Field Office (JFO), p. 108
- Joint Information Center (JIC), p. 90
- Joint Information System (JIS), p. 90
- Major Disaster Declarations, p. 116
- Media Monitoring, p. 223
- Media pool, p. 109
- National Weather Service (NWS), p. 114
- News Desk, p. 122
- Operational Period, p. 101
- Planning Section, p. 93
- Program Liaisons, p. 125
- *Recovery Times*, p. 125
- Research and Writing, p. 124
- Situation Unit, p. 93
- Stafford Act, p. 115

Crisis Communications

After the 1991 East Bay Hills fire around the Oakland, CA area, the United States Fire Administration noted, "The public must be warned to take protective or preventive actions or to evacuate an area that is in imminent danger. There should be procedures to provide for rapid activation of the public information system and close coordination with the incident commander."[3]

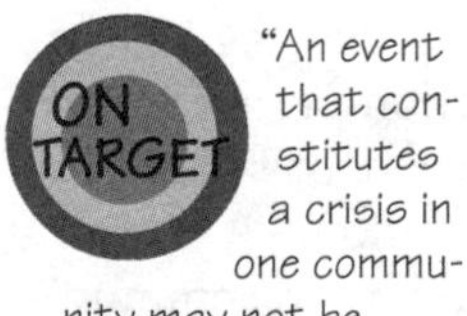

"An event that constitutes a crisis in one community may not be considered a crisis in another."

These types of crises often have several factors in common. Multiple agencies are often involved because the event has affected a large area and/or the crisis requires significant resources to manage. This type of crisis lasts longer, from several hours to weeks or months. Lives are disrupted; this may simply be loss of power, or it could be loss of all possessions, severe injuries, and/or property damage.

When considering how to plan for a crisis, answering a few simple questions may help guide you through the process. What is a crisis in your community? What type of crisis have you endured? As a citizen, were you adequately informed about the crisis? What were the good and bad points about the crisis from your perspective as a citizen? What can you learn from this experience?"

Once you have an understanding of how a crisis affects you and your community, then you may begin making plans to deal with crises when they occur. In nearly all cases, during a crisis our performance level is not at its peak. We think less clearly, need more tools to get the job done, and have less time to do this critical job.

Whole books have been written on this subject, but in essence, managing a crisis from the PIO perspective means taking several basic steps. Start by realizing you should not do this alone. You need to form a crisis communications team. The more complex the issue, the bigger the team must be to manage the situation. Sometimes this team may be part of a **joint information system (JIS)** working out of a **joint information center (JIC)**.

You should analyze the situation with the team, by reviewing the basics of an appropriate news story: who, what, when, where, why, and how. Determine whether the crisis is real or perceived. Should there be immediate press releases, perhaps a news conference, or is there a need to activate the **emergency alert system (EAS)**?

The analysis may point you toward your **Emergency Operations Plan's (EOP's) Emergency Public Information Annex**. The annex may contain appendices, which will guide you through the steps needed to manage different crises. If these guides do not exist, you will need to create them.

The emergency public information annex often includes several key sections.[4] The *purpose* is a broad statement outlining why the annex exists. The section on *situations and assumptions* describes the environment and some of the uncertainties present when the plan was developed. The annex should also contain a *list of responsibilities and organizations assigned* under emergency public information. Later in this chapter, we will discuss JICs. The need for strong administration and logistics will become apparent. Emergency public information should address these topics as well.

Each annex should address plan development and maintenance, which will guide the PIO through a regular process of reviewing and updating emergency public information. Finally, a section on authorities and references will include any references to local, state, or federal law applicable to the delivery of emergency public information.

If the crisis involves your organization, you should begin communication with your constituents as soon as possible. Communicate often, and when there is no more information to communicate, stop. The media will often want to drag a story out, especially if they believe you have not been forthcoming about the situation. If your agency is being investigated by an outside agency, work with the communications personnel from that agency, as well as your legal council to determine who will speak on what topic.

Forming a partnership with the media can be beneficial in many types of crises. The media have a vested interest in providing the public with information. If this is a disaster-related crisis, the media may be the best source to provide life saving information.

Before a crisis happens, you should develop a plan. This plan may be the Public Information Annex of the Emergency Operations Plan, or it may be a separate document outlining the key issues involved in crisis communications. This information should include a listing of your crisis planning team. At the very least, it should be made up of your agency's CEO or Chief Officer, additional information officers, the attorney from your agency, and perhaps PIOs from other community agencies.

In developing your **crisis communications plan**, you must clearly state and agree that the public information officer has the authority to perform the requirements of the job. When the going gets tough, the PIO is the best person to lead the crisis communications effort. The PIO has developed the trust of the media outlets, and has the contacts. Suddenly replacing the primary media contact with a superior in the organization can be detrimental to overall media relations, and may appear to be a means of hiding something.

As important as the external crisis communications plan is, you cannot forget that one of your constituencies is the employee group that makes up your organization. Your plan needs to include communication not only with the media, but also employees and perhaps even their families. The internal crisis communications plan should include a mandatory notification list, an on-call schedule for the primary contacts of those covering the crisis, and specific assignments for the crisis team. Your plan should address timelines for establishing contact with the people on your list.

Media contacts are a critical consideration in developing a crisis communications plan. Among for the points of information you should disseminate about contacting the media during a crisis, include information regarding who may speak to the media and when the contact should occur. Written communications are a good way to begin the process as well as a tool that will allow for documentation of the information you have released.

While it is obvious that your communications list will include the media, it should also contain government officials as well as an internal contact list. It may also include key nongovernmental organization (NGO) community leaders.

To contact the media, your plan should contain editor, assignment editor, and producer contact numbers, along with an information gathering form for you to use in obtaining the necessary information about the crisis and some prewritten news releases to be used for specific crises. These could include natural disasters and hazardous material emergencies.

While on the scene of a crisis, important information must be communicated regarding the situation at hand, and life safety issues may need to be addressed in the initial stages of the emergency.

Crisis communications do not necessarily end when you leave an incident. You may want to plan for communications later in the day,

FIGURE 6-1
News Reporter at Crime Scene

perhaps to update the information you released earlier in the crisis, or to work with regional or national media that may have picked up the story. The need to communicate will likely last for several days.

Always consult with legal counsel before you give out any additional information. Be aware that any communication must include the facts related to the incident and that information related to the vehicle unit numbers, crew members, and/or any equipment involved in the incident or the location of the incident may be sensitive.

When notified of a crisis, verify the initial report of the incident. Any emergency responder knows that what they find when they arrive at an incident is not always what they were called out for. Sometimes it is worse than expected, but most of the time the incident is less severe than expected.

Once you have determined that the crisis is real, your crisis notification plan should be activated, and superiors within your organization should be notified according to the plan. If other agencies are affected, begin early, and stay in regular contact with them. Your plan should provide you with guidance about where the PIO will be located. Some PIOs will go to the incident scene, others to a command post. This may be dictated by the incident commander.

When communicating information to the media, begin by issuing a brief incident alert to the news agencies. Inform and coordinate with the other PIOs from the other agencies.

During the early phases of a crisis, up-front communication is important; however, there are times when communications may need to be delayed to gather facts. You should keep in mind that the media will be looking to get information from wherever they can, so you will not be able to ignore the press, because they will not go away. There is nearly always a feeding frenzy circulating around a crisis, and it is your responsibility as a public information officer to "feed the beast."

"The media are an important ally in a crisis situation."

At a crisis incident, the lead information officer should request an early briefing from the incident commander. If warranted, a JIC will be established, and contact with the media on the scene organized. Briefings, which may be in the form of a press conference, should be scheduled at regular intervals. If you tell the media you will be at the briefing location at 3:30 P.M., you should be there *ON TIME*! If you are late, your credibility will be diminished.

Any major incident will garner media attention. The days of the single reporter with a notepad are long gone, and the modern media will arrive on scene with any combination of electronic newsgathering equipment. In addition, there may be media arriving from a long distance, perhaps bringing larger vehicles, which will allow them to send and receive satellite signals. You will need to establish a media area, close enough to the incident to allow them to get the story, but not close enough to interfere with incident operations. Once you determine the location, identify and mark the area with temporary signage.

With the help of the **Incident Command Planning Section's Situation Unit** and other members of the JIC, develop a display board to post incident information, photos, and the latest press releases. The display board area can also be used as the briefing area for the incident. Briefing times should be posted in this media staging area.

When conducting a briefing or press conference, limit what you say to the media before you have the facts. This is a very stressful time. Emotions are at a peak! Members of the media and emergency workers may overreact. The media want to get the story quickly. The PIO wants to provide information in a timely fashion, but that is not always possible.

"When planning for a crisis, you should analyze what mistakes you or others in your agency could make that could elevate a minor incident to a national one."

During this time of stress, the PIO and perhaps emergency workers often perceive that the media are interfering with incident operations by asking questions, using bright lights, and sometimes by just being there.

Those operating at an incident know that any mistakes being made will be caught on video tape and could potentially be embarrassing. All media can become national media. Whether through Internet phones, satellite transmission, or even photo cell phones, there is a good chance that the story will become a national, or at the very least, a regional story.

You will be busier after the crisis than during it. There will be items to catch up on from your daily activities that have had to wait because of the demands of the crisis. Your physical and mental health may be adversely affected by the stress of working through the crisis. Watch for signs and symptoms of critical incident stress. (See Chapter 5.) This may be the time to use a network of information officers so that some can rest while others are working. A fatigued information officer *WILL* make an incorrect statement or an omission that can escalate the crisis. You may have to become a manager and delegator, instead of a hands-on person, for a brief period surrounding the crisis. You may need to schedule statements and briefings after rest periods. The media want accurate information, and a well-rested information team can provide that better than one that is fatigued.

Eventually, your crisis will end. However, the process of crisis communications is not over. There are still some important tasks to complete. All PIOs involved in the crisis should analyze the event. The analysis should start with a review of plans to determine whether the team followed all the elements of the crisis plan and whether problems resulted after adopting any of those elements. If the plans were not followed, determine why.

The National Incident Management System (NIMS) emphasizes the importance of critiques and sharing of lessons learned.[5] Your incident review should not become personal. Every person and organization should improve after taking time to review the crisis communications work; a successful critique of a crisis should be forward looking. Those who supervise information officers may also be invited to participate in the critique, but must follow the same guidelines.

The communications review should be written and should provide readers with an accurate assessment of the successes and failures of the media relations effort. It is important to remember that a critique is not all criticism; it is a constructive review of how an incident was handled.

Each organization should conduct regularly scheduled training for at least supervisory personnel, but the preference is to train as many employees as possible. You may even consider holding educational sessions on how to handle the media. This can go a long way toward enhancing partnerships being formed with the media. Many organizations are encouraging a "speak about what you know" policy, which encourages cooperation with the media. However, this type of policy should be accompanied by some media training.

When Mistakes Are Made

Despite their best intentions, reporters, editors and, yes, even information officers make mistakes. The actions taken to correct these mistakes are crucial to maintaining solid media relationships.

When mistakes are made, there are several courses of action to take. Each course of action is dependent upon the situation, and requires careful consideration.

Do Nothing

If a reporter has made a mistake in a story, your best course of action may be to do nothing. By challenging the mistake, you may be opening yourself up to more questions than were initially asked.

Case Study

You are the PIO for an emergency management agency. A reporter has received a tip from an area resident that the emergency management agency has not dealt with certain flood prone areas. You discuss the issue with the reporter, and explain those areas have not yet come due on a master calendar of mitigation project priorities. The reporter writes the story and misinterprets the information you provided, stating the areas are not a priority to emergency management. What the reporter does not know when the story is written is that the emergency management agency has missed three deadlines for federal grants to deal with the specific issues of the areas in question.

This case study should prompt you to think about the following questions:

1. If you ask the reporter to correct the story, will additional questions open up the emergency management agency to further review?
2. Is the information about the missed grant deadlines more damaging than the way the story was written?
3. Will the audience that read the story be the same one that reads the correction, if one is written?
4. Is a meeting with the neighbors in the affected areas a better way to handle the misinformation than trying to get the reporter to clarify the story?

When determining the action to take when a mistake is made in a story written about your agency, there are general considerations you

Box 6-1 Example of News Story: Does It Tell the Whole Story?

"Emergency Management's Delayed Response: Did it cost a life?"

Witnesses say it was too late for a 59-year-old area resident when County Emergency Management finally showed up at an evening fire. "I can't believe it took them so long to get here," said a bystander who wished to remain anonymous. "The volunteer fire department had to get that poor woman out of the fire." She told reporters that when Emergency Management people finally did arrive—some say 30 minutes after the 9-1-1 call—they arrived in an SUV, with no equipment and no manpower."

Although this story may be accurate, it is not factually correct. The person interviewed either did not have the facts or misinterpreted them. The fact is that Emergency Management has nothing to do with emergency response and had no responsibility or authority to provide first response and rescue. What the bystander reported was an incomplete view of the situation, and the story could lead to a higher public expectation than can be delivered.

should review. Do you want the story to live and grow legs? This refers to the additional stories being written about an issue or additional issues creeping into a story line. Ask three public safety workers about response times and you will get three different interpretations. Question a citizen about response times and you will get yet another set of opinions. These differing opinions can become a new story.

When Hurricanes Katrina and Rita slammed into the U.S. Gulf Coast, they devastated thousands of square miles. Media coverage of the events focused on the slow response of the government. The media accurately reported this slow response, but incorrectly interpreted it because of public sentiment. The federal government is not a first responder to disasters, yet the media coverage created a public expectation of this first response. Many actual first response activities were conducted; however, they received little or no coverage from the local or national media.[6]

Talk to Reporters

A friendly phone call to a reporter to discuss the problem may be the best course of action. Most reporters do not intentionally misrepresent what they heard in an interview. Their interpretation may have been colored by a misunderstanding of the point you were trying to make.

You should consider the reporter's history. Is this the first mistake? Have you been down this road before?

Even after the discussion, do not expect a retraction. These are rare. You might get a correction, but corrections are not usually seen or heard by the same audience.

Meet with Reporter's Editor, Manager, or Owner

While meeting with the reporter's boss is an option, you want to tread carefully. How would you feel if a reporter went over your head, and reported problems directly to your boss, instead of initiating a conversation with you first? Some news outlets require all complaints be brought to the editors. This would be a matter of policy and is often done to ensure that issues are handled correctly.

Regardless of whom an issue is discussed with, the conversation should be professional, not adversarial. Too often, the "power of the uniform" is used as a trump card in these conversations. Uniforms are nice, but a reporter's future stories will probably be more effective. Never forget the importance of relationships when dealing with a media problem.

Inform State Media Association or Media-Emergency Coalition

There are ethics policies for many journalistic organizations. The Radio-Television News Director's Association is one example of a professional media organization with a strong ethics code. The ethics code preamble says journalists "should operate as trustees of the public, seek the truth, report it fairly and with integrity and independence, and stand accountable for their actions."[7] Most states have some media organization, often affiliated with national groups. Local, state, and national press clubs are such groups.[8] Taking an issue to this level is a major step, and one, which might not yield any results. Most of these organizations are non-regulatory in nature. There might be some unofficial mediation offered, but bringing a local issue to a state or national organization is asking for a broader spotlight to be shown on the problem.

Go to the Competition

"Mommy, look what Jimmy did!"

While running to a media outlet's competition might seem like a logical solution to a problem, the action trivializes it. It turns a complicated issue into a "consumer product" complaint. Indeed, the media target consumers. Understanding what the audience wants allows the media to present a product designed to increase viewers, readers, and listeners. This brings in additional advertising revenue, which then results in better budgets for pay and equipment, as well as better market research, all of which give the media outlet an improved understanding of the market. Using news stories to "one-up" competitors might be advantageous to the media outlet, but certainly is not advantageous to the PIO's agency.

Another problem with this approach is the varied audiences served by the media outlets. Going to the competition might not get your story to the audience you want.

When attempting to get the correct story told, you should determine the story angle you are looking for. One media outlet has already made a mistake with a story on the subject in question, and there is no guarantee that a new outlet might not make the same mistake.

Finally, make sure that going to the competition is simply not motivated by revenge. This only serves to create more problems, and it is not a good way to build long-lasting relationships.

Take Legal Action

Taking legal action is a last resort. This will often require proof there has been a negative impact from the story. Legal proceedings can be very expensive and last for years. You should only consider this alternative if you have exercised all the other options.

Aside from the issues just discussed, the dissemination of emergency public information might be delayed while you deal with the issue of an incorrect story.

If a media outlet has a vendetta against your organization, there is not much you can do but hold your head high, continue positive efficient service, and hope that the public realizes the difference between fact and exaggeration.

Media Relations at the Scene

The terror attacks of 2001, hurricanes striking the coastal beaches, a state trooper assaulted by a suspect, a house fire in the neighborhood—what do these incidents have in common? All of them are incidents where a public information officer will interface with the media at a scene. The media will trumpet these incidents as "live, local, or late breaking," or whatever the catchphrase of the week is.

These are also examples of incidents in which the "media" may be a "**citizen journalist**." Citizen journalists are regularly promoted by major media networks and are people who are encouraged to provide stories on specific subjects or simply to present stories for possible

"Citizen journalists create a new challenge for PIOs. The success and ease of use of camera cell phones, Internet blogs, home video editing equipment, and technology yet to be released is allowing citizens to potentially become recognized news media members."

network use. MSNBC, Fox News, and CNN, the popular cable news networks, often use reports from citizen journalists during disasters and other emergencies. Citizen journalists are the 21st century version of the common practice of news departments encouraging the audience to provide news tips. News departments have also used "stringers" journalists who provide stories, but who are not employees. The new trend is using citizen reports, including repeat calls to these citizens for updates. Citizens are even providing still photos or videos of incidents for use on newscasts. The use of citizen reporters is certainly faster and less expensive than using skilled journalists; however, for the PIO, these citizen journalists can report inaccurate information, causing potential hazards resulting in injury or even death.

Poynter Online's Steve Outing notes that ". . . there's plenty of confusion about citizen journalism. What exactly is it? Is this something that's going to be essential to the future prosperity of news companies?"[9] Dan Gillmor has even penned a book on citizen journalism: *We the Media*.[10]

Today, a PIO should not be surprised when news is reported by citizens. As discussed earlier in the chapter, the means by which a story's inaccuracy is addressed is done on a case-by-case basis. However, you might never be able to track down a citizen journalist to reeducate him or her on a story's inaccuracy. Regardless of the sources used by media outlets, it is the PIO's responsibility to provide information to the public in a timely manner, allowing people to take action to save lives or property. Being on scene will enable a PIO to interact directly with the mainstream media, perhaps setting straight problems caused by inaccurate citizen journalist reports.

Journalists do look for officials at incidents. Even if a news outlet refuses to use an "official's" statement as gospel, the outlet desires the information you have. Journalists want the life and death information for use by their audiences

Several characteristics of an emergency scene contribute to effective media relations. The most obvious is the "news" nature of many emergency scenes. The media want to tell the story, and the PIO can be there to assist them. Emergency scenes are often visual and full of human-interest stories. Critical lifesaving information needs to be presented along with frequent updates, which the media will want to report.

To best present the media with this information, the PIO should rely on the skills used in day-to-day media contact. Personal relationships help with calming the chaos often present at an emergency scene, but more importantly, the skills used in developing these relationships can be used to quickly build new ones at an emergency scene.

When working at an incident, both the media and the PIO have special needs. The media need the information quickly, while the PIO needs access to the incident commander to get the information approved for release. Both media and PIOs may need technology. The media will bring equipment for live broadcasts, and the PIO may need equipment to conduct large briefings. Larger incidents call for more equipment.

Responding to an Emergency

When a PIO responds to an emergency, common practices should be adhered to. Many of these mirror the common responsibilities outlined in the basic principles of the incident command system. They include the following: what to do prior to leaving for the assignment, the need to check in at the incident or event, common responsibilities, and demobilization responsibilities. The information contained in this section is taken from the National Interagency Incident Management System basic incident command system (I-200) curriculum.

General Responsibilities

The PIO's approach to an emergency incident must be organized in advance. Every PIO should develop a **go kit** containing media policy documentation, field operations guides, prewritten press releases, and other material appropriate for typical incidents. This material will be based on the discipline that the PIO works in.

Among the equipment that the PIO should include in a go kit are a cell phone, pager, PDA/Palm Computer, digital or film camera, audio recorder, notebook computers, and e-mail access.

If the PIO is being deployed to an incident away from the home base, the travel kit should include personal items such as medications, professional contacts, personal emergency contacts, and any special equipment plus other items as needed. Toiletries should also be included as well as books, magazines, and items that can be used for relaxation during downtime.

When alerted to respond to an incident, whether it is local or distant, review your emergency assignment. Take into account specific issues involved in the task. Does the response have inherent dangers? What are the media like? Does the incident have national significance? Has a JIC been established? What role will you play within the JIS?

Should you be assigned a position within an incident command structure, which requires decision making, you should have a clear understanding of the authority you have for your agency while at the incident. Efficiency at an emergency depends on the ability to make rapid decisions. For an incident commander and a PIO, this ability can save lives.

Whether the PIO is using standard operating procedures or a written plan developed during an incident, there should be some basic

Box 6-2 Information Needed Prior to Departure for Incident Assignment

- Incident type and name or designation.
- Incident check-in location.
- Reporting time.
- Travel instructions.
- Communications instructions.
- Resource order number or request number (if applicable).
- Your unit's radio designation.

communications procedures that the PIO will follow. This will include, but not be limited to, the procedures developed for communicating with the media. These procedures will be outlined by the JIS plan being used. Some may be formal written plans, others may be verbal plans that the PIO and incident commander agree on.

As outlined in Chapter 5, stress at an incident can affect a PIO's ability to perform. One of those stressors is family members, a concern for their safety and their ability to contact you in an emergency. The victims of many incidents may be members, or relatives of members, of the PIO's agency. To ease some of the tension of being separated from family during an emergency, PIOs should ensure that family members know their destination and how to contact them.

Traveling to an "emergency" can be as simple as walking down the hall to an established briefing room or as complicated as meeting a military transport that will take you to a remote location where you will work. Regardless of the situation, understanding the travel plan and any pickup arrangements is vital. As the PIO, you hold an essential position within an incident command structure, and if you do not arrive on scene when expected, there may be greater implications later as the incident progresses.

Additionally, if you drive a company (agency) vehicle, familiarize yourself with the regulations regarding traveling to an emergency. If you use emergency warning devices (lights and sirens) use due regard as you travel to the incident. Get to the scene safely!

If you are replacing another PIO at a shift change, or being replaced by someone for a similar reason, key elements must be addressed during that transition, starting with a discussion of the current situation. Other important information that should be imparted during a shift change includes information about job responsibilities, identification of coworkers, the location of the work area, eating and sleeping arrangements, obtaining support, and **operational period** work shifts. You should exchange an **Incident Action Plan (IAP)** and, if available, an **ICS-209 Incident Summary** form. (See Box 6-3.)

Box 6-3 ICS Form 209

INCIDENT STATUS SUMMARY
FS-5100-11

1. Date/Time	2. Initial ☐ Update ☐ Final ☐	3. Incident Name	4. Incident Number

5. Incident Commander	6. Jurisdiction	7. County	8. Type Incident	9. Location	10. Started Date/Time

11. Cause	12. Area Involved	13. % Controlled	14. Expected Containment Date/Time	15. Estimated Controlled Date/Time	16. Declared Controlled Date/Time

17. Current Threat	18. Control Problems

19. Est. Loss	20. Est Savings	21. Injuries	Deaths	22. Line Built	23. Line to Build

24. Current Weather WS Temp WD RH	25. Predicted Weather WS Temp WD RH	26. Cost to Date	27. Est. Total Cost

28. Agencies

29. Resources																							TOTALS	
Kind of Resource	SR	ST	SR	ST	SR	ST	SR	ST	SR	ST	SR	ST	SR	ST	SR	ST	SR	ST	SR	ST	SR	ST	SR	ST
ENGINES																								
DOZERS																								
CREWS Number of Crews:																								
Number of Crew Personnel:																								
HELICOPTERS																								
AIR TANKERS																								
TRUCK COS.																								
RESCUE/MED.																								
WATER TENDERS																								
OVERHEAD PERSONNL																								
TOTAL PERSONNEL																								

30. Cooperating Agencies

31. Remarks

32. Prepared by	33. Approved by	34. Sent to: Date Time By

(Continued)

Box 6-3 ICS Form 209 (continued)

General Instructions

Completion of the Incident Status Summary will be as specified by Agency or municipality. Report by telephone, teletype, computer, or facsimile to the local Agency or municipality headquarters by 2100 hours daily on incidents as required by Agency or municipality (reports are normally required on life threatening situations, real property threatened or destroyed, high resource damage potential, and complex incidents that could have political ramifications). Normally, wildland agencies require a report on all Class D (100 acres plus) and larger incidents (unless primarily grass type in which case report Class E (300 acres or larger). The first summary will cover the period from the start of the incident to 2100 hour the first day of the incident, if at least four hours have elapsed; thereafter the summary will cover the 24 hour period ending at 1900 (this reporting time will enable compilation of reporting data and submission of report to local agency or municipality headquarters by 2100 hours) daily until incident is under control. Wildland fire agencies will send the summary to NIFC by 2400 hours Mountain Time.

1. Enter date and time report completed (mandatory).
2. Check appropriate space (mandatory).
3. Provide name given to incident by Incident Commander or Agency (mandatory).
4. Enter number assigned to incident by Agency (mandatory).
5. Enter first initial and last name of Incident Commander (optional).
6. Enter Agency or Municipality (mandatory).
7. Enter County where incident is occurring (optional).
8. Enter type of incident, e.g. wildland fire (enter fuel type), structure fire, hazardous chemical spill, etc. (mandatory).
9. Enter legal description and general location. Use remarks for additional date if necessary (mandatory).
10. Enter date and Zulu time incident started (mandatory—maximum of six characters for date and four characters for time).
11. Enter specific cause or under investigation (mandatory).
12. Enter area involved, e.g. 50 acres, top three floors of building, etc. (mandatory).
13. Enter estimate of percent of containment (mandatory).
14. Enter estimate of date and time of total containment (mandatory).
15. Enter estimated date and time of control (mandatory).
16. Enter actual date and time fire was declared controlled (mandatory).
17. Report significant threat to structures, watershed, timber, wildlife habitat or other valuable resources (mandatory).
18. Enter control problems, e.g. accessibility, fuels, rocky terrain, high winds, structures (mandatory).
19. Enter estimated dollar value of total damage to date. Include structures, watershed, timber, etc. Be specific in remarks (mandatory).
20. Enter estimate of values saved as result of all suppression efforts (optional).
21. Enter any serious injuries or deaths which have occurred since the last report. Be specific in remarks (mandatory).
22. Indicate the extent of line completed by chains or other units of measurement (optional).

(Continued)

Box 6-3 ICS Form 209 (continued)

23. Indicate line to be constructed by chains or other units of measurement (optional).
24. Indicate current weather conditions at the incident (mandatory).
25. Indicate predicted weather conditions for the next operational period (mandatory).
26. Provide total incident cost ot date (optional).
27. Provide estimated total cost for entire incident (optional).
28. List agencies which have resources assigned to the incident (mandatory).
29. Enter resource information under appropriate Agency column by single resource or strike team (mandatory).
30. List by name those agencies which are providing support (e.g. Salvation Army, Red Cross, Law Enforcement, National Weather Service, etc. mandatory).
31. The Remarks space can be used to (1) list additional resources not covered in Section 28/29; (2) provide more information on location; (3) enter additional information regarding threat control problems, anticipated release or demobilization, etc.(mandatory).
32. This will normally be the Incident Situation Status Unit Leader (mandatory).
33. This will normally be the Incident Planning Section Chief (mandatory).
34. The ID of the Agency entering the report will be entered (optional).

Documentation during emergencies is a key component of incident management and a PIO is not exempt from paperwork. Basic guidelines are to be followed in this regard, as much of the PIO's work is subject to scrutiny after action reports and other incident reviews are filed.

All PIOs should become familiar with and regularly use the **ICS-214 Unit Log** form. This form provides places for charting work activities and subordinating staffing activities, as well as notes about any issues that may arise. Since documentation may become part of later legal proceedings, it should be either printed or typed (computer entry) to assure legibility.

The date and time should be entered on all forms. The date format that should be used is month/day/year, while time is always reflected in military (24-hour) style.

All blanks on a form should be filled in. If there is no information for the blank, use an "NA" to stand for "not applicable."

When an incident is complete, or you are being relieved by another person, you will be required to follow a demobilization plan. The plan may be in written form on an incident command system **ICS-221 demobilization checklist** form. (See Box 6-5.) First, make sure that your work is completed or that any incomplete work is outlined for completion by the appropriate person.

Next, brief subordinates regarding demobilization, evaluate the performance of your subordinates prior to their release from the incident (as required by agency policy), and return any incident-issued communications equipment or other nonexpendable supplies.

Box 6-4 ICS Form 214

UNIT LOG	1. Incident Name	2. Date Prepared	3. Time Prepared
4. Unit Name/Designators	5. Unit Leader (Name and Position)		6. Operational Period

7. Personnel Roster Assigned		
Name	ICS Position	Home Base

8. Activity Log	
Time	Major Events

9. Prepared by (Name and Position)

Box 6-5 ICS Form 221

DEMOBILIZATION CHECKOUT

1. Incident Name/Number	2. Date/Time	3. Demob. No.
4. Unit/Personnel Released		
5. Transportation Type/No.		
6. Actual Release Date/Time	7. Manifest? ☐ Yes ☐ No Number	
8. Destination	9. Notified: ☐ Agency ☐ Region ☐ Area ☐ Dispatch Name: Date:	
10. Unit Leader Responsible for Collecting Performance Rating		

11. Unit/Personnel

You and your resources have been released subject to sign off from the following:
Demob. Unit Leader check the appropriate box

Logistics Section

- ☐ Supply Unit ____________________
- ☐ Communications Unit ____________________
- ☐ Facilities Unit ____________________
- ☐ Ground Support Unit Leader

Planning Section

- ☐ Documentation Unit

Finance Section

- ☐ Time Unit

Other

- ☐
- ☐

12. Remarks

13. Prepared by (include Date and Time)

(Continued)

Box 6-5 ICS Form 221 (continued)

Instructions for completing the Demobilization Checkout (ICS form 221)

Prior to actual Demob Planning Section (Demob Unit) should check with the Command Staff (Liaison Officer) to determine any agency specific needs related to demob and release. If any, add to line Number 11.

Item No.	Item Title	Instructions
1.	Incident Name/No.	Enter Name and/or Number of Incident.
2.	Date & Time	Enter Date and Time prepared.
3.	Demob. No.	Enter Agency Request Number, Order Number, or Agency Demob Number if applicable.
4.	Unit/Personnel Released	Enter appropriate vehicle or Strike Team/Task Force ID Number(s) and Leader's name or individual overhead or staff personnel being released.
5.	Transportation	Enter Method and vehicle ID number for transportation back to home unit. Enter N/A if own transportation is provided. *Additional specific details should be included in Remarks, block # 12.*
6.	Actual Release Date/Time	To be completed at conclusion of Demob at time of actual release from incident. *Would normally be last item of form to be completed.*
7.	Manifest	Mark appropriate box. If yes, enter manifest number. *Some agencies require a manifest for air travel.*
8.	Destination	Enter the location to which Unit or personnel have been released. *i.e. Area, Region, Home Base, Airport, Mobilization Center, etc.*
9.	Area/Agency/ Region Notified	Identify the Area, Agency, or Region notified and enter date and time of notification.
10.	Unit Leader Responsible for Collecting Performance Ratings	Self-explanatory. *Not all agencies require these ratings.*
11.	Resource Supervision	Demob Unit Leader will identify with a check in the box to the left of those units requiring check-out. Identified Unit Leaders are to initial to the right to indicate release. Blank boxes are provided for any additional check, (unit requirements as needed), i.e. Safety Officer, Agency Rep., etc.
12.	Remarks	Any additional information pertaining to demob or release.
13.	Prepared by	Enter the name of the person who prepared this Demobilization Checkout, including the Date and Time.

If transportation home from the incident has been arranged by others, report to the assigned departure points on time or slightly ahead of schedule. As appropriate, stay with your group until you arrive at your final destination.

Media Staging Area

Even before the media arrive, a PIO should consider establishing a media staging area. This area should accommodate the media's need for parking and setting up the live broadcast equipment area, as well as a place for them to attend news conferences and prepare stories. While establishing an incident perimeter is crucial to efficient incident management, this perimeter cannot be used to keep the media out if the public is allowed into an area. Whatever areas the public has access to must also be open to the press.

When establishing a media area, safety of the press is a primary concern and the staging location should keep them clear of the effects of the incident. This is not an opportunity to create artificial hazards, just to keep the media back from an incident.

An additional safety concern is the presence of overhead wires. The live broadcast trucks will have tall masts that allow point-to-point transmission of broadcast signals. Contact with the wires can be deadly for the crew in the vehicle and for those near the wires.

The larger the incident, the larger the media area needs to be. During presidentially declared disasters, the U.S. Department of Homeland Security's Federal Emergency Management Agency (FEMA) will establish a **joint field office (JFO)** containing a JIC. Somewhere within the JIC, there will often be a media center, including a broadcast division with satellite uplink facilities. This may limit the need to establish larger parking areas for each station's live broadcast vehicles.

If the media staging area is affiliated with a JIC, JFO, or incident command post, security for the host facility must be part of the plan. The media cannot be allowed to have access to management locations unless such access is expressly planned for. While you do not want to restrict access to officials, there are times when the official's attention must focus on the incident, not on the media. Remember that the media will have nearly as many pieces of equipment at a major incident as the police, fire, and EMS personnel, so space is a consideration as well as proximity to the scene.

"The media will get the story. The PIO should assist so that the process can be completed safely."

A media staging area should be located so that it does not infringe on access to the scene by emergency responders or interfere with the work being conducted. Major incidents also often draw political leaders and policy makers. The media staging area should be accessible to them. Don't forget that you, too, must be able to gain access to the media.

There are also creature comforts that should be considered for long-term operations. Restrooms, food, electrical outlets, and phone-line access are necessary for the press to function. These amenities are often provided in JICs.

Once a safe and accessible location has been determined, the media staging area should be clearly marked and the media notified of its location.

It is important to remember that the media will get the story, but as the PIO, you must consider the type of information that you do not want the media to have. In some cases, restricting visual access can protect the lives of responders, although laws governing freedom of the press make restricting access difficult. The media all have access to live broadcast capabilities including their own cameras on towers or buildings, as well as traffic cameras used in many communities. Some media outlets either own or rent helicopters. It is better to expect pictures to be taken than work to restrict the access.

With respect to media aircraft, PIOs should coordinate their activity with the Air Operations Branch in the incident command structure to avoid any conflicts between incident and media aviation crews.

Preplanning with the media can prevent some dangerous situations from becoming more dangerous. Many communities have worked with the media to develop a mutual understanding of the need for certain restrictions to the scene during incidents such as a hostage situation or an undercover raid, or when serving a surprise warrant. These can all become deadly for public safety responders if the element of surprise is compromised. Television can become an intelligence-gathering tool for suspects as well as public safety officials.

The media need regular "official" updates. These updates will entice them to stay close to the staging area, but members of the press will wander. Scheduled, on-time briefings will allow you to get the correct message out, allowing it to be balanced with the other information obtained by reporters. These media briefings, also known as news conferences or press conferences, are used when individual interviews are impractical, an incident has communitywide impact, numerous agencies are involved with messages to deliver, or the subject is of interest to all levels of media. Most importantly, such briefings allow all of the media to hear the *same message* at the *same time*.

"When working at any incident, PIOs must keep in mind whom they work for: the agency, not the media."

When operating at an incident, the PIO has specific needs including access to workers, administrative, and legal staff. He or she must be involved in management briefings and have the trust of coworkers. Of course, this trust is developed over time, and eventually, as with any incident position, the PIO becomes an expected, welcome presence.

A controversial, yet sometimes necessary method of providing media with access to restricted or dangerous areas is to establish a **media pool**, or perhaps more correctly stated, allow a media pool to form.

Media pools consist of representatives from broadcast and print news departments who are escorted into a scene by a field PIO and must share what they bring back with all other media present. The pool members are chosen by the media, not the PIO or other incident source.

A pool should be used only if there is no viable way to get the media the information that they are requesting, such as photos and first-hand scene descriptions. If a pool is used, the PIO or a representative should escort the media members and advise them of any potential safety issues they might encounter. (The media frequently believe that they accept the risk inherent at an emergency scene, but rarely have any training on how to recognize the hazards.)

Media pools are not appropriate for use at every incident and should not be used as a tool to make the PIO's job easier. These pools will not eliminate requests for individual interviews, however, under certain circumstances this may be the best way for the media to get the story.

Problems at an Incident

The National Highway Traffic Safety Administration's (NHTSA) public information guide for law enforcement lists several problem scenarios at an incident. These include

- providing no information;
- providing the wrong information;
- losing your cool; and
- playing favorites.

The dangers of these problems are clear. Providing no information does not mean that the press will simply leave the scene. The media will get information from whatever source they can find, and that information will become the basis for the story.

In the heat of a crisis, incorrect information may be provided, but this is usually corrected as the incident progresses. Providing the wrong information to the media without correcting it can have devastating effects.

On September 8, 2005, Canadian news organizations reported the overnight death of former Quebec Premier Lucien Bouchard. He was alive and well.[11] Perhaps one of the most devastating informational mistakes happened in early 2006. On January 4, 2006, the 1:29 AM CNN headline shouted, "Family members say 12 miners found alive."[12] The headline was repeated by newspapers across the country. A little more than two hours later, the headline was "Official: 12 of 13 miners dead."[13] Overheard conversations were misinterpreted and repeated to reporters. This inaccurate information release caused deep psychological harm to the families. It is a classic example of the need to have a solid media relations plan in place at any incident.

While home video of you losing your cool might make for good party fare later in life, being immortalized on professional video tape is not pleasant. Losing your cool with the media can be interpreted by the public as lack of control over incident management. As the face of an incident, the PIO represents everyone working the incident. Such an emotional outburst may also be interpreted as a sign of lying or manipulating the truth. "Clear thinking is the first step to stopping your outbursts. If you stop and think before you act, your life will be more in control—in *your* control."[14]

Playing favorites when providing information at an incident will cause you problems in the future. The local media will always be the local media, and they will be present long after others leave. Fairness in providing base information cannot be compromised. While certain media outlets may have their own "hook" for a story, the base information should be shared with all.

Use care to balance the need to meet deadlines and issues of safety. The PIO must work with the media to keep them safe while trying to meet deadlines. A little information can go a long way when the deadline is just minutes after an incident occurs. The "live, local and late-breaking" theme used by many media outlets, coupled with "team coverage," will force you to act fast, but that does not mean acting unwisely or unsafely.

Emergency Public Information

"Emergency Public Information Objectives:

- Recognize communications technology available to both media and PIOs during an emergency
- Describe the purpose of the Emergency Alert System (EAS)
- Describe the PIO's role in a Presidential disaster"

Emergency public information is a form of crisis communications. The crisis can be any incident requiring immediate dissemination of information that will save a life.

During an emergency, the public *needs* certain information. It *desires* other information. It is important to balance the necessary with the desired information. This balance goes to the basics of public information. PIOs should provide information needed to save lives, protect property, and call people to action.

Disseminating and managing emergency public information requires most of the skills a PIO will use on a daily basis; however, the pace of activity is greatly exaggerated. These activities include maintaining communications with other PIOs, as well as assuming responsibilities within the incident command system. This may be at the incident command post, in the EOC, at the city hall or in a JFO.

The Select House Committee reviewing the 2005 response to Hurricanes Katrina and Rita identified new challenges perhaps unpredicted by emergency public information practitioners. In its report, the committee

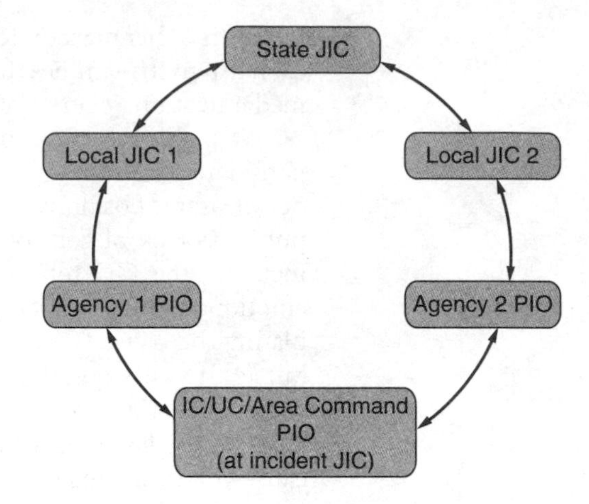

FIGURE 6-2
Diagram illustrating the communication flow between Joint Information Centers as outlined by NIMS

questioned whether or not the relationship between the messages being issued about evacuation and the severity of the approaching storm were effectively communicated.[15] Margaret Sims, vice president of the Joint Center for Political and Economic Studies, is quoted in the report emphasizing the importance of messages being delivered by "someone you trust."[16] Additionally, Linda Aldoory, director of the Center for Risk Communication Research at the University of Maryland, notes that those people who created the messages may not have recognized that the audience would encounter physical or access barriers in attempting to follow the emergency public information recommendations.[17]

It has been said before in this book, but bears repeating here, that a PIO should network before any crisis occurs. The ability to deliver emergency public information in an effective manner is enhanced when there are several team members working together. This networking also builds the PIO's contact list, which should be frequently updated. Together with your contacts, learn about the Emergency Alert System (EAS) and how it can be used effectively in your community.

Today's PIO works in a high-tech world. E-mail is fed through a BlackBerry™, files are shared via the Internet, and news stories are broadcast with cellular phones. While this may be the norm, when an emergency strikes our common means of communicating emergency public information may be lost. This was best illustrated during the hurricanes of 2005. When Katrina and Rita slammed into the Gulf Coast of the United States, nearly all communication systems were lost. When power was lost in a large portion of the northeastern United States during a blackout on August 14, 2003, many communication lines were either taken down by the loss of power, or jammed by citizens trying to use them. When a PIO must disseminate information under these conditions, creativity and "out-of-the-box" thinking must be used because, for at least a time, there is a new and unfamiliar "normal" to work in.

Methods of communicating might include distribution of hand fliers, face-to-face community gatherings and door-to-door meetings with neighbors in an affected community. There might be large bulletin boards used to place the information. PIOs will work with community relations personnel as they move through the community making personal contact with disaster victims. The use of portable public address systems or ones on emergency vehicles or even bullhorns might enhance the ability to deliver this information. Commercial warning systems exist that incorporate warning sirens, and public address systems can be strategically placed around a community. An Internet search for "Emergency Public Address Systems" will yield millions of references. These systems may be incorporated into a community's emergency warning plans and might be funded through grants or donations. While most depend upon electricity to function, some are solar powered or may be outfitted with a generator for use during power outages.

FIGURE 6-3
Emergency Warning System

One method of communicating emergency public information is to use the Emergency Alert System (EAS). This system is a tool for use by the President to warn the nation of an emergency. With a history dating back to 1951, it has evolved into a robust technological system used by emergency managers across the country. The EAS replaced the **Control of Electronic Radiation System (CONELRAD)** and **Emergency Broadcast System (EBS)** in 1997 and makes use of digital technology to enhance emergency messaging.

In the 1950s, the Federal Communications Commission (FCC) established the CONELRAD to alert citizens of a pending nuclear attack. An alert tone would be broadcast on radio stations, then most would go off the air, or move to official emergency frequencies of 640Khz or 1240Khz on the AM band. Radios were manufactured with triangles at those frequencies to allow for easier identification of them. The common frequencies were used to throw off direction-finding equipment. The CONELRAD system was scrapped and the EBS system implemented in 1961, after the Cuban missile crisis.[18] Each radio station in the country had a sealed envelope next to the newsroom teletype containing authentication codes. In a nuclear emergency, the teletype would receive a message with the codes listed. Weekly tests of the system were implemented, and those tests remain a part of the EAS program today.[19]

"The EAS is a valuable tool for PIOs in times of emergency."

The EBS system relied on broadcast station operator intervention, wherein the operator would actually shut down the transmitter for a few seconds. Receivers tuned to that frequency would detect this interruption in signal and open a special receiver, allowing the emergency tone and information to be broadcast across the radio band. EAS now uses digital technology and has many advantages during an era when many radio stations are completely automated.

The digital system allows messages to be tailored to certain geographical areas, such as counties or cities, and also for specific emergencies. The **National Weather Service (NWS)** uses the same signaling system and can access the EAS receivers to broadcast emergency information. The NWS also uses special weather radios to provide emergency information.

Since January 1999, cable systems that have 10,000 or more subscribers have been a part of the EAS. Updates and changes to the system have been made by the FCC as recently as 2005. These changes have improved the EAS use of digital technology.

The EAS can be a valuable tool for PIOs providing emergency public information to constituents. Depending on your home agency, you might have jurisdiction over the local EAS. You should always be familiar with the local EAS broadcast outlets and the emergency management agency in your community so that you have a thorough understanding of the local EAS. Learn who has the authority to activate the EAS. Gather an understanding of any pre-event messages the system contains, and suggest others that might be appropriate. There are many advantages of the modern EAS, including automatic operation which "allows broadcast stations, cable systems, participating satellite companies, and other services to send and receive emergency information quickly and automatically even if those facilities are unattended."[20] The FCC's fact sheet on EAS notes that the system requires two independent sources for emergency information, thus making it more likely that such information is received and delivered to the citizens.

Another advantage of the current system is the ability to have the message available in a second language.

Today's Emergency Alert System is designed to be a partnership among all those involved in issuing and transmitting emergency warnings. These partnerships guide state and local plans and help them to conform to EAS rules, thus ensuring that all agencies have the same understanding about the system and its capabilities.

Use of the EAS is often outlined in a community's Emergency Operations Plan emergency public information annex. This annex will also include other policy and logistical information necessary for the PIO during a disaster.

Disasters and Emergency Public Information

Presidential disaster declarations are more common that people think. A check of the U.S. Department of Homeland Security's Federal Emergency Management Agency Web site will provide a listing of the latest declarations. Many who review these are surprised at never hearing about the problems in a declared area. As a PIO, you might be involved in a federally declared disaster at some time in your career. Understanding the disaster system will not only benefit you when state and federal personnel descend on your town, but prior to their arrival. These practices should be easily adopted by PIOs for daily use.

The main Federal disaster law is the **Stafford Act**. According to the FEMA Web site, "There are two types of Declarations provided for in the Stafford Act: Emergency Declarations and Major Disaster Declarations." Both declaration types authorize the President to provide federal disaster assistance. However, the cause of the declaration and type and amount of assistance differ.

- **Emergency Declarations**: An Emergency Declaration can be declared for any occasion or instance when the President determines that federal assistance is needed. Emergency Declarations usually supplement state and local efforts in providing emergency services by helping protect lives, property, public health, and safety, or by lessening or averting the threat of a catastrophe in any part of the United States. The amount of emergency assistance is capped at $5 million per single event. If additional assistance is needed, the President must report to Congress.

- **Major Disaster Declarations**: The President can declare a Major Disaster Declaration for any natural event, including any hurricane, tornado, storm, high-water event (e.g., a tidal wave), wind-driven water event (e.g., a tsunami), earthquake, volcanic eruption, landslide, mudslide, snowstorm, drought, fire, flood, or explosion, that the President believes has caused damage of such severity that it is beyond the combined capabilities of state and local governments to respond. A major disaster declaration provides a wide range of federal assistance programs for individuals and for the public infrastructure, including funds for both emergency and permanent work."[21]

If you are involved in an official emergency or disaster, you will be working with state and federal public affairs personnel. At the federal level, and often at the state level, the term "public affairs" will include PIOs, as well as other groups involved with communications, such as congressional affairs and community relations. FEMA now refers to the public affairs function as **external affairs**, which encompasses media relations, community relations, congressional relations and intergovernmental relations. External affairs is Emergency Support Function (ESF) number 15. Many states have also adopted this concept. These public affairs personnel often have years of experience working disasters and providing emergency public information. They can provide you with a good educational experience before you have to work in a disaster situation.

A natural disaster often forces communities to dust off their emergency operation plans and put into practice response and recovery strategies that may have never been tested. If the plan has been updated within the last decade, the emergency public information annex should include references to establishing a JIC. PIOs from police, fire, and emergency medical service agencies may get together to discuss how they will present information to the media. However, these three agencies are just scratching the surface when it comes to establishing a complete JIC.

When a disaster occurs, representatives, responders, and leaders from many levels of government will be involved. At a federally declared disaster, at least Federal, State, County, and Local governments will be represented. Nongovernmental organizations (NGOs), such as power companies, will be involved in the incident. Voluntary organizations active in disasters (VOAD) and volunteer agencies (VOLAG) will be present and often bring along their own PIOs to represent their organizations.

Box 6-6 Statements Made During News Conference Using Concepts of JIC/JIS.

Fire PIO: "The fire started in a bundle of clothes left too close to a space heater."

EMS PIO: "There were no injuries as a result of the fire; however, two firefighters have been treated for heat exhaustion."

Police PIO: "Traffic will be diverted around the area for the next 24 hours. Alternate routes include Bath Street and Smith Avenue."

When asked about the fire during an independent interview later during the event, a fire chief, briefed by his PIO, was able to tell reporters, "The fire started in a bundle of clothes left too close to a space heater. There were no injuries because of the fire; however, two firefighters have been treated for heat exhaustion. Traffic will be diverted around the area for the next 24 hours. Alternate routes include Bath Street and Smith Avenue."

The communications and information management section of the NIMS refers to a JIS and JIC. These concepts have been used to manage information during disasters for many years, however, the establishment of NIMS in 2004 was the first official federal mandate of the system by the Department of Homeland Security. The design of the JIS, according to the NIMS standard, will provide PIOs and incident commanders with "an organized, integrated and coordinated mechanism for providing information to the public during an emergency."

The NIMS training document issued by the Federal Emergency Management Agency says that "Using the JIC as a central location, information can be coordinated and integrated across jurisdictions and agencies, and among all government partners, the private sector, and nongovernmental agencies." It is important to understand the concepts involved with a JIC, and the system that makes it work, because this system has been shown to be the best way to provide potentially lifesaving information during emergencies.

Another key advantage of the JIS is that it ensures that decision makers and the public are fully informed throughout the duration of the response.

"Without a JIC, getting coordinated information out is hampered."

When JICs have not been established, there is evidence of difficulty in disseminating coordinated information. The after-action report completed by the Arlington County, Virginia, Fire Department after the terrorist attacks on the Pentagon on September 11, 2001, clearly illustrates this point. The report says, "the failure to establish a JIC proved to be an impediment to the presentation of coordinated, factual, and timely public information. There was not a central point of interface between the media and the agencies involved in the response."[22]

Much like the NIMS concept of unified command, jurisdictions and responding agencies work together to manage information flowing from

FIGURE 6-4
TV reporter interviews uniformed fireman

an incident by using the JIC. While the JIS establishes policies, procedures, and standard guidelines under which the PIOs from the various agencies work together and cooperate, the JIC provides a location for these PIOs to work.

The JIS can be as simple as a face-to-face discussion between the PIO and incident commander establishing the information release guidelines or a more complex system consisting of several rooms of PIOs working on specific aspects of the incident information gathering and subsequent release to the media.

The NIMS system suggests that the JIC have an organizational structure that incorporates a research team, a media team, and a logistics team. It suggests the creation of a liaison position as well to allow a jurisdictional press secretary to function.

During a major incident, there may be more than one JIC established. As an incident grows in scope, additional resources are needed and different levels of government become involved. Each of these layers might create a JIC consisting of representatives from all agencies that are involved in the response and recovery at that level. These JICs must communicate with each other to allow for coordination of the messages.

One key component of a JIS, and perhaps a difficult one to understand, is the concept that each entity, while part of a JIC, maintains its

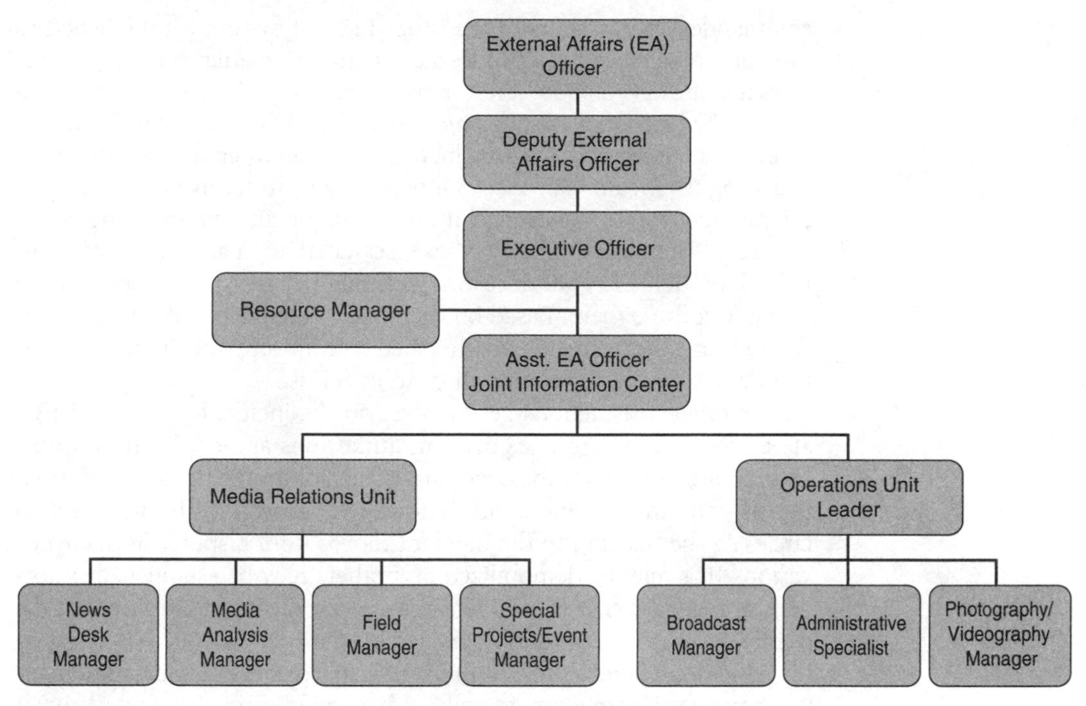

FIGURE 6-5
FEMA JIC Organization

"During an emergency, the public must receive one coordinated message."

own identity, yet conforms to the policies and procedures of the JIS. In other words, when police, fire, and EMS departments' information officers work together on an incident, they agree on a lead spokesperson, develop a plan for release of information, and then implement that plan. Should there be discipline specific information to be released, usually the JIC members defer to the appropriate discipline to release the information. However, since everyone is in the same location, information is shared prior to the media briefing. Thus, all PIOs hear, understand, and can deliver the same message.

In an emergency, this can be crucial. If the incident commander has decided to evacuate an area, and those participating in the JIC know that this emergency public information has to be released, then evacuation can proceed without incident. However, if another agency is providing information to the media that many volunteers are needed at the disaster site, the influx of volunteers and evacuees are going to meet at the perimeter, potentially impeding the ability of the evacuees to reach safety.

The development of the JIC should begin when an emergency is reported. Responding agencies, based on established policy, dispatch an information officer to the scene. The PIO interacts with the incident commander and meets with the other PIOs. A system is established to provide emergency public information to the media. Nonemergency messages are also crafted, and the media are briefed. As the incident escalates, the JIC is moved into a more permanent facility and divided into several functional areas which include a research team, a media team, and a logistics team. The research team begins to receive requests from the public for information and inquiries about rumors involving disaster issues. These rumors are further researched, their authenticity is confirmed or denied, and decisions are then made about the need to publicly address them. Based on the policies established by the JIS, media inquiries are directed to the media team and the incident commander clears all information prior to its release.

As other jurisdictions get involved in the incident, additional JICs are established, as are lines of communications among the JICs. Information is shared, joint messages are issued, and the release of information is coordinated. State and Federal JICs soon join the information circle. As the reaction to the incident moves from response to recovery, various JICs may be demobilized and others may be established. Information is always shared, and releases are coordinated to ensure that the public receives one common message.

When developing a JIS, PIOs should consider the personnel involved; how information is collected, verified, and distributed; what information is collected and by whom; methods of distributing information; rumor control; and coordination of information among PIOs. The JIS should include policies that guide the group, a discussion of how internal and external rumors are managed, and what relationship will be established between the Emergency Operations Center (EOC) and the JIC. How critical issues are discovered and how information is released are also part of the JIC/JIS operation.

"You cannot manage the media, but you can manage your JIC/JIS."

As with any organization, strong, trained leadership is required to make a JIC function at its highest level. Proper management of both internal and external group dynamics, as well as stress assistance (helping one another), not only extremely important to the success of incident information management; it is vital!

A successful JIC will allow agency spokespersons to remain autonomous, while sharing pertinent information. Within the JIC, no agency has authority over another, and there is teamwork among the JIC members.

When considering the function of a JIC, it is more important to understand the reason a JIC is established rather than a more formal organization. JICs are established to assist the public information team in providing the best information in a timely manner. This function is best accomplished with a strong JIS and a solid JIC organization. Reviewing the organization of a FEMA JIC can provide a base for organizing local JICs.

Box 6-7 PIO establishes, and operates within, the parameters established for the JIS

"The PIO establishes and operates within the parameters established for the Joint Information System—or JIS.

The JIS provides an organized, integrated, and coordinated mechanism for providing information to the public during an emergency.

The JIS includes plans, protocols, and structures used to provide information to the public. It encompasses all public information related to the incident.

Key elements of a JIS include interagency coordination and integration, developing and delivering coordinated messages, and support for decision makers."[i]

[i]NIMS I-700 Course Guide.

Joint Information Centers, FEMA Style

A FEMA JIC is established to assist the agency in providing support to state and local governments in a disaster. Often located within the JFO, the FEMA JIC consists of several positions. Flexibility of the system allows for some or all to be staffed. FEMA recently created position task books, which outline the tasks performed by each position. The National Wildfire Coordinating Group[24] (NWCG) also has task books for the PIO position. Although some components used in a FEMA JIC may not be applicable to a local government agency, the local PIO may, at some point, be working within the FEMA JIC. FEMA conducts a course titled "Advanced Public Information Officer" that teaches PIOs how to operate in a joint information setting. An additional online course titled "Emergency Support Function 15 (ESF 15), External Affairs: A New Approach to Emergency Communication and Information Distribution" is available on the FEMA Independent Study Web site. It covers the various components of ESF 15, including the JIC.

The new FEMA ESF 15 organization alters the JIC organization somewhat, allowing for greater expansion with larger incidents. As in any incident management system, this concept is expandable and contractable. To a lesser or greater extent, nearly all functions occur during most operations. Several functions may be performed by one person; or, at a larger incident, additional personnel may be required to accomplish all tasks.

The external affairs function is defined by the following major responsibilities:

- Planning and products
- Joint information center

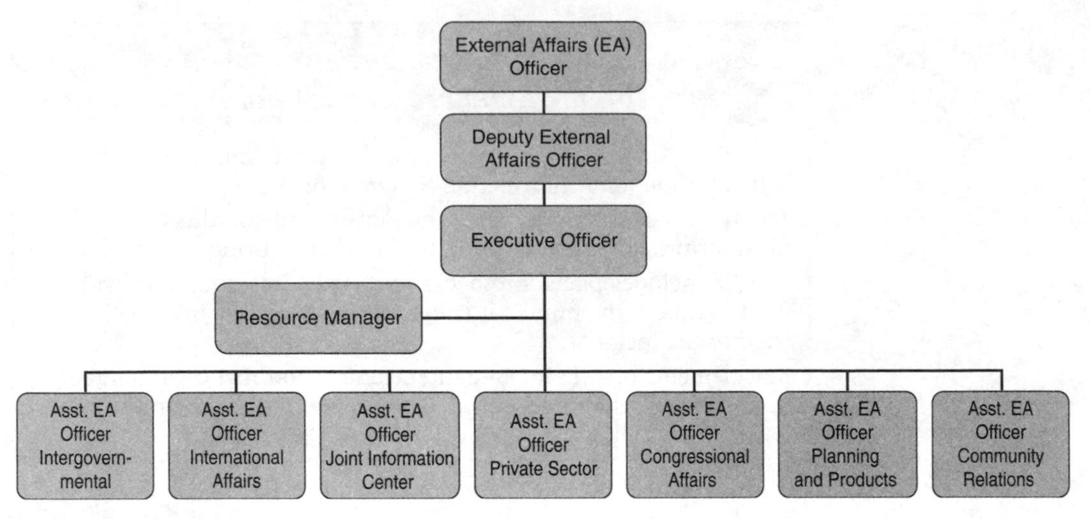

FIGURE 6-6
ESF 15

- Private sector
- Community relations
- Congressional affairs
- Intergovernmental affairs (tribal, state, and local)

ESF 15 is led by an external affairs officer. This position reports to the federal coordinating officer in a JFO, just as a PIO reports to the incident commander in a standard incident command organization.

All the positions within this organization are important; however, this chapter will concentrate on the JIC and on planning and products. The tasks within these designations are most likely to be used by the local-jurisdiction PIO. Both units are led by a "unit leader," a standard title within the incident command system. The various components within these units have a "manager" assigned to them.

Joint Information Center

The new JIC organization (see Figure 6.5) consists of two units: media relations and operations. Media relations is further divided into the **news desk**, media analysis, **field operations**, and special projects/events. Operations is divided into broadcast, administration, and photo/video.

The JIC is responsible for distributing products to the media. It does so using face-to-face contacts (field), answering questions and scheduling media interviews (news desk), and producing broadcast segments, including photographs and videos (broadcast and photo/video). The messaging is developed by products and planning.

Other key positions include the following:

News desk personnel answer inquiries from the news media. They provide press releases and work from fact sheets to answer questions accurately. This staff will also arrange interviews with certain key personnel, based on guidance from the lead PIO.

Field operations consists of PIOs working at the site of the disaster. In a large-scale disaster, they also have the responsibility to meet with local media outlets, establish relationships with them, and provide materials needed by specific outlets.

Media analysis provides an ongoing review and evaluation of the coverage given to the disaster. This is one of the primary goals of the JIS as described in the NIMS document: "The PIO handles media and public inquiries, emergency public information and warnings, rumor monitoring and response, media monitoring, and other functions required to coordinate, clear with the appropriate authorities and disseminate accurate and timely information related to the incident, particularly regarding information on public health and safety and protection."[25] These tasks are performed in support of the incident commander. The information obtained through **media monitoring** will help to determine whether the media are reporting the information released through the JIC. More importantly, it will provide guidance on the accuracy of information being reported. Media monitoring should be a part of the daily activity undertaken by a PIO, but must be a part of any JIC operation.

In a large JIC, a separate area for **broadcast operations** might be established. Within the area, interviews and briefings can occur, and video news releases, as well as **B-roll** video, can be produced and provided to the media. Those working in this area are often former broadcast journalists. During major disasters, FEMA produces programming for cable and satellite delivery sometimes called the "Recovery Channel."

In establishing a JIC, there may be partners who have little or no understanding of JIC functions or the incident command system. Training should be established to provide "just-in-time" education programs for these new JIC partners.

Day-to-day PIO job functions include setting up special events such as news conferences, media tours, or program announcements. Within the JIC, the special events team is activated when similar activities will be needed as they relate to the disaster.

All one has to do is look at the FEMA Web site to learn about the work of the photo documentation personnel.[26] Both still photography

FIGURE 6-7
Example of a Mitigation Photo

and video photography are used during disasters, not only to tell the story of the victims and responders, but also to create a historic record of the event. These photos can show successful mitigation efforts (see Figure 6-7) or unique damage patterns.

Planning and Products

The planning and products unit (see Figure 6-8) has absorbed several of the previous JIC organizational elements while adding others. The unit is subdivided into three support areas: strategy/message, liaison, and creative services (research and writing, the Web, *Recovery Times*, graphics).

As issues emerge at an incident, they are often picked up by the liaison, who works with the various other entities doing their jobs at the incident. (In a JFO, the liaison function might include the public assistance program.) The strategy/message team determines the method of addressing the issue and hands it off to the creative services team, which creates products such as press releases, brochures, and talking points. In addition, Web page content, as well as newsletter stories, may be developed.

Some other key tasks within products and planning include the following:

The **research and writing** group has the responsibility for all written material. All materials developed by research and writing must be

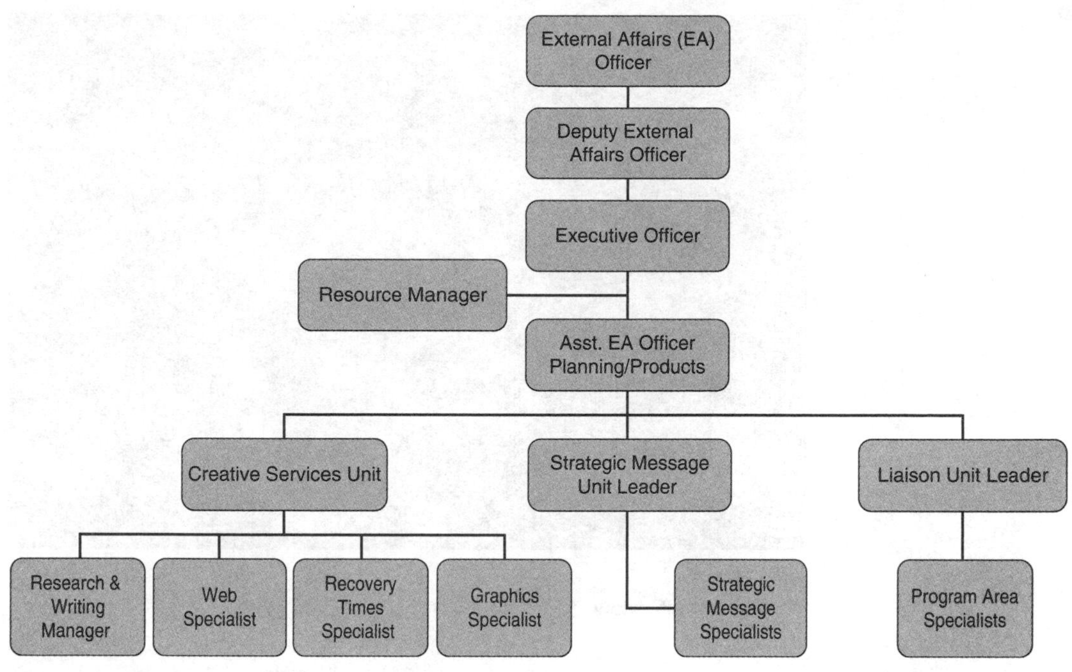

FIGURE 6-8
Planning and Products

approved through policies outlined in the JIS plans and, ultimately, by the incident commander, prior to their release.

Those assigned to **editorial production** should have exceptional writing skills. They will produce all written material developed by the JIC for release. This material includes press releases, fact sheets, and special brochures necessary for the delivery of a message associated with a particular disaster.

As noted in NIMS, the PIO must coordinate the release of accurate information, and the **program liaisons** assist with that function. They work with the various local, state, and federal disaster relief program groups, such as public assistance or housing. They can highlight issues faced by these groups, which can result in press releases or fact sheets that can clarify specific issues facing the public.

FEMA publishes a newsletter called ***Recovery Times*** during disasters as a method of communicating with victims. The publication contains pertinent information for disaster victims and is usually distributed by the community relations personnel stationed at the **disaster recovery centers (DRCs)**.

This text makes several references to the various constituencies served by a PIO. One of them is the multilingual community. When an emergency arises, communication materials must be developed in several

FIGURE 6-9
Multilingual interview

languages so that all of the affected constituencies can receive and understand the information. Throughout the external affairs function, the multilingual theme is emphasized. Press releases, the *Recovery Times*, and other material are translated into languages appropriate for those needing service within a disaster area. (See Figure 6-9.)

In the establishment of a JIC, gathering all the players involved in an incident is the first step toward success. Agreeing on the JIS plan will facilitate accurate, timely, and coordinated delivery of the information. Establishing other work areas within the JIC should occur only as necessary. The JIC can be flexible, with more areas opened and staffed in a complicated event and fewer in a simpler one.

The criteria for a successful JIS are applicable to a PIO's daily job activity: Get the RIGHT information to all of the *RIGHT* people at exactly the *RIGHT* time *SO* that *THEY CAN MAKE THE RIGHT DECISIONS*.

Summary

Working under stressful situations created by emergencies and crises can result in mistakes made by agencies or PIOs. Planning for such events can limit mistakes and greatly improve the efficiency of providing information to the public at a time when they need it most. Emergency public information can save lives, the ultimate goal of a PIO. The NIMS promotes the JIS as a way to enhance emergency public information. A PIO should develop a complete understanding of NIMS, JIS, and the inner workings of a JIC.

Of all the topics presented in this book, this one is likely to undergo the most changes in the near future. From technology to doctrine, the methods a PIO uses to communicate during an emergency are going to change. You Tube and other Internet video-sharing services are now a part of the daily lives of Americans; thus, a PIO will soon need to be aware of and use these services, as well as streaming video, cell phone alerts, and other technological methods, as standard methods of communications.

FEMA is working to improve the public information system as described by NIMS and will be releasing final job aids for PIOs. These can be obtained at the FEMA Web site as they become available.

REVIEW QUESTIONS

1. Which federal document outlines the PIOs responsibility in a disaster?
   a. The Constitution
   b. The National Incident Management System
   c. The Stafford Act
   d. None of the above

2. Within a Joint Information Center, agency PIOs maintain their autonomy, while still providing coordinated incident information.
   a. True
   b. False

3. Reporter errors can occur because of
   a. A misunderstanding during an interview
   b. Incorrect information provided by a PIO
   c. Editing by superiors within the news department
   d. All of the above

ENDNOTES

1. http://abcnews.go.com/US/story?id=1469171
2. Lee Wilkins. 1993. "The Mass Media, Disasters and Risk: Entwining Communication and Culture." pp. 118–130 in *Proceedings of the United States—Former Soviet Union Seminar on Social Science Research on Mitigation For and Recovery From Disasters and Large*

Scale Hazards, edited by E.L. Quarantelli and Konstantin Popov. Newark, Delaware: Disaster Research Center, University of Delaware. (p. 122)

3. Technical Report Series: The East Bay Hills Fire Oakland-Berkeley, California; United States Fire Administration, (p. 82)
4. U.S. Department of Homeland Security's Federal Emergency Management Agency, "State and Local Guide (SLG) 101: Guide for All-Hazard Emergency Operations Planning," http://www.fema.gov/plan/gaheop.shtm
5. NIMS, Department of Homeland Security, March 1, 2004. p. 40
6. http://www.fema.gov
7. www.rtnda.org/ethics/coe.shtml
8. Florida Press Club—http://www.floridapressclub.com; Syracuse Press Club—http://www.syracusepressclub.org; National Press Club—http://npc.pres.org
9. Poynter Online, June 15, 2005, The 11 Layers of Citizen Journalism, http://www.poynter.org/content/content_view.asp?id=83126
10. Dan Gillmor, *We the Media* (2004, O'Reilly)
11. http://www.regrettheerror.com/2005/09/networks_argue_.html
12. http://www.cnn.com/2006/US/01/03/mine.explosion/index.html
13. http://www.cnn.com/2006/US/01/04/miners.intl/
14. Don't Lose Your Cool, by Aysha Hussain; http://www.psychologytoday.com/rss/pto-20060308-000003.html
15. Select House Committee on Hurricane Response. 2006, p. 20
16. Alison Stateman, Time for a Change? What Hurricane Katrina Revealed About Race and Class in America, *PUBLIC RELATIONS STRATEGIST*, Oct. 1, 2005
17. Alison Stateman, Time for a Change? What Hurricane Katrina Revealed About Race and Class in America, *PUBLIC RELATIONS STRATEGIST*, Oct. 1, 2005
18. http://www.piedmontcommunities.us/servlet/go_ProcServ/dbpage=page&GID=00134000000973802080999925&PG=00139000000976071566049464
19. http://www.akdart.com/ebs.html
20. http://www.fcc.gov/eb/easfact.html
21. http://www.fema.gov/media/fact_sheets/declarations.shtm
22. Arlington County After-Action Report Annex A Page A-32
23. http://www.learningservices.us/fema/taskbooks/
24. http://www.nwcg.gov/pms/taskbook/command/piof.pdf
25. National Incident Management System, p. 45
26. http://www.photolibrary.fema.gov/photolibrary/index.jsp

CHAPTER 7

Speaking to Groups

Objectives

- Define the importance of effective public speaking skills for a PIO
- Describe the common "fears" held by public speakers
- Review the tools available for those who make presentations

CASE Study

The community organization begins to gather for its monthly luncheon. You watch as the crowd heads toward the buffet line, and you notice that the mayor and a local city council member are talking with the chief executive officer of the area's largest employer. The person walking in the door picks up the name tag indicating that she is president of a neighborhood watch group.

Your presentation is complete; attendees gather around you and begin pressing the mayor and council member to increase the budget for your department. The politicians inquire about programs you spoke about and pledge to improve funding and communications with your office.

Case Study Questions

1. How did the PIO in this case study benefit from this presentation?
2. What are three tools that the PIO might have used during this presentation?
3. Did the presence of the public influence politicians attending the luncheon?

Introduction

While working with the media is important to a PIO, the community relations aspect of the position can bring some of the most rewarding results. Speaking to both organized and spontaneous groups of people is becoming an ever-important role of a PIO.

During emergencies, speaking to small groups may be the only way to disseminate public information. When traditional methods of communicating are interrupted, these **"town crier"** type of meetings harken back to a time when television and radio were nonexistent, and cell phones weren't even part of science fiction.

Community groups carry tremendous influence with elected officials. They can also become your best advocates when promoting programs or **key messages**.

Speaking to groups allows an organization's representative to simultaneously inform a large number of people, provide an official position on specific issues, and make corrections to published or broadcast reports. These presentations can also serve to provide publicity for specific programs or address safety issues. They provide a forum to discuss a crisis or incident. They can help save lives by helping people prepare for imminent incidents such as a hurricane or wildfire.

"The message contained in a successful public presentation will extend well beyond the audience in the room."

Group presentations might also be used as part of an overall program launch such as an injury prevention program. A news release might be provided at the public session for the benefit of the media. Prepublicity might bring stories about the public attending the meeting to learn of the program being introduced.

Of all the positive benefits public speaking can bring to a PIO, perhaps the least understood and most significant is an expanded audience. The audience attending the presentation will take the message back to family and friends. In "Street Smart Public Relations", John Bud, Jr. calls this the "ripple effect." He says "**word of mouth** is the real communications catalyst."[1]

KEY TERMS

- Bullet points, p. 137
- Extemporaneous, p. 136
- Key messages, p. 130
- "Town crier", p. 130
- Word of mouth, p. 130

Stress and Public Speaking[2]

The potential benefits of speaking to groups are often outweighed by the stress these public environments frequently bring upon a speaker. Those not used to speaking in public believe it is inherently stressful. Most

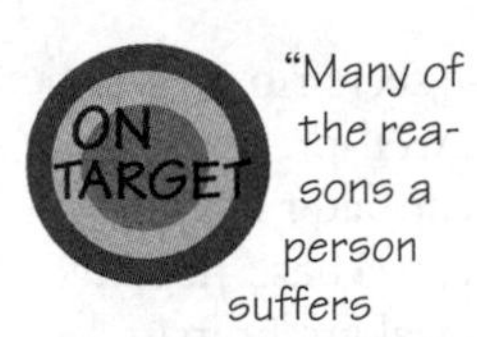

"Many of the reasons a person suffers stress before, during, and after a public speaking engagement are mirrored when the person is interviewed by reporters."

who regularly speak to groups learn that it is not that stressful. A PIO or any other public speaker does not have to be perfect to succeed. The most brilliant people can deliver the perfect speech, yet not be successful at persuading the audience.

One reason many public speakers fail and suffer the resulting stress is because they try to cover too much in a short presentation. This common mistake results in the audience trying to understand and digest too many thoughts at once. If audience members cannot understand the point of the message, they will not pass it on, thus breaking the word-of-mouth chain. This diminishes the impact of a public presentation.

Not clarifying the purpose of the presentation can also cause a speaker stress. This stressor can be eliminated or minimized by knowing your audience, the subject you are speaking about, the venue, and the format. The more public speaking you do, the more topics you will become familiar with, making it less likely that you will be unclear about a topic that is new to you.

Many speakers expect to receive something from the audience during the presentation. When the audience doesn't deliver, the stress level increases. A public speaker should plan to give the audience something, rather than the other way around. An audience attends a public event, whether formal or informal, with a purpose in mind. In the case of a presentation by you, the PIO, they are ready to hear what you have to say on the given topic. Most often, the audience does not come with the knowledge or experience to provide valid input to the speaker. They expect to get that knowledge from you. Your role as a speaker is to meet the expectations of the audience.

While trying to meet these expectations, you should avoid the stressor of believing you can please everyone. A speaker will rarely receive unanimous approval from a crowd. This does not mean you were not a successful speaker. You may have provided the audience with the best information, in the best manner, and still not have pleased certain segments of the audience.

"Trying to emulate your favorite public speaker can be your downfall and will increase your stress."

Audiences often come to a public meeting with preconceived notions on the subject. These may be incorrect ideas developed through rumors, misinterpreted news reports, or experience relayed through multiple parties.

There are thousands of very good public speakers across the country, and we have all heard several of them. As they speak, the little voice in the back of our head tells us, "this is the person to be like." This emulation can be your downfall because you are not that speaker. You are you!

Each of us develops our own style. Our voices are different. Our approach to the audience is personal. Your personality and the characteristics that make you who you are will show in your presentation. In certain circumstances, being personally revealing and humble can instantly win an audience.

When standing before an audience, the worst-case scenario is for the presentation to bring negative outcomes. While even well-prepared and well-researched speeches may have a bad outcome, a speaker cannot let that have a major influence on his or her nervousness. These negative outcomes rarely occur, mostly because good public speakers prepare by thoroughly researching the subject on which they plan to speak.

When speaking before a group, there are many variables. You have control over very few of them. Do not stress over things you cannot control. You can control your material, your knowledge of the subject, and your presentation method. You cannot always control technology, the audience, or the venue. You can make contingency plans. You can bring less technical presentation materials as a backup for projector-driven slideshows. While a speaker should know how to use a microphone, sound systems do fail. If this happens to you, have a plan in place. (Perhaps you could simply speak louder, move closer to the crowd, or even use a bullhorn.)

"An artist's only concern is to shoot for some kind of perfection, and on his own terms, not anyone else's."[3]

The behavior of your audience can easily raise your anxiety level. While most people who attend a public presentation want to be there and learn from the speech, there are some occasions when an audience is required to attend, and on those occasions the audience may not be friendly. Often, you know this because of the subject at hand. Discussing decreases in service, increases in expenses, or other unpopular decisions is never fun, but these sessions should be looked at as opportunities rather than challenges. Winning over an audience under negative circumstances is a special feeling.

Regardless of the presentation, your downfall may be what most might consider the smart thing to do for a public speaking engagement—over preparing. In the case of a public presentation, too much preparation can be overkill. The key to being ready to make a presentation is to learn and understand the material, not memorize it. When a spontaneous question arises and interrupts the tempo of your talk, you may be unable to return to the thought you were presenting when you answer the question. When you learn your subject matter and understand the implications of the presentation's content, the spontaneous questions will become a welcome addition to the program.

When you prepare, you become the "expert" in the room. In fact, when you answered the phone requesting your presence at the event, you became the expert. A community group or other organization will call on you to make a presentation because there is already a perception of expertise. That perception might be developed from members attending previous presentations, from television and radio appearances, from reading newspaper articles, or because of other marketing done by your agency.

The most critical person at any presentation is the speaker. After all, you know the subject. You know when you make a mistake. You have a

feel for whether or not the audience reacted the way you wanted. Few speakers encounter an audience as well versed on the subject as they are. When you do encounter such an audience, personality can win your audience over. Your "human" side can make the difference. Harness the urge to be smug and arrogant. Be informative and genuine. Make people want to invite you home for coffee.

Nervousness

ON TARGET "A little nervousness is natural; too much is detrimental. Controlling your nerves is critical to a successful presentation."

There are many well educated scholars who have researched the nervousness experienced by public speakers. Nearly any reference you review will tell you this nervousness is natural. Some will contend it is even healthy, because it shows you care about doing well. There is a limit, however, and too much nervousness can be detrimental to your presentation.

Toastmasters International, an organization that teaches public speaking techniques offers many suggestions to those who must deliver presentations. Local chapters can be a valuable place to learn these techniques. Much of this chapter is based on these proven tips and tricks.

Start getting your nerves under control when you accept the assignment. Learn as much as you can about the audience and about what is expected from your program. How long will your presentation be? Will you need audio/visual aids? Should you prepare handouts? Is the event being recorded? Will the media be present? Can you invite the media?

By walking around the room in which you will speak, you will begin to understand its peculiarities. Are there dead spots where it may be difficult to hear? Is there a public address system, and does it work? Will there

be someone from the facility to set up and work the public address system controls? Do you know how to set up the system? Is there a backup?

If you are using audio/visual displays this walkabout can help you determine the proper size needed to ensure that they are visible. Is the text on your slides the correct size? Is there a computer projector, or do you have to bring one? Will your computer connect to the venue's system? If you will use audio aids in your presentation, how will you connect them to the public address system?

Prior to your presentation, practice it, but don't memorize the information and wording. Learn it. Memorization can make you sound stiff and unbelievable. Sometimes this stoic style of presentation leads to a perception of mistrust. The audience might feel that you are "reading" a speech instead of telling them information about the subject. Simply stated, know your material.

There are some basic relaxation techniques which can help you prior to delivering your talk. Many studies have shown exercising will relieve stress.[4] Deep breathing techniques also seem to help prior to delivering a public presentation.[5]

On the day of the presentation, you might become familiar with your audience by greeting them at the door. Sitting amongst the crowd, if possible, will allow you to develop a personal relationship with some of the audience members. You might learn about hobbies, likes, dislikes, and what these audience members want to learn from your presentation. This developing "friendship" can help you in making your presentation. If you know the people you are speaking to, you are better able to carry on a conversation with them. This improves your presentation by turning it into a conversation with acquaintances instead of a speech to strangers.

When you are to be interviewed by the media, a good practice is to visualize your success. This advice also holds true with regard to speaking in public. Think about your voice, the pace of your delivery, and the reaction of the audience. Remember, you can control your voice and delivery pace, not the audience, so don't let your "dream" distract you if it doesn't come true.

Those attending your presentation want you to succeed in your delivery. People do not come to a program to watch you fail. The audience is looking for you to be interesting, informative, and knowledgeable about the subject. If it fits your personality, you can be entertaining with your delivery. Do not force comedy into your presentation. Someone who is not naturally funny trying to do comedy is painful to watch. Comedy must also be appropriate for the subject and the audience.

When delivering your presentation, use caution with the medium you are using to enhance the message. Speakers often fail in their efforts to present a program because they concentrate too much on the medium while the message suffers. Between attempting to get the remote to work and spinning graphics on the projected slide, you may lose the audience because the people begin to believe that they are at a circus instead of an informative program. Do not use equipment and presentation tools you are not familiar with. When making one of history's greatest speeches, the Gettysburg Address, President Abraham Lincoln never used a slide show, chart, or photo. He let the words speak for themselves.

"Harness your nervous energy and transform it into vitality and enthusiasm."[6]

Like most skills we learn in life, public speaking is one that improves with experience. As a PIO, you should embrace opportunities to speak before groups. You should seek out these opportunities by establishing a speaker's bureau within your organization. This will allow you to present your agency's programs to various community groups throughout the year. The more often you make a presentation, the better it and you will become!

Box 7-1 Public Speaking Principles[i]

- Speaking in Public is NOT Inherently Stressful
- You Don't Have to be Brilliant or Perfect to Succeed
- All You Need is Two or Three Main Points
- You Need a Purpose That is Right for the Task
- The Best Way to Succeed is NOT to Consider Yourself a Public Speaker!
- Humility and Humor Can Go a Long Way
- When You Speak in Public, Nothing "Bad" Can Ever Happen!
- You Don't Have to Control the Behavior of Your Audience
- In General, the More You Prepare, the Worse You Will Do
- Your Audience Truly Wants You to Succeed

[i] *How To Conquer Public Speaking Fear*, Morton C. Orman, M.D., © 1996–2002, M.C. Orman, MD, FLP.

Your Presentation

Now that you have a better understanding of the potential causes of stress as it relates to your presentation, let's review the content of that talk.

How will you deliver the information? You could write a script and read it to the audience or memorize the content and recite it. Another option is to be completely **extemporaneous**. Whatever comes to mind will be what the audience hears. Many speakers will chose a combination of these presentation methods. There are advantages to each of these methods.

The speech read to an audience can be boring for the listener. However, when the content is a direct quote from someone else, or an official policy statement, this type of delivery may be necessary to avoid mistakes and confusion.

Memorizing a speech, as noted earlier, can cause the presenter to appear robotic and stiff during the presentation and doesn't allow for any deviation.

Extemporaneous presentations can be a valuable tool. If a PIO always has messages ready for delivery, a spontaneous opportunity to address a group can allow extemporaneous speaking skills to shine. The key to success with this type of presentation is to always have a message to deliver. Completely extemporaneous presentations can, however, be dangerous if they have no set message. The speaker may begin to ramble and cause the audience to lose interest because the subject matter is disjointed.

Whichever method you choose for your presentation, there are basic skills to master that will enhance your delivery style. As you do more public speaking you will learn which presentation style fits you best, however you must be yourself when delivering your speech. Vary your voice so as not to be monotone. Emotions should be natural, not forced. Making eye contact with members of your audience, especially those you are trying to influence the most, can go a long way in making your presentation successful.

Start developing your presentation by establishing some objectives. Objectives can be developed in several ways including the ABCD method:[7] audience, behavior, condition, and degree. This method has you review who the people in the audience are, what behavior you expect of them after the presentation, under what condition they will hear your message, and, finally, how much you want the audience to be able to accomplish. Once you have decided on your objectives, begin developing an outline for your presentation. This can be done using a commercial computer program such as Microsoft's PowerPoint or by jotting down a few notes. The outline's content should meet the objectives you have established and allow you to present the message within the prescribed time frame.

Once you have refined the outline, determine whether any audio/visual props will be needed, and gather those. Remember to make sure that they are the appropriate size for the room in which you will deliver the program.

It is now time to practice your speech, refine the message, and finalize any "slideshows" you will use.

Don't forget the basic format of any presentation:

Tell them what you are going to tell them; then tell them; and, finally, tell them what you told them.

Presentation Tools

This chapter will not attempt to teach you how to create slides, charts, or other visual aids. It will give you some options to use during your presentations.

There are many tools you can use to enhance your presentation. Many have learned that, of all the tools available for use in a presentation, the most important tool is the one you choose not to use.

Slideshow Software—Modern computers bring a great deal of variety to the visual aspect of your presentation. They offer "slideshow" software by several vendors, which will make it easier for you to emphasize points, show photos and graphs, and display short video clips as part of your program.

While these software marvels have many bells and whistles, the tricks can take over the program, and the audience may miss your message. Another danger of relying on these programs is the chance of equipment failure. Computers fail, projector lights burn out, and the venue may not have a screen large enough to display your creation.

Avoid writing long sentences and reading from the slide. Use **bullet points**, and talk about the points as you present the material. To make the most effective visual presentation, choose the predesigned templates offered by the various software programs. These have the proper proportioned text, graphics, and colors. Some offer slide transitions, which will enhance your presentation.

Overheads—In this day and age of computer-driven presentations, many scoff at the "old-fashioned" overhead projector, but when a computer or some other type of equipment crashes just before a presentation to the mayor's staff, an "overhead" can be your best friend. "Overheads," otherwise known as clear letter-sized "transparencies," are made using a modern printer or by simply writing on the surface. The finished product is placed on the lit surface of an overhead projector which displays an enlarged image on a screen or wall. While rarely used as a primary mode of presentation enhancement, these "old fashioned" transparencies are a backup for you in the "can't live without" category.

Charts—Charts can be an important part of a presentation. when they are created in the correct size and manner. The chart, which can remain on

stage as long as necessary, can be referred to often during your program. Sequential charts can show the progress of a project or funding differences.

Charts can be produced in color, which can be expensive, but color charts are more appealing to the audience. Attempt to develop charts that are not time sensitive. (The same goes for the display boards discussed next.) These charts will last through many presentations and be more cost effective.

Display Boards—Few speakers use large display boards today, opting instead to use wall-sized screens with computer-generated slides projected onto them. These display boards can serve a useful purpose before and after a program. By placing the boards near an exit or entrance, your audience can view additional items such as photos or program promotional elements.

Regardless of what audio/visual enhancement you choose, let the message of your presentation be the focal point, not the multimedia bells and whistles.

Speakers' Bureaus

Speakers' bureaus allow an agency to highlight key programs using the personnel most familiar with them. Teaching these subject matter experts proper public speaking techniques can increase the number and variety of presentations your agency can offer to the community. Community groups are always looking for speakers, and the topics are not necessarily issue based.

Your speakers can help improve your agency's public image by putting a friendly face to a common logo. Never forget the rank and file who work for your organization. Whether it is the paramedic on an ambulance, a police officer walking a beat, or a firefighter on an engine, these people are the daily public speakers for your organization!

Summary

A PIO will be called on to speak in front of groups. It might be a group of managers, citizens, or media. Knowing and understanding the common methods of delivering these presentations will limit anxiety and go a long way toward improving the PIO's persuasiveness.

REVIEW QUESTIONS

1. List three common causes of stress for a public speaker.

2. List three suggestions to ease the nervousness public speakers often feel.

3. A standard method of making a presentation includes
   a. Telling the audience what you will tell them
   b. Telling them
   c. Telling them what you told them

   _________True _________ False?

ENDNOTES

1. John Bud, Jr, *Street Smart Public Relations,* p.48, Turtle Publishing Company, Lakeville, Connecticut, 1992.
2. *How To Conquer Public Speaking Fear,* Morton C. Orman, M.D., © 1996–2002, M.C. Orman, MD, FLP.
3. http://creativequotations.com/one/456a.htm
4. http://www.holistic-online.com/stress/stress_exercise.htm
5. Marianne Ross, Ph.D., Copyright 1994–2006, www.selfhelpmagazine.com, Pioneer Development Resources, Inc.
6. Toastmasters International—ten tips for successful public speaking.
7. Heinich, et al., 1996.

CHAPTER 8

Marketing Your Agency

Objectives

- Define the PIO's market
- Identify the products that your agency could market
- List the components of a marketing plan

The news is filled with stories about criminal activity in your community. There are shootings, burglaries, and vehicle thefts. The mayor is after the police chief to "get something done."

In a meeting back at headquarters, the police chief grills his senior staff, asking, "Why are we having these problems?" His staff tells stories of increased arrests, a high percentage of unsolved homicides, and failed "Neighborhood Watch" meetings. Department morale is at an all time low. "We work so hard and get no recognition. We hold these meetings and no one shows up. What are we to do?"

The chief enlists the help of a local marketing consultant. A plan is developed and implemented. Soon, Neighborhood Watch groups are established all over the city. New reports now show a decrease in criminal activity in neighborhoods and progress of the detectives in solving violent crimes. The mayor holds a public meeting to praise the police department, and department morale soars.

Case Study Questions

Marketing involves promoting and selling a product that an audience needs. Match the product with the audience as depicted in this case study.

Product	Audience
____ 1. Neighborhood Watch Groups	a. Mayor
____ 2. Positive Publicity for police	b. Media
____ 3. News stories promoting decrease in crime	c. Citizens

Introduction

While many do not believe that there is a need for **marketing** in emergency management or for a public safety agency, there is no doubt that PIOs perform vital marketing functions every day. Much of what has been discussed in previous chapters of this text are portions of a comprehensive marketing strategy. This chapter will attempt to fill in some of the missing pieces of the marketing puzzle.

If you think about it, the definition of emergency public information—providing the public with the right information at the right time to allow them to make the right decision—can be easily adapted to describe a marketing plan.

When we market to our audience, we have to understand its needs and wants, and then satisfy those needs through products and services. In an emergency, we know what needs the public has, yet they may not perceive them as a need. Our efforts must be focused on convincing the public that there is a need and then presenting the public with a product to satisfy that need.

To explain this concept, let's compare a consumer product and an emergency management issue.

High-definition television (HDTV) is the next major trend in high-end consumer electronics. Soon, the long-standard analog television (TV) signals will go dark in favor of digital television signals. Broadcast television stations and networks have made the transition to digital transmitting equipment and are touting the improved signal quality. At the same time, cable television and satellite TV providers are competing with varying claims regarding how they carry these new HDTV signals.

The challenge facing the HDTV industry is to convince the public to buy the new products. Certainly, a deadline for the end of analog television looms as an incentive, but consumers still have to be shown the advantage of the products. Marketing campaigns depict increased clarity, greater programming options, and decreasing prices.

For the emergency management example, we'll discuss the challenge of convincing citizens to evacuate prior to storms. As of this writing, many studies are still being conducted to try to understand why people did not evacuate when category five hurricanes were heading toward their residences. Max Mayfield was the director of the National Hurricane Center in 2005 when the hurricanes Katrina and Rita struck the Gulf Coast. At the 2006 National Hurricane Conference, Mayfield told the opening session that he believes that 1969's Hurricane Camille killed more people in 2005 than it did in 1969. His premise is that many Gulf Coast residents did not evacuate in 1969 and survived Camille. In 2005, these same people either chose not to evacuate or passed their survival stories on to relatives who, in turn, decided to stay through Katrina and Rita. Many did not survive. They did not have a perceived need to leave the area because they did not believe they were in danger.

When it comes to evacuations, emergency managers have to convince the public that lives are in danger. The message must be one of "it is going to happen," not "remember what has happened in the past."

"Marketing is a vital component of public safety."

To achieve this mindset change, emergency managers may employ basic marketing techniques over a long period. These techniques can help the citizens better understand their "need" (life threat) for the "product" (evacuation) and, in turn, "buy it."

There are countless examples that show why marketing is necessary in public safety. Perhaps a challenge the marketing industry faces is convincing public safety providers that they need to market their services. When you need a loaf of bread, you have a choice of grocery stores, bakeries, and brand names. All these companies must convince you that their bread is the best. When you have a crime, you call 9-1-1, and the police arrive. When you are injured, you call 9-1-1, and the paramedics arrive. When you have a fire, you call 9-1-1, and the fire department arrives. There is no need to shop. Most people do not even ask about the quality of the police, fire, and EMS services in their community when they buy a house. Many never think about these entities until they have a problem. "They will always be there!"

Of course, while public safety agencies strive to answer every call in a timely fashion, it is becoming more and more challenging. Budgets are being cut, requests for service are increasing, and in some localities, it is becoming a challenge to maintain staffing at minimum levels. Could these challenges be because of poor marketing? Does a product fail because of poor marketing? Do college classes fail to attract enough students because of poor marketing? An analysis of these questions will most likely conclude that the answer is yes.

KEY TERMS

- Advertising,[1] p. 145
- Assumptions, p. 147
- Direct marketing,[2] p. 150
- Five "P's" of marketing, p. 145
- Marketing, p. 142
- Mission statement, p. 147
- Publicity,[3] p. 150
- Public information, p. 142
- Public relations,[4] p. 145
- Public service announcements, p. 146
- Vision statement, p. 147

Marketing Defined

The American Marketing Association says, "Marketing is the process of planning and executing the conception, pricing, promotion, and distribution of ideas, goods, and services to create exchanges that satisfy individual and organizational goals. Through the use of marketing, individuals and groups create and exchange products and services with others in order to create value or satisfy wants and needs."[5]

Of course, in order to understand this definition, one must look at its components and place them in the context of emergency management and public safety. In order to market a product, you have to admit you have customers. Which comes first, the product or the customer, is debatable. For professionals working in emergency management, admitting residents of the service area are customers is for some, a challenging but necessary leap.

Emergency management and public safety agencies have a long list of customers including citizens, facilities within the jurisdiction, politicians, and agency employees. The list is similar to the list of a PIO's constituents discussed in Chapter One of this book.

Once we identify who the customers are, we have to understand our product. This is where complacency sometimes clouds our vision. Public safety agencies were born out of need. If we never had fires, fire departments would not have evolved. Even the types of fires the fire service responds to today are different. They have adjusted the "product" they deliver. The "cop on the beat" has morphed into "community-oriented policing."

Emergency medical services (EMS) evolved from the days of "ambulance drivers," when the term "paramedic" wasn't even in the dictionary. The 1966 white paper "Accidental Death and Disability: The Neglected Disease of Modern Society"[6] was, in essence, a consumer review for a product need, which was to develop an EMS system where one did not exist.

Now comes the challenging part of this discussion. Exactly what does an emergency service agency have to sell? We have already established that people will call us when they are in trouble. So, what else could we possibly have to "sell"? In fact, there are many "products" public safety agencies can "sell." In some cases, "sell" can actually mean developing a revenue stream for the agency, not just providing a concept for people to "buy in to."

Among the many emergency service products are the all-important concepts of personal preparedness and prevention. In disasters, citizens need to be prepared to be on their own until help arrives. The U.S. Department of Homeland Security's Federal Emergency Management Agency (FEMA) recommends that the public prepare for at least 3 days of being on its own. A marketing plan can be developed for this product.

Police departments are promoting a program called "watch your car," which encourages etching vehicle identification numbers (VINs) on windows and placing a sticker on the car. The VIN etching is a deterrent to criminals who want to steal your car for parts, and the window sticker tells the police to stop the vehicle if it is seen on the road during certain early hours of the morning. This program can be successful only if a marketing plan is developed and implemented to get citizens to mark their cars.

Public Information, Public Relations, or Marketing?

There are differences between public information, **public relations**, and marketing. Public information is mostly reactive; public relations is proactive; and marketing is an ongoing process of planning and execution of the plan. The PIO has a role, if not sole responsibility, for all three within the context of the job.

Marketing uses **advertising**, the media, the Internet, and graphics as part of an overall plan. Often, the marketing plan consists of public information and public relations activities. A typical marketing plan might include a strategy of constant "Good News" stories, mailers to residents about a specific program, and a speaker's bureau circuit of community groups.

"The five "P's" of marketing apply to emergency management and public safety."

While there are some variations on this theme, marketing is generally defined by what is commonly known as the **five "P's" of marketing**:[7] people, price, product, promotion, and place. Do the five "P's" of marketing relate to emergency management and public safety? Absolutely!

People

As discussed earlier, the people that a PIO works with cover a wide range, and whom the PIO addresses depends on the subject at hand. One day "people" could mean a neighborhood that has been affected by a hazardous material spill or crime spree. The next day it may mean "selling" the chief executive officer (CEO) on a new public awareness campaign. To develop an effective marketing plan, you must understand the "people."

Price

If a PIO works for a government agency, price does not necessarily seem to apply, unless you are tasked with the annual pilgrimage to the local legislative body to plead for your share of shrinking tax dollars. Price is an absolute consideration any PIO must take into account if they are to be successful at marketing a concept.

No matter what the project is, there are costs. It could be the cost of evacuating a neighborhood. There will always be economic factors to consider. While the decision to evacuate rests on others' shoulders, the dissemination of the message rests on yours. Eventually, you will be asked to explain cost recovery for those who have been displaced. There will be questions about reimbursement and, more than likely, a need to "sell" various constituencies on the fact that the decision you made was correct, that it saved lives, and that there is no way to put a value on a life.

Product

Entire books can be written on the "product" a PIO has to sell. In some cases, the product might be convincing the CEO that the PIO's position is vital to the organization. Development and promotion of individual public safety campaigns, news stories, and policies and procedures for working with the press are just of few of the many "products" a PIO works with daily.

Promotion

Once the PIO identifies the "people" and the need they have, develops a "product" to meet that need, and determines the "price" of that product, it must be promoted. The PIO can promote the product through news stories, community group meetings, flyers mailed to area residents, or a series of public meetings. In some cases, the promotion involves soliciting local media outlets for free airtime and developing **public service announcements**.

Place

In standard marketing, the place is considered to be the location where a product is sold. When you walk into a department store, there is a reason that the merchandise on the floor is there to greet you. It is not a random placement. With this in mind, the PIO should consider the proper place to sell the product. If the product is a "start-a-Neighborhood Watch campaign," then the place to sell the product might be a neighborhood church or school gathering.

The Marketing Plan

Every marketing plan has a specific template. This outline can be used for nearly any project a PIO is working on. The template follows a general outline and includes the following parts:

- overview
- objectives
- market discussion
- market segments
- market segmentation
- discussion of needs and requirements
- sales goals
- product definition
- distribution channels
- competitive analysis
- communications strategy
- expense budget
- discussion of sales and marketing resources available
- measurement and evaluation
- keys to success
- conclusion

"Follow a template to develop a marketing plan."

While the preceding template may seem complex, following it can help you separate out the great ideas from the mediocre ones.

Overview

No plan can be developed without providing a brief overview and description of the project. This overview should consist of goals, **assumptions** you are working under, and a description of the actions you will take to achieve your goals.

If your organization has a **mission statement** or **vision statement**, your plan should include it, and the program should match that statement's intent. Mission and vision statements are common in the corporate environment; however, few exist in the public safety world. For decades, police agencies have labeled their cars with "To protect and serve" as a slogan. The Phoenix Fire Department is famous for its mission statement, "Prevent harm, survive, and be nice." These statements can be important as they help guide you in developing your marketing and promotion plan. It will help you define your service philosophy, the audience, why you want to serve them, and the manner in which you will serve them. This statement may also explain why your organization exists in the first place.

Objectives

When developing objectives for your plan, they should be measurable, attainable, and applicable to your project. Develop your objectives with the available resources in mind. You may want to land a person on the moon, but when you are still struggling to get the training wheels off the bicycle, it will be a monumental task.

A Discussion of Your Market

The marketing plan must address the concerns of the supervisors to whom you present it. One reason for concern is often a misunderstanding of the market. To circumvent this misunderstanding, include a market discussion in the plan. Identify the needs of groups of people, and show how the product will meet those needs. This will help the decision makers understand why you selected a particular product or marketing plan.

Market Segments, Market Segmentation Strategy, Discussion of Needs and Requirements

You can probably never understand too much about the needs and requirements of your market. Every market is different, and as the audience varies, so will the needs. The media may have one set of needs, while the citizens may have another. These different market segments should be explained in the marketing plan, and each segment's needs should be defined.

A good example of understanding diverse market segments was shown in TV ads for a major bank. The ads illustrate how one picture can have different meanings to different people, emphasizing the importance of knowing cultural differences. Similar cultural differences influence the meaning of a statement or gesture. Handshakes, the proximity of one person to another, and even the type of clothes one wears may affect how a message is received.

In Chapter 1, the topic of a PIO's constituency was discussed. Review this chapter as you begin to look at your audience and market segment.

Sales Goal

While the "sales" goal you are trying to achieve may not mean collecting money from customers, there should be some type of numeric goal set for your project. This goal might simply be a minimum number of people to reach with a new message. You should also set sales goals within each market segment and even among each product line, if there is more than one.

Product Definition

The marketing plan should clearly outline what you are selling. A good exercise is to discuss what makes this product unique. You should be able to explain why the customer would "buy" the product.

In the earlier example of forming a Neighborhood Watch group, you would explain how this group is unique for the target audience and what benefits they attain in adopting the idea.

"Target Marketing"

Distribution Channels

A common mistake made by marketers is not understanding the audience's preferred method of product delivery. When you understand how the audience wants to receive your product, service, or message, then you can develop an effective strategy to deliver it.

When establishing a Neighborhood Watch group, you might consider running public service announcements on a local radio station encouraging people to attend the meeting. Running the announcements on your favorite station might not be the best method of delivery because the targeted audience does not listen to that station.

By talking with neighborhood leaders, you would be able to ascertain the best station on which to place the message.

Competitive Analysis

When you work for a public safety agency, you rarely have direct competition; however, there are significant levels of competition for an audience's time. There are so many issues and activities today that people make very careful choices about how they allocate their time. In the marketing plan, reviewing competing interests may help in forming new alliances, thus helping you accomplish your objectives as well as another agency's.

Natural competition exist among individual public safety entities. The fire service has often had heated battles with third-service or private emergency medical service providers. These are competitors. PIOs can learn from competitors that are successful at promoting their messages. Review their strengths and weaknesses, and any unique customers they serve.

Communications Strategy

Perhaps the most important part of the marketing plan is describing how you will communicate your message. There are dozens of methods to communicate the message to your chosen audience. These include advertising, public relations, **publicity**, **direct marketing**, direct mail, a trade show exhibition, Internet marketing, outdoor marketing, and sponsorships.

Direct mail is an extremely effective means of reaching a specific audience. This type of message delivery allows you to target a specific zip code, a block or a street, or an entire municipal boundary. The brochure, letter, or package mailing should be coupled with another type of message delivery such as a news story, a follow-up phone call, or flyers posted in neighborhood locations.

You should understand that each method of message delivery has advantages and disadvantages. Direct mail companies can help you with the specifics of this type of message delivery. An advertising agency can assist with all types.

Expense Budget

How much money do you have to spend on this project? If you do not know, you need to find out. A marketing budget can help you determine which parts of your plan you can afford and which ones you cannot. You should be prepared to fight for the important part to be funded. Pick your battles carefully, think about all the alternative methods you might use to alter your plan, and spend less money while still achieving goals.

Above all, you have to have realistic expectations about what you can spend and what you can accomplish with the budget you have. You also have to understand the tools you have to work with. If you are required to do all the design work on the new brochure, you should have the proper computer software to complete the task. If you need 3 hours a day to make presentations to community groups but only have 1 hour, your expectations will have to change.

Discussion of Sales and Marketing Resources Available

To ground everyone in the real world you work in, your marketing plan should include a discussion of your resources. Both financial and human resources can affect the overall plan. Explain your marketing infrastructure and build realistic expectations for the plan.

Measurement/Evaluation

If your objectives were correctly developed, they should be measurable. In your marketing plan, you should explain how the objectives would be measured. When measuring the plan's success, you should devise a strategy to change and improve on your plan. The method of evaluation should be predefined evaluation tools.

Keys to Success/Critical Issues

The final part of your marketing plan should be a discussion of the most important parts of your plan. Outline the parts that will make or break success of the plan. Discuss the absolutely essential tasks that your plan must accomplish. Make sure that the plan completely describes why these items are essential.

Summary

The marketing plan is a marketing device in itself. You must sell the boss on the concept in order to get the plan in place. The plan then must then be salable to the customer. Marketing is not as easy as this chapter may lead you to believe. Perhaps the best course of action is to employ the professionals. After all, when the smoke alarm sounds, we want the public to call the fire department. An advertising agency can help your marketing be more successful. In addition, community coalitions can often be more helpful. Municipalities and not-for-profit organizations might be able to get a professional advertising firm to donate some time for a project as a community service.

Above all else, planning can make for successful public safety campaigns. The plan gives you something to measure success against and improve on when it comes time for the next project.

REVIEW QUESTIONS

1. Public information, public relations, and marketing are different terms for the same thing.

   _________True _________ False?

2. A marketing plan should include objectives and measurement tools.

   _________True _________ False?

3. List three projects for which you could develop a marketing plan.

ENDNOTES

1. http://www.managementhelp.org/ad_prmot/definition.htm, Carter McNamara, MBA, PhD, Copyright 1999.
2. http://www.110creative.com/kb/terms/direct_marketing.php, Copyright © 1999–2005 Lorentz Consulting, LLC, Dallas, Texas.
3. http://www.managementhelp.org/ad_prmot/definition.htm, Carter McNamara, MBA, PhD, Copyright 1999.
4. Public Relations Society of America (PRSA).
5. American Marketing Association.
6. National Academy of Sciences and the National Research Council in 1966.
7. Action Plan Marketing, http://www.actionplan.com; http://www.marketingteacher.com/Lessons/lesson_marketing_mix.htm, May 27, 2006.

CHAPTER 9

Case Studies in Public Information

Objectives

In this chapter, the reader will

- Learn from a PIO's experience in working with the media during disasters
- Develop an understanding of the skills necessary to be an effective PIO
- Review techniques for using research to develop key message points

Introduction

The National Information Officers Association (NIOA) is a professional organization for Public Information Officers. Members regularly receive newsletters containing pertinent information on legal rulings involving the media and PIOs, articles outlining the best practices in providing public information, and first-person accounts of incidents in which they have played a major role.

This chapter contains several articles from NIOA that reinforce the information presented throughout this book.

These articles are reprinted with permission of the authors and the National Information Officers Association.

KEY TERMS

Coast Guard public affairs (PA) personnel, p. 157

Key messaging, p. 162

Maximum disclosure, minimum delay, p. 157

"Push/pull" system, p. 158

Sample size, p. 160

Sound bites, p. 174

Stakeholders, p. 157

The five C's: crime, corruption, catastrophe, conflict, and color, p. 177

The 3R's for 3S and 3D contexts, p. 172

Case Study One COMMUNICATING IN A CRISIS

Analysis by Lt. Robert Wyman, 8th District
United States Coast Guard
May/June 2006 NIOA News

Watching Hurricane Katrina head across Florida as a Category 1, and then back into the Gulf of Mexico on Aug. 25, one couldn't help but feel bad for the people of Florida who appeared to be in the crosshairs of yet another hurricane.

But by Aug. 26, as Katrina slowly tracked west, that sympathy shifted to concern, and the interest in the news and weather took a dynamic shift. As it became clear that Katrina had zeroed in on New Orleans and the Louisiana/Mississippi coast, the 8th District Public Affairs staff shifted from being consumers of the news, to being responsible for reporting the news of the Coast Guard's involvement in Katrina.

"We knew each other and I think that made a lot of difference."—CNN Producer on the Coast Guard's approach to media relations during the response to Hurricane Katrina.

By the night of Aug. 29—as the extent of the flooding and damage became clear; as the unprecedented operational response swung into full gear; as the first dramatic videos of operations were broadcast; and as several hundred local, national and international media outlets began calling—the Coast Guard's public affairs policies would be tested at every level, and perhaps more so than at any other time in our Service's history.

The Instant News World

The evolution of the Internet, along with the media's push to show live coverage, has created exponential changes in the public's expectations and demands for news. "A disaster such as Katrina is exactly the wrong time for agencies to start establishing relationships with media organizations," said Mike Ahlers, senior producer, CNN. "That's where the Coast Guard came out on top. They had established relationships with CNN reporters and producers such as myself long before the disaster, and that paid off during Katrina. We knew who to call, and the Coast Guard knew who to call. We knew each other, and I think that made a lot of difference," Ahlers said.

The 8th District Katrina response Web site, http://www.uscgstormwatch.com, was viewed by almost 2.3 million people during the response. No longer does anyone wait for the evening news or the morning paper. Instead, there is a broad expectation by all publics and **stakeholders** that timely and accurate information will be available around the clock.

This unprecedented visibility of the Coast Guard, and 24-hour interest in operations, placed significant strain on the limited personnel assigned to fill the "information" role of the various incident commands. Meeting all of those demands, while simultaneously shielding operators from the media crush and trying to avoid impacting Coast Guard operations, was a constant challenge.

Meeting the Demand

One of the principal goals of the Coast Guard's public affairs program during a crisis is to be both the best source of information as well as the first source—otherwise known as **maximum disclosure, minimum delay**. This approach to releasing information has historically done an exceptional job of keeping the public informed, and continually reinforces the proactive approach to public affairs at all levels of the organization.

"A team of public affairs professionals working alongside an incident commander can assist in proactively feeding the media's need for information."

To best do this, 15 **[Coast Guard] public affairs [PA] personnel** were initially assigned to gather and distribute Coast Guard information, capture video and photographic documentation of operations, coordinate media requests for interviews and ride alongs and complete the other requirements of the "information" role at the various Coast Guard incident commands in Alexandria, LA, Mobile, AL, and St. Louis, MO.

This number of PAs grew during the response with upwards of 40—almost half of the entire rating [that is, half of those assigned as PAs]—serving in support of Katrina and Rita response operations. Although providing this number of personnel from such a small rate was challenging, providing a team of full-time public affairs professionals alongside the incident commanders was instrumental in proactively feeding the information machine.

"During the Hurricane Katrina response, we were overwhelmed with media requests from all markets—radio, television and print," said Capt. Terry Gilbreath, the commanding officer of Marine Safety Unit Morgan City, LA, and an incident commander during the hurricane response. "We would not have been able to manage this massive public affairs effort without an assigned public affairs team. Their assistance following Hurricane Katrina was invaluable in organizing, coordinating and preparing for numerous media interviews and broadcasts."

In an event of national significance, such as Katrina, where there is 24-hour global interest, if the demands for information are going to be met, it is imperative that a **"push/pull" system** be in place. News and imagery constantly are "pushed" out by the PA staff through press, photo and video releases; there were more than 150 such releases of information during the response.

Just as critical, however, is the "pull" aspect, which provides a centralized place where all stakeholders can go for their informational needs. The 8th District response Web site filled this need and created a virtual meeting place where interested parties gathered their own information. It also gave visitors a chance to electronically submit questions, concerns, or opinions.

One e-mail read: "In a time the nation and its citizens are crying for help, you have come through with courage and compassion. The nation and people of Louisiana and Mississippi are indebted to the Coastguards' (sic) hands of humanity laboring tirelessly in their time of need. With immense appreciation for all that you do. You truly make the difference. God bless each and every one of you. You are the best!"

The Coast Guard always has had an open relationship with the news media. We trust that they will do their best to accurately interpret the information we provide and report the news fairly. Because of this long-established relationship, the media know they can come to the Coast Guard for information and for spokespersons. Selecting spokespersons was easy, as the Coast Guard has always had a culture of communicating to our various audiences. This culture of communicating is reinforced through policy, policy that empowers every Coast Guardsman to speak on that for which he or she is responsible. This programmatic approach is invaluable in a crisis, especially one in which there are almost as many members of the media in the field as there are responders. Whether it was a boat crew coming out of a flooded neighborhood after a grueling shift, or an aircrew setting down at an air field, when the media showed up with cameras rolling—almost without exception—every member of the Coast Guard spoke professionally on what they did, why they were there, and why it was important.

"Having the ability to show an agency's efforts is invaluable."

And lastly, having the ability to show our efforts, though operational photography and video of our operations, is invaluable, not only for the immediate short-term media use, but also for the long-term historical needs of our service. In addition to embedding Coast Guard PAs aboard aircraft and boats, we also embedded media at almost every level of operations, including on more than one occasion giving 24-hour access at Air Station New Orleans to a documentary film crew working with the Weather Channel who said that ". . . it was an honor and a privilege to meet and talk to so many of you during this historic moment for the United States Coast Guard. Thank you so much for giving us access to so many of your people at such a critical time for our country. I can assure you that you will be more than pleased with the final product."

"Actions always speak louder than words."

The Long-Term Impact

Actions always will speak louder than words. The amazingly heroic and dedicated efforts throughout the organization resulted in the saving of more than 34000 lives. The public affairs response, however, contributed to helping the public better understand the "why" behind every Coast Guard man's and woman's efforts. By being aggressively proactive with outreach; by diligently working toward shooting imagery and embedding the media to show the public what the Coast Guard was doing; by making Coast Guard rescuers available to the media; and by empowering all responders to speak to what they were doing, the public affairs program helped increase the public's awareness and understanding of the Service. It helped build credibility in the Coast Guard's abilities, it created new relationships while strengthening existing ones, it met the demand for timely, accurate information, and ultimately it helped to reassure the American public that efforts were underway to help the impacted people of the Gulf Coast.

The long-term impact of this visibility on the Coast Guard as an agency is incredibly difficult to gauge and may never be known. But immeasurable value can be found in the hand-colored "thank you" card from a 4th-grader in Fremont, Calif.: "Dear Coast Guard, it is good to save people because they could have died. The hurricane did a lot of damage, and you saved a lot of people. If I had to call anyone a hero, it would be you."

Case Study One Questions

1. Media relations should be established
   - **a.** After a disaster occurs
   - **b.** During a disaster
   - **c.** Before a disaster
   - **d.** Only when necessary
2. Feeding information to the media as well as making it available on the Internet is considered
   - **a.** Too time consuming
   - **b.** Too expensive
   - **c.** Not possible
   - **d.** A "push/pull" system

Case Study Two COMMUNITY SURVEYS—DOING THEM RIGHT (PART 1 OF 2)

By Judy Pal
Communications Manager City of Irvine, California
January/February 2006 NIOA News

Most police agencies have adopted a community-based style of policing that puts the public's needs first and makes proactive, problem-solving policing a priority. In attempting to connect with the community, many departments are turning to an age-old marketing tool—the survey. For an agency that has never done one before, or attempted to do one itself, it can be a formidable process.

There are a couple of very basic things to consider before embarking on this kind of research, including whether or not to undertake the job internally. From personal experience, it's something I don't recommend for a number of reasons—the most compelling being the fact that few departments have adequate staffing capabilities to conduct and analyze a survey. Hiring an outside agency to do the work also avoids a risk of community misperception that results may be manipulated internally.

Sample Size

Once you've decided to move ahead with the initiative, you must first determine how many people you need to survey to get credible feedback data, or in marketing terms, what your **sample size** will be. For a mid-size department, a sample of 500 is usually adequate. However, be aware of the fact that the smaller the sample size, the lower the survey's accuracy will be. You also have to determine the type of survey that will be most effective for you, including considering the pros and cons of doing a phone or mail survey. Any survey is worthless if not sufficiently representative of your community.

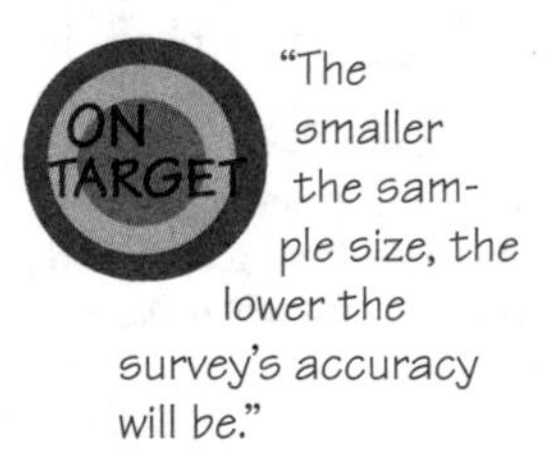

Mail vs. Phone

To obtain a sample of 500 households, you will have to mail out anywhere between 3000 and 10,000 surveys. Response to average marketing surveys range from 3 to 21%. If you are in a smaller community and policing is a high-profile issue, you may have a higher return, but not likely more than 33%.

The biggest consideration for mail surveys is your sample demographic. If you mail your survey out with the water bill, for example, you will only reach homeowners. Apartment dwellers, renters, people who have wells, etc., would all be left out. Depending on your region, this may seriously skew the demographic results, i.e., you would get response from average to higher income homeowners, between the ages of 25–65.

If you decide to do a mail survey, your best bet is to do a mail drop in each of your postal or zip code areas—ensuring you cover urban, suburban and rural areas, including homes, apartments, low-income housing complexes, etc.

"Don't forget to develop surveys in languages spoken by all constituencies."

Language is another issue to consider. In some cities, like Toronto or New York, surveys must be produced in a number of different languages to ensure a wide range of ethnic citizenry is represented. Then, of course, there's the problem of people not bothering to check their mail carefully, fill out the survey and find a mailbox to send it back.

When it comes to phone surveys, the biggest drawback is cost. Be prepared to spend between $10,000 and $20,000 on a survey. However, the advantage of a phone survey, reliable and controllable collection of data, is well worth it.

First, surveyors have the opportunity to screen respondents to ensure an accurate proportion of all your identified demographics are represented—by geographic area, income level, language spoken or age. Once an appropriate number of respondents have answered the survey from one demographic group, that group can be screened out from further calls so that you can hear from others. (Of course, there is a marginal demographic skew in that your survey would only reach people with phones.)

Best of all, instead of waiting for surveys to be delivered, and hoping people mail them back; your wait-time for results is much shorter. In most cases, a survey will take less than a week to conduct, and results should be back to your department within two to three weeks after that.

What about web-based surveys? Any opportunity a community has to interact with its police agency is a positive thing. However, it is wise not to place a lot of confidence in results from this type of questionnaire. The likelihood of demographic skew of respondents is enormous and the old adage about the "squeaky wheel" applies to on-line surveys. You'll get a lot more people complaining about your service, than comments from satisfied customers; if your department is doing its job . . . it's an expected quality of service, not often worthy of positive comment.

Question Development

It's up to your department to formulate the basis of the questions being asked. Is there a specific issue you need feedback on? Are you trying to establish a baseline satisfaction index from which to work? Are you trying to determine if your department's goals and objectives are in line with your community's priorities for safety?

Once a baseline study is done, it's only valuable if follow-up surveys are conducted on a regular basis to monitor positive or negative change. It's a good idea to include a number of questions that will be repeated each time. Establish a "Police Satisfaction Index" with five to ten basic questions that can be repeated on each survey your department commissions. This allows you to effectively illustrate improvements in customer service over time.

It's also smart to conduct internal communications audits around the same time your external survey is being done. It's an opportune time to find out if your officers' goals are in keeping with the expectations of the community they serve. For the most part, people want three things: to be safe in their home, to be safe on the streets and for their children to be safe in school. That means good customer service, high visibility, proactive crime prevention programming, and excellent traffic enforcement—extremely valuable information when budget time rolls around!

COMMUNITY—WORKING WITH RESULTS (PART 2 OF 2)

Community Surveys—Working with results

By Judy Pal Communications Manager, City of Irvine, CA

March/April 2006 NIOA News

Congratulations! Your department has conducted its first community survey and, as a result, you've been able to identify excellent feedback in some areas and define a few key areas of improvement. Now what? Before writing up a news release lauding the good news, think carefully how best to utilize this valuable information.

Sure, it feels good to release positive information about your department's good relationship with the community . . . but is there a better use for the numbers that, in the long run, will be more strategically beneficial? Absolutely.

I strongly believe survey results are nothing to brag about. They are, quite simply, an invaluable tool for improving your service, gauging positive or negative changes in community perceptions, and providing solid evidence for **key messaging**.

The only time you should consider releasing survey results is if they yielded positive responses to counter negative perceptions the media and/or citizens have about your department or police officers. If, for example, there was recent press accusing your department of racial profiling, publicizing survey results indicating 98% of respondents reported being treated fairly by police would seem beneficial. However, releasing this information could be a double-edged sword because typically you would then be asked to provide statistical data of the survey demographics—and if a good number of respondents were not visible minorities, your 'positive story' takes a nosedive.

Instead, consider using survey results as a supporting foundation for your strategic planning process. This information can be extremely useful in helping make and support decisions regarding allocation of resources, budget increases and additional hires. Elected officials understand, and more importantly respect, survey numbers. The stats can also be used in your communication to staff about why management has made decisions to implement, alter or remove certain programs. Being able to provide police officers with "hard evidence" of why changes are made helps employees better understand organizational change.

But perhaps the most important way survey feedback can be used is in providing rational, reality-based fact to support key messaging. For example, Halifax Regional Police (HRP) in Nova Scotia, Canada conducted town hall meetings each year in its three jurisdictional areas. Year after year, the issue of police visibility came up and citizens were always asking for a higher police presence in their neighbourhoods. In 2001, HRP conducted its bi-annual community survey two months before the town hall meetings in order to define specific issues management would most likely be queried on during the open meetings. One question was prepared specifically to address the issue of visibility. The survey asked, "How many police officers do you believe are on patrol in the HRP jurisdiction at any given time?" Response varied from 25 to 100 officers, with a full 65% of respondents citing the number was upwards of 50. In truth, about 28 uniform officers were at work at any given time.

With these facts in hand, management was able to convey the message that the department must indeed be providing a high-level of visible service to its citizens, since more than half the people of the region felt there were many more officers on patrol than there actually were. It gave citizens pause for a reality-check, and an opportunity for management to dig deeper into the real and perceived needs of the community.

"A baseline survey provides an excellent measure of the status of customer service and quality control."

The stats also provided an opportunity to dispense some well-deserved praise for often-beleaguered officers for being 'out there' and visible in the community, as well as a strong base from which to work when municipal councillors approached staff about providing increased patrols in their regions.

Finally, once a baseline survey is conducted, it provides an excellent measure of improvements (or deterioration) in customer service and quality control. In today's fiscal environment of activity-based costing analyses, and "show me proof" budget allocations, providing solid, independently-corroborated evidence of customer satisfaction goes a long way in helping a department win buy-in for its strategic business planning process and funding requirements.

Case Study Two Questions

1. Mail surveys of between 3,000 and 10,000 people will yield an average of
   - **a.** 2,500 responses
   - **b.** 500 responses
   - **c.** 50 responses
   - **d.** 1,000 responses
2. Community surveys can assist an agency in
   - **a.** Targeting messages
   - **b.** Improving customer service
   - **c.** Winning by-in for funding requirements
   - **d.** All of the above.

Case Study Three STARTING YOUR FIRE DEPARTMENT PUBLIC INFORMATION OFFICER

By Chris Kear, Assistant Chief & PIO
Hillcrest Fire Company #1-Spring Valley, New York
January/February 2006 NIOA News

ON TARGET "Every fire department should have a designated public information officer."

The question is; should my department have a public information officer? The answer is quite simple, yes. Each and every fire department from the smallest rural to the largest city should have a designated public information officer. Whether your department designates one or adopts a directive, SOP or even the assumption that the chief or officer in charge takes on the role, is the first step in the right direction. In this article I will be discussing choosing the PIO, defining the PIO role, and getting the PIO started.

Choosing the PIO:

Selecting the right person for the role as Public Information Officer is extremely important. The individual chosen will be the department's liaison to the media. In departments that require a full time PIO, they will be constantly in contact with media outlets. Smaller departments in particular volunteer departments can possibly have a more limited role due [to] the fact that their availability on a daily basis may be limited. Therefore the volunteer fire department officer, who may be in charge of an incident, might be required to fill the role of PIO.

In addition to my current position of Assistant Chief, I also fill the department's role as PIO. I have held this position since 1992 and have worked with all the officers who have held rank higher than me throughout the years. There have been many times that I have held both the role as incident commander and PIO. There have also been times that I have worked with the media when I have responded to an incident and when I have not. In addition, I have taken a step back when the

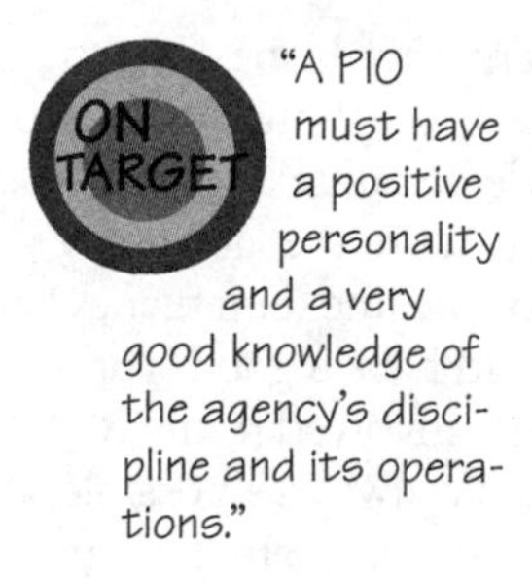

"A PIO must have a positive personality and a very good knowledge of the agency's discipline and its operations."

Chief or incident commander have felt comfortable enough to speak with the media when I have been available.

Flexibility is important. Just because your department has designated a PIO does not mean that they must perform those duties 24/7. Let's face it. There are some Chiefs that like to talk to the media and there are some that do not. That's ok. There is no rule that the Chief must always speak and disperse information. That's why the position of PIO is formed and is part of the incident command system.

Now how do you choose the right person? The right individual must have a positive personality and a very good knowledge of the fire service and its operations. We do not want to delegate this role someone who is not people friendly or to someone who has one year in the fire service. The PIO is there to provide information and answer questions, so having a tough personality or adopting the attitude that the media are just information/gold diggers or story tellers will not look favorably on the fire department. Just as we do not want someone who has limited fire service knowledge providing information on fire department operations. The PIO must provide accurate and knowledgeable information to give the fire department credibility. So be wise, choose an individual who you can trust that when speaking with the media has only the intentions of making the department look good, even in bad situations.

Defining the PIO Role

This should be relatively easy. However, you do not want to be too particular or not specific enough. This position should have some type of boundaries for both the PIO and for members of the company. First off, do you want your PIO to handle both incidents and non-incidents? We are talking about providing information on structure fires (emergency incidents) and advertising for a fund raising event or parade (non-emergency events). This could be considered line vs. house.

"Agency members must understand the role of the PIO."

Most departments have an individual who handles both types of incidents/events. This is made easier because in most cases the media outlet that is dealt with is usually the same as are your contacts.

With this said and the role defined, each member of your department must understand the purpose of the PIO.

They should understand that your job is to get the information out or make it available so that your department gets media exposure. This exposure to the public if done correctly makes the department look good. Officers, both house and line (President and Chief) should take advantage of having a PIO and be creative in what information that they feel is necessary to the public.

When information is provided to any type of media outlet, whether is gets printed/broadcast or not, your attempt at 'getting the word out' should be known to all department members. This is easily done on a monthly basis by providing a report at your company meeting.

Your effort to publicly expose your department should be known. When dealing on the house (non-emergency) level, the house officers must know that they can depend on you to provide accurate and timely information to the media. They should know that you are the 'go to guy' when it comes to public exposure. This should go for the line (emergency) side too. The Chief and higher ranking officers should have a good working relationship with the PIO. Some might want to be involved in the PIO process at incidents and some may want to stay as far away as possible. The PIO needs to get a feel for each officer as to the role that each one wants to play during incidents in regards to providing information.

As I previously said, some officers like speaking with the media and some do not. But please, always try to make yourself available to your officers, members or the media itself. Setting some rules for your department in reference to dealing with the media is important. It should be understood that no one but the incident commander, chief or PIO can provide information about an incident to someone of the media. Many times after an incident the media will call the firehouse and start asking questions about the incident.

A department member who thinks their intentions are good or whom feel that the opportunity of being the paper the next day is too good to pass up may provide inaccurate or inappropriate information. Not everything about an incident should be provided. The investigation may be ongoing. There could be firefighter injuries. Owner/occupant names might not want to be provided.

So how do we curtail this? Start by developing a directive or SOP. My department has a posted directive that states that no member shall speak with anyone from the media at anytime. If a person should call the firehouse looking for information, they are to take their name and phone number and pass it on to the PIO, chief or officer in charge. They are to provide no information about any incident that the department may have responded to. Speaking of not providing information, we prefer not to comment on police or medical information. If we are providing information about an extrication, patient injuries or the accident investigation should not be commented on. Just as we would not want a paramedic to give details about our operations we should not tell the media that the driver sustained head trauma and had severe bleeding. The exception of course would be a department which provided both fire and medical service and had a single PIO.

"All types of media have deadlines which need to be observed."

Getting Started:

After being appointed or assuming the role as PIO, you need to develop a foundation of contacts and education. Both of these areas are easy to put together. The contacts that you should begin with are the local ones in your area. This may be the local newspaper(s), radio stations and television/cable networks. A simple phone call to these media outlets with an explanation of who you are will probably get you a list of contacts with phone and fax numbers. They may also break down the geographical areas and reporter interests/responsibilities (public safety, education, political) that each one may cover.

Also make sure that you inquire about deadlines. All types of media have deadlines. This all can be faxed or mailed to you or you could even pick it up so as to introduce yourself. Do not be afraid to ask for business cards also. They are small and can be carried with you at all times. These local contacts are the most important because you will be dealing with them on a regular basis.

Larger media outlets, like in bigger cities will likely provide contact information but on a smaller scale. Generally there is only one contact usually for a reporter who covers a distinct area like a county or region. The larger media outlet can be contacted by finding their phone number on the internet, major newspaper or even by watching the nightly news where at times they show their phone number so the public can report information to them. Fax numbers are not always provided but you can ask for it when you call for additional information. Your local government should also have contacts for all local and larger media outlets.

Your dealings with the larger media outlets will more than likely be at a minimum. What is considered interesting news to you may not be to a larger network or newspaper. Generally they will be contacting someone from your department if they hear of an incident that is newsworthy. Many times they will contact the local government, police department or other agencies that may have responded to inquire about the incident and obtain information on how to get in touch with you.

All this contact information should be consolidated into a book or master copy and kept with you at all times. Copies can also be made where you can keep one at home, in your vehicle, firehouse or even a master on your computer. Having this handy at all times will make your job easier when it comes time to get your information out on a timely basis. When all the above is said and done it is now time to formally introduce yourself.

This can be done by drafting a letter on department letterhead introducing yourself with an explanation of the role you will obtain as department PIO. Provide phone and fax numbers for yourself, firehouse and even your workplace if that is possible. The most important is your cell phone. This is a number where you should be reached most of the time. Remember that taking on this role means that you need to be reachable and available most of the time. Deadlines do not wait. If you are unavailable at a certain time, retrieve the messages quickly and return that call. You do not want the reporter assuming anything about your incident or them contacting just anyone for information.

Remember, your job as PIO is not just to get the information out, but to make your department look good.

Case Study Three Questions

1. Career or volunteer fire departments should appoint a PIO or develop policy to address the role of PIO as it is outlined by the Incident Command System.
   a. True
   b. False
2. Media deadlines are important for a PIO to know and meet when disseminating information.
   a. True
   b. False

Case Study Four POSITIVE RELATIONS WITH MEDIA HELPS DURING TRAUMATIC EVENTS

By Mike Tellef,
President NIOA Peoria Police Department
January/February 2006 NIOA News "999—Officer needs help urgently!"

It's the dreaded call that springs a police PIO into immediate action. It means an officer has been critically injured or killed. It means news of far-reaching or even tragic consequences is about to go out to the community. It means we must leap into the fray, sort out the facts of a breaking and possibly confusing drama, then handle the inevitable onslaught of questions, not only from the press and public, but fellow department members.

Such circumstances sadly struck home December 17, 2005, for the first time in the 51-year history of the Peoria Police Department. At about 4:30 AM our officers responded to a shooting call and upon arriving at the scene witnesses pointed out the suspect vehicle leaving the scene and after a three mile chase the suspect vehicle stopped in the middle of a major roadway. With six officers surrounding the suspect vehicle with a felony stop the suspect bailed out of his car shooting at the officers. One of those bullets struck Officer Bill Weigt just above his vest, severing his spine [and] leaving him paralyzed from the mid-chest down. Our officers returned fire killing the suspect. At the original call location a 21-year old male was found dead from gun shots. The coverage of the incident was as we would expect but the surprise came from the way the media in the Phoenix area covered the wounding of Officer Weigt.

It all started the night of the shooting. Officers, department members, their families and friends gathered at John C. Lincoln Hospital in Phoenix for a candle light vigil. All of the local TV stations were there as well as newspapers. All of the reporters were very respectful of the event and did not push their way into the ceremony but were shocked when I invited them in. They did not "hound" department members for interviews and when I told them which officers were available to be interviewed they honored my request. The media truly treated this event with the dignity and respect it deserved. Over the following weeks they kept the injured officer, his family, and what they were going through in the public eye while at the same time going out of their way to respect the family's privacy. They had their suspicions as to what the officer's injuries were and had heard rumors but never once released anything until I went public with his condition on December 20th at the family's request.

There have been numerous benefits to help Bill and his family with expenses not covered by industrial compensation insurance and they have promoted them and shown up at them to cover the story. Again, they have never pushed anyone for information about the incident; they have stayed with how is Bill and his family. When Bill's family came out to speak to the media the way in which they were treated was just outstanding. Since the shooting I have received numerous phone calls, e-mails and blackberry messages from the TV stations' assignments desk and reporters wishing Bill the best and offering their prayers. The Arizona Republic published an editorial regarding the incident and the dangers police officers face on a daily basis and Brent Whiting, the public safety beat writer for the Arizona Republic, did an opinion piece that was fantastic. In all there has been about 26 television, 4 radio and 8 newspaper stories done regarding Bill, his family and events supporting them. Here we are a month and an half later and anytime there is a fund raising event for Bill and his family the promoting of it and the coverage is excellent.

The shooting of Officer Weigt came at the end of a string of one tragic event after another, many involving kids.

- Nov 23: double fatal crash with two 19-year olds dead at scene
- Dec 1: Fatal crash in which a four-year old was ejected and killed and five-year old sister critical injured with two other sisters with minor injuries
- Dec 2: adult male critically injured when he stepped in front of a truck in a construction zone
- Dec 4: adult male fatally injured in a car crash
- Dec 14: trailer fire killing 1 adult and 3 kids (one of the kids was just involved with our Shop with a Cop event on December 10)
- Dec 17: homicide of a 21-year old male and Officer Weigt shot with the suspect being shot and killed by other Peoria officers

There is only so much a department and its employees can withstand in a short period of time. We like to think we are strong and can

"The media always have the last word."

handle all of this and we can with help. But imagine how much more difficult it would have been if we had a hostile relationship with the media in the Phoenix area.

The relationship with the media starts with you. You as a PIO MUST make the effort to maintain a positive relationship which is not always easy. Some people on both sides are just set on making life miserable for each other, but in the long run the only one who loses every time is the public safety department. REMEMBER the media always has the last word.

Case Study Four Questions

1. The injury or death of an agency employee will most likely bring significant media coverage.
   a. True
   b. False
2. The media may often report rumors as facts if a PIO does not come forward with truthful statements in a timely manner.
   a. True
   b False

Case Study Five ATTENTION TO DETAIL, ACCOUNTABILITY CORNERSTONES FOR TODAY'S PIO

By Shell Armstrong—Contributing Writer
September/December 2005 NIOA News

Years ago, emergency responders were warned to avoid the media—they were the enemy. Over the last two decades, that philosophy has undergone a huge transformation, and necessarily so, said Richard Kirkland, the former director of the Nevada Highway Patrol.

"When I started in government service, we were told that you stayed away from the press," he said. "In media relations classes, we were told that the press was the enemy, don't talk to them." When Kirkland reached the Federal Bureau of Investigation's National Academy, the change began. "Then they told us to talk to them but don't tell them too much," he said.

The real epiphany for Kirkland came while he was with the Reno Police Department. After a fellow officer was arrested on Peeping Tom charges, the police chief opted to allow the officer to resign and keep the story quiet. "Of course the whole sordid story got out anyway, and the story that got out was substantially worse than what actually happened," Kirkland said.

For the next 10 days, the department danced with the media trying to correct the facts, he said.

We didn't gain a thing by handling the situation the way we did," he said. "We ended up looking like we came from the long line of people who protect bad officers." Any suggestion to just tell the press the truth, Kirkland said, was shouted down.

The chief had an epiphany of his own in the aftermath of the incident: He appointed Kirkland the department's public information officer. "Either I wasn't saying enough or I was saying too much," he said. "It was a nightmare."

But the experience reinforced Kirkland's appreciation of the importance of public information and education systems. It also helped him hone his PIO system when he assumed the police chief role. A successful PIO system, Kirkland said, trains, teaches and then extends the authority for the spokesman to gather and dispense information, be accountable for getting the details right and, when mistakes happen, admitting and correcting them.

"(Agencies) have to rely upon PIOs in 99.9 percent of the cases to handle it and release the information," Kirkland said. "The PIO in turn has to have the ability to be tough and smart enough, to know there are going to be mistakes and, when there are, admit the error."

"If you can't remember the past, you are destined to repeat it."

Because the initial information is rarely completely correct in developing incidents, PIOs have to be tenacious in seeking information and pay extreme attention to details. "It's better to tell the press, 'We have some information but we are still gathering info.'

When you have all the facts, you are going to be pretty darn close to your initial statement." But when the wrong information is released to the press, PIOs have to set the record straight. "We are going to have the wrong information and people are going to tell us the wrong information," Kirkland said. When that happens, he said it is vital that agencies undergo intensive examination of how information was gathered. "If you don't, it will be like the great philosopher chiseled in stone said, 'If you can't remember the past, you're destined to repeat it.'"

Lack of attention to detail and accountability are crippling for public service agencies, Kirkland said. "You are the messenger; you can't afford to be sloppy or lazy in getting to truth before going to the media or the public. It is essential that you ensure the information you give is correct. If you don't have credibility with the people we protect and serve, you can't function. Know that you have got to make decisions and you are going to make enemies. Just don't make the same mistake twice."

Case Study Five Questions

1. A PIO must be accountable for providing accurate information.
 a. True
 b. False

2. Select the **incorrect** statement.
 a. PIOs do not need the support of their agency
 b. PIOs will receive and report inaccurate information
 c. If an inaccurate report is provided by a PIO, the report should be corrected
 d. PIOs must pay attention to detail

Case Study Six STAYING 'ON MESSAGE' IN TOUGH TIMES A CHALLENGE FOR PIOS

By Shell Armstrong—Contributing Writer
September/December 2005 NIOA News

When times get tough, public information officers are often lightning rods for the ire of the community and the media. The challenge for messengers is to stay attuned to the different audience: the message receivers, seekers and challengers, said Dr. Gordon Blush, Ed. D., of Target Productions, Inc. "There are a lot of similarities between the three, but they do come in different colors," he said. "You have to pick up on what clues they've given you."

To be effective communicators, Blush theorizes that PIOs can apply **the 3R's for 3S and 3D contexts**. Translated, he said, that means acknowledging the realities of the situation to yield greater readiness to become more effective in your responsiveness to the situation. "The reality is that stuff happens," Blush said. "The frustration and conflict arise because of the real issue: Who is getting what." Keeping humans' universal needs (the need for control and wanting to be understood on one's own terms) can help allay power struggles, which are the basis of all relationships, he said.

"The message delivered to the public by a PIO should not demotivate them."

"People do things for their own reasons, not yours," Blush said. While developing their message, PIOs should remember that they probably cannot directly control others' behavior, especially if the PIO is the perceived authority figure in a situation. Rather than seeking to motivate people, Blush said PIOs will do better not to demotivate them with the message. Learning to read and understand people's behaviors will give PIOs the "power position" in managing communications.

In determining one's readiness, Blush said PIOs must consider the conditions prior to the event. "Prior experiences, information and events will all profoundly shape listeners' perceptions, expectations, needs and wants."

The ability to read behaviors and craft messages accordingly is a very useful tool in a PIO's arsenal, he said. "The more of these behavioral tools you have, the higher your potential for success in dealing with the demands of the tough situations you handle."

Realizing that connections have consequences in the struggle for control can help PIOs develop effective leadership skills, he said. "Keep in mind everyone needs a sense of control, and that you cannot control how someone else thinks, feels or behaves," Blush said. "What you can control is your own response behaviors."

That combination, he said, will produce greater cooperation from others and more control for PIOs in difficult situations. PIOs who can accurately read behaviors (verbal and non-verbal communications) and use intentional behaviors to influence the communication environment will help defuse volatile situations.

"At press conferences, you are badly outnumbered by the media," Blush said. "Using behavior literacy and leadership balances the communications and relationships and helps control the power struggles and usual 'noise.' Establishing this balance is in your best selfish interest professionally and personally."

The leadership strategy—balancing the other person's needs and wants with your behavioral leadership—takes emotion out of the equation, he said. "It gets the person thinking about possible outcomes instead of fighting for control."

Case Study Six Questions

1. According to the article, PIOs serve as messengers. They must be in touch with the following three audiences.
   - **a.** Police, fire, and EMS
   - **b.** Citizens, politicians, and children
   - **c.** Message receivers, message seekers, and message challengers
   - **d.** Believers, pacifists, and activists
2. If a PIO understands people's behavior
   - **a.** The PIO will be in the power position in managing communications
   - **b.** It will not make a difference in delivering the message
   - **c.** The PIO will understand the weak position he/she is in
   - **d.** The PIO will be able to control people's minds

Case Study Seven TURNING COPS INTO PIOS

March/April 2005 NIOA News
By Wayne Shelor,
NIOA Immediate Past President Clearwater, FL Police Department PIO

More and more often, these days, PIOs are culled from the ranks of the media; all sorts of American agencies and organizations are hiring specialists who have the training and (most importantly) the experience to anticipate and deal with the occasionally oppressive demands of the media.

Here in 2005, trained civilian specialists have become the spokesperson of choice for hospitals and governmental agencies . . . except in the field of public safety, where—nationwide—the majority of PIOs are still sworn officers or certified firefighters representing their agencies.

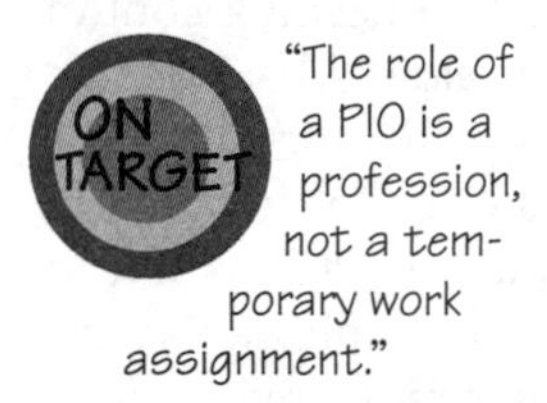

Some of the best, most effective PIOs I've known in law enforcement were sworn law enforcement officers—cops who were given the complicated and sensitive task of media relations.

Over the years of working with and watching these professionals, I've found a commonality among those cops who succeed as PIOs: unlike some of their peers, the most successful officer/PIOs embraced their work as a profession, rather than a temporary assignment.

Captain Rod Reder left the Hillsborough County Sheriff's PIO office in January (he's now the Deputy District Commander for a Patrol District) after a $5\frac{1}{2}$-year stint as PIO in a media market that absolutely thrives on public safety news. Over that time, I watched Reder excel as a PIO, largely because he threw himself into the job, and because he never believed he arrived with all the answers.

Whether his agency was attacked for the way it conducted a sensitive, high-profile investigation, was scrutinized after a deputy died in a single-car wreck en route to a call, or was questioned by editorialists and columnists over how it conducts business, Reder was always—always—prepared and forthcoming.

He learned to speak in intelligent, digestible **sound bites** instead of cop jargon, he treated reporters like professionals (including many who hadn't earned it), and went to great lengths to learn about both the inner workings of the media and the tried-and-true techniques of information dissemination.

After the events of September 11, 2001, Reder worked with Florida Department of Law Enforcement PIO Rick Morera to chair a state-wide Terrorism Task Force committee, and they created a state-wide PIO information exchange/preparation platform for emergency response unlike any other in America.

"Rod was a great PIO," said Debbie Carter, HCSO's civilian PIO and one of the senior law enforcement spokespersons in Florida. "He was a quick student and didn't have a problem asking for someone else's opinion.

Rod was the first to tell you that he didn't have a clue what it meant to be a PIO until he was assigned here."

The greatest strengths sworn officers bring with them when they become a PIO are their experience and training as a cop. But much of what they are taught about being a cop flies in the face of being an effective PIO: cops are taught to never expand on a thought or question when testifying in court—just give a simple, narrow answer. But Reder always took the time to dissect and detail common policing theories and practices when educating the media. Cops are told by lawyers not to admit a mistake ("It might be used against us in court."), but Reder realized the value of coming clean and winning over the Court of Public Opinion now, and leaving civil litigation to the lawyers.

And Reder learned early on how a trusting and accommodating PIO-media relationship could advance investigations, and even help solve crimes.

"The PIO craft must be learned over time."

"I noted very quickly how important the police/media relationship is," he recalled, "and I used the media. I saw the advantage of working with them."

Like now-retired Pinellas County Sheriff's PIO Lieutenant Greg Tita and my own recently retired partner, Sergeant Doug Griffith, Reder was one of the most respected and involved cop/PIOs in the Tampa Bay region. They all devoted long hours to learning about the PIO craft and offered up novel, innovative ideas to embellish the profession. And they each used their parochial skills and techniques to reach out to the community through the mass media.

As cops, they were very effective PIOs, largely because they looked at it—they lived it—as something more than a temporary assignment.

Perhaps the most difficult part of the officer-to-PIO transition for cops is learning how to take off the badge or star and wrap themselves in the garb of a "spokesperson." And since that "uniform" often comes with a three-circle target on it, it can be a frightening change for a law enforcement professional. But that's another story for another time.

> ***A postscript:*** *A public safety agency using the PIO function (writing, visibility, pressure, research, quick-thinking, etc.) as an administrator grooming tool may be a good and effective idea. At HCSO, civilian Debbie Carter has trained three sworn officers as PIOs over the years, deputies who were routed through the PIO function as part of their preparation for higher rank. All arrived as Sergeants; their present ranks are Captain, Colonel and—as of January 2005—Sheriff David Gee, himself, with whom I worked as a PIO on occasion.*

Case Study Seven Questions

1. PIOs should use jargon when communicating with the media because it improves credibility.
   a. True
   b. False
2. The person acting as a PIO does not need formal training because just trying to assist the media will be seen as a positive, and the media will not pressure the person.
   a. True
   b. False

Case Study Eight PUBLIC'S PERCEPTION DEFINING ISSUE FOR AGENCY'S IMAGE

By Shell Armstrong—Contributing Writer
September/December 2005 NIOA News

The first seven seconds of any encounter can define an agency's image forever.

Despite an emergency response agency's best effort, failing to plug into what the public is thinking can be a department's downfall, according to public relations guru Judy Pal.

Following the tragic events of Sept. 11, 2001, the public perception of police, firefighters and medical responders changed tremendously. "The public redefined who they consider heroes to be since 9/11," she said. "Your image is a whole lot more impressive since then."

Although overall rescue workers are riding a high, individual departments only have a small window to impress today's fickle public. And, Pal says, the clock is ticking.

"It is a fact that most people don't see police officers face-to-face that often," Pal said, quoting a recent survey. "They make their decisions based on what they see in the media."

To ensure a good public image, she said, it is essential to work on building a good relationship with the press. "Certainly what we do matters, but what the public perceives we do matters more." And that, Pal says, is often driven by what they see on TV and in the news.

"When something good happens to you, you'll tell one or two people," she said, "but when something bad happens you are going to tell everyone over and over again. Law enforcement has to deal with perception every day, and the media plays a huge role in the public's disconnect between reality and perception."

On TV shows, major crimes are solved within an hour, usually by plainclothes detectives, said Pal. Newscasts carry the globe's most gruesome crimes, leaving many to believe violent crime is on the rise in their neighborhood, Pal said. “The perception is that crime is horrible, when in reality the media’s spin is ‘If it bleeds, it leads’,” she said.

Conversely, a survey released in January indicated 93 percent of people believe news media is not fair in its coverage, Pal said. “It’s nice to know the public thinks that but it still doesn’t affect their perception about what is going on in their own backyards.”

That’s where PIOs can help effectively shape a department’s image. By understanding the media’s needs—one of **the five C’s: crime, corruption, catastrophe, conflict and color**—PIOs can pitch stories that help cultivate a good public image.

“Good PR can build a good public image, but you have to have a public image in place before you can start doing PR,” she said. “What good PR can’t do is build on things that are non-existent. If your department is corrupt or is not doing its job, good public relations is not going to do anything.”

Editor’s Note: In November, Judy Pal became the City of Irvine’s Communications Manager.

Case Study Eight Questions

1. Public opinion is more based on
   - **a.** Perception than action
   - **b.** Action than perception
   - **c.** Only facts
   - **d.** None of the above
2. Good public relations
   - **a.** Can’t fix a corrupt agency
   - **b.** Can hide a corrupt agency
   - **c.** Are not possible for public safety agencies
   - **d.** Are not a PIO’s responsibility

Case Study Nine SMALL SC COMMUNITY PIO CAUGHT IN THE SPOTLIGHT AFTER THE COUNTRY’S SECOND WORST TRAIN COLLISION

By Shell Armstrong—Contributing Writer
September/December 2005 NIOA News

At 3:50 p.m. Jan 6, Thom Berry got the call: A 42-car Norfolk Southern freight train had slammed into a parked train in downtown Graniteville, S.C., and at least one of three tank cars contained chlorine.

With that small bit of information, members of the state's Department of Health and Environmental Control, of which Berry serves as the director of Media Relations, responded with a "full turnout."

"My thinking when I first got the call was 'swallow hope.' I knew this was going to be an event that would be much wider in scope than Aiken County would be able to deal with and even what we as the State of South Carolina might be able to deal with," Berry said.

What South Carolina's emergency responders, along with personnel from 106 outside agencies, did encounter was America's second largest rail disaster, and the deadliest train wreck involving hazardous materials in nearly three decades, he said.

The large freight train's conductor rounded a bend at 41 mph when he saw an open switch running into the smaller pump and cars, Berry said. Investigators believe the switch was inadvertently left open by the night crew. "(The engineer) had 17 seconds from the time he recognized the open switch until he collided with the parked train. Experts say it would have taken a half-mile to stop that train; he didn't have anywhere near that."

When the trains collided, the cars containing the chlorine came to rest buried in a twisted heap at Avondale Mills, a denim textile plant. One of the cars sustained a gash in its side and began to leak toxic fumes. Berry said it took over three hours to confirm the cars' contents with Norfolk Southern.

"Prior to this incident, there was a move afoot to have the placards tagging the cars with toxic chemicals removed to prevent a possible terrorist strike," he said. "If there had been no placards it could have potentially been much, much worse."

Nine people were killed, including the freight train engineer, from inhaling chlorine gas. About 250 people required medical attention, and 5,400 residents of Graniteville had to evacuate their homes, Berry said.

The first responders to arrive at the wreck were members of Aiken County's volunteer fire department. By the time the chief of the 45-person force arrived, the chlorine cloud had begun to spread. The fire department, located about 400 feet from ground zero, housed all the protective gear but was completely inaccessible.

"The station was totally lost," Berry said, because the chlorine converted to hydrochloric acid as it came in contact with moisture and metal. "Sadly, the first three people transported from the scene were firefighters trying to get to the station who unknowingly drove right into the cloud."

"PIO's need to understand the Incident Command System."

With the fire chief out of commission, the command role fell to the Aiken County sheriff. Understanding the incident command system became an important lesson for all of those involved, Berry said.

Initially, residents were told to "shelter in place." The small community's volunteer firefighters and Sheriff's Office battled the chlorine cloud for just over an hour before the State of South Carolina, and subsequently the National Response Center, was notified. "That was probably lesson number one," Berry said. "Be sure to notify as quickly as you possibly can."

"Reverse 9-1-1 is a valuable method of delivery for Emergency Public Information."

After the NRC call went out, emergency personnel from South Carolina and Georgia rushed to the scene to provide assistance.

It quickly became clear that Graniteville's 5,400 residents would have to be evacuated. A recorded 911 message instructed people in the cloud's path to report to the parking lot of the University of South Carolina's Aiken campus, Berry said. There, a triage and decontamination center were set up to process residents.

Not surprisingly, few of those who evacuated visited the decon site. "Many people in the area did not take advantage of the shelter; many did not even go to the parking lot for medical help," Berry said.

Approximately 95 percent of those treated medically self-reported to area hospitals, including facilities over 50 miles away, he said. "Lesson number two: Make sure you notify every hospital in the area and then keep them posted on what is happening," Berry said.

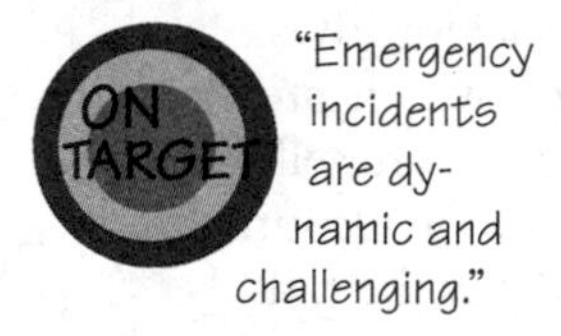

Throughout the incident, Berry said he and Aiken County Sheriff's Office PIO Lt. Michael Frank held regular press conferences, concentrating on the needs of the electronic media. "We were trying to supply the media with the latest information we could provide because the situation was very dynamic and changing all the time," he said.

Fact sheets broken into sections based on topics—security, public safety, health, environmental issues and the like—were distributed to the press. In addition, officials held a series of community meetings to update evacuees. The sessions were held daily for the first three days.

A final issue Berry said responders ran into at the shelter was pet care. "Many people wouldn't go to the shelter because their pets weren't welcome," he said. "Think about the situation with pets because that may come back to haunt you."

Case Study Nine Questions

1. Emergency scenes are dynamic and
   - **a.** Require PIOs to wait for all information before holding a press conference
   - **b.** Require PIOs to hide the incident from the media until all the facts are known

c. Require PIOs to provide frequent updates to the media
d. Therefore the media will not be interested until all work is complete

2. Fact sheets, press conferences, and community meetings should not be used during emergencies.
   a. True
   b. False

Case Study Ten AGENCY'S MESSAGE CRUCIAL TO LANDING FUNDING, SUPPORT

By Shell Armstrong—Contributing Writer
September/December 2005 NIOA News

"Selling their agency is contingent upon sharing their message—a pivotal role for PIOs."

Competition for taxpayer dollars, legislative resources and public support has police and fire chiefs re-examining the value of effective public information officers.

Tualatin Valley (Ore.) Fire Chief Jeff Johnson, Nevada Dept. of Public Safety (Parole and Probation) Chief Amy Wright and Metropolitan Nashville Police Chief Ronal Serpas agree that selling their agency is contingent upon sharing their message—a pivotal role for PIOs.

"Police and fire are competing for tax dollars, which are finite," Johnson said. "You'll find that people who win the game are selling their services more aggressively, better maintain integrity and accountability and have learned to communicate with people who pay the bill."

To best explain an agency's motives—"Why we do what we do, why we spend money the way we do, and why we deliver the services the way we do"—Johnson said it is critical that the PIO be included on the innermost circle of the command staff. "(PIOs) have to understand not only what the decision is, but why you made it; what were the other considerations when you made it," he said. The payoff—financially, legislatively and in the court of public opinion—will make all the difference in an agency's success or failure, the trio agree.

At Nevada's Department of Public Safety, Wright said PIOs are a vital resource. Beginning with recruiting and retaining the right personnel, she said the agency strives to sell its professionalism. Internally, PIOs also train top administrators when difficult issues arise. "In our business, it does sometimes go wrong," Wright said. "And when it goes bad, it goes very, very bad."

Maintaining open communication lines—within the agency and publicly—is essential in tough times, she said. Getting administrators to recognize the connection between PIOs and positive public perception—the lifeblood of taxpayer-funded agencies, including police and fire departments—is a constant battle, however. "There is still a tremendous resistance within the command staff to keep the PIO as a peer,"

Serpas said. "I have to resend messages to the PIO regularly because they don't think to do that. That's pretty ignorant on their part because the PIO has to be as knowledgeable with every facet of our organization. . . . Either one of us could get stuck with the microphone at any time."

The price for failing to sell an agency can reach beyond local funding, too, Serpas noted, recalling his role with the New Orleans Police Department. "We did a horrifically poor job with the media," he said. "We played right into their hands. We were ignorant and we were stupid and we were dumb and we got portrayed across the world as the most corrupt and incompetent police department in America."

The lessons learned in New Orleans were the backbone of Serpas' stay with the Washington State Patrol. "I had given my heart and soul to (New Orleans) before I retired," he said. "I realized we can't win this fight just by telling the facts; we were going to win by engaging in it and being out front."

The real challenge law enforcement and fire officials face, the three said, is selling a positive message to inexperienced reporters more interested in "National Enquirer-like" stories. "There's no investigative reporting going on and there's no coordination of information," Serpas said. "(News outlets) hire reporters for the day and tell them to go find the story. (Stations) are basically running with whatever they've got in front of them that day."

Building relationships between PIOs and revolving reporters is a tremendous challenge. "It is not what we have come to know as folks that you can create a relationship, some confidence and trust with," he said. "You can't have fair and honest reporting . . . that comes from a relationship of trust." To reach the masses, Johnson said agencies are having to think outside the box.

Direct education programs have given way to exponential education: media, newspapers, bus billboards and the like. "The fact is the people who need the education the most don't have time for classes anyway," Johnson said. "I can't reach 400,000 people 20 people at a time without having more community educators. So, I look for more creative ways to reach people."

Having a public information officer attuned to the agencies mission and inner workings is critical to sharing a department's story. "Sometimes we get so close to the forest that we can't see the trees," Wright said. "(PIOs) are able to bring that balance to the discussion. Then you weigh it all together and move forward."

Case Study Ten Questions

1. A PIO has no role in selling an agency's message.
   a. True
   b. False
2. PIOs typically work with only one reporter from a specific news agency.
   a. True
   b. False

Summary

These case studies from Public Information Officers are a microcosm of the information you can learn from networking with professionals. Working locally, regionally, and nationally with other PIOs is always a rewarding and educational experience. Conversations over coffee will yield many examples of good and bad practices from which PIOs can learn, thus enhancing their performance.

CHAPTER 10

Legal Issues
Facing the Public Information Officer

Objectives

- Describe the legal implications of releasing information to the media
- Name the provisions of the Health Insurance Portability and Accountability Act (HIPAA) as it relates to information release
- List the implications of the Freedom of Information concept as is relates to information release
- Identify effective policies relating to the legal rights of media access to a scene

CASE Study

A 9-1-1 call is received from a noted celebrity. A female is unconscious at the residence. Police patrol units, fire department first responders, and an emergency medical service crew are dispatched to the scene. A media outlet hears the call on a scanner and sends a crew to the incident. Meanwhile, the news department sets a crawl on the bottom of the television screen announcing that there has been a request for emergency help at the celebrity's house.

The assignment editor places a call to the PIO of the fire department, police department, and EMS agency, as well as the 9-1-1 center, trying to find out what is happening.

Case Study Review Questions

1. Which agency cannot confirm a response to the residence?
   a. Police
   b. Fire
   c. EMS
   d. 9-1-1
2. The agency from Question 1 cannot release the information because of which regulation?
   a. HIPAA (Health Insurance Portability and Accountability Act)
   b. FOIL (Freedom of Information Law)
   c. FOIA (Freedom of Information Act)
   d. RTNDA (Radio and Television News Director's Association)
3. The media can be kept in a separate area from the public so that they can't take pictures in a public venue.
   a. True
   b. False

Introduction

The PIO has no time to relax. The desire to "just do the right thing" is not enough for today's PIO. Many laws exist that govern the work a PIO performs, and those laws change. PIOs must know what laws pertain to them and to the release of information. In this chapter, you will learn some of the basics of the law and how it affects your job. You cannot be sure that all parts of this chapter are current, since the laws can change frequently, and some of these ideas may have different legal definitions depending on where you live and work. The chapter will provide you with many ideas about where to look for specific legal policies and some discussion items. It will also discuss some media plans and how these can be used in your favor or against you.

A PIO and the PIO's agency can be taken to task for disparaging comments made in public. Statements relating to a criminal suspect, a victim of a motor vehicle crash, or the owner of a property can be negatively interpreted. By understanding this, a PIO will be able to phrase statements so that libel and slander are avoided. One of the many issues a PIO must grapple with is the patient confidentiality issue, especially since the introduction of the **Health Insurance Portability and Accountability Act (HIPAA)**.

ON TARGET "Choose phrasing of statements carefully to avoid legal action."

KEY TERMS

Freedom of Information Act (FOIA), p. 185

Freedom of Information Laws (FOIL), p. 192

Good Samaritans, p. 189

Health Insurance Portability and Accountability Act (HIPAA), p. 184

Libel, p. 185

Protected Health Information, p. 188

Slander, p. 185

Legal Terms for the PIO

The PIO must learn what laws cover information that must be released, as well as what must not be released. It is often confusing, because many interpretations of new laws are done by lawyers. Unfortunately, the court decisions needed to back up those differing opinions are not always available, and sometimes court challenges are necessary to formalize and interpret exactly how these laws affect a PIO's actions. The best advice is to always work with your legal representatives. A solid relationship with the agency attorney can save you much aggravation in the future.

There are a number of terms that apply to the legal aspects of an information officer's job. These include **libel** and **slander**. These words refer to written or spoken untruths or statements. Slander is spoken ("s" for "spoken") and libel is written. Both indicate words that falsely and negatively reflect on a living person's reputation.

The **Freedom of Information Act (FOIA)**, a series of legislative acts and laws passed by both federal and state governments, ensures that the public has access to certain records. These laws are constantly being reviewed for proper application and ease of use for the public (and the media). PIOs may be subject to one of more of these laws. Check current local, state, and federal FOIA regulations often to remain up to date. FOIA laws are sometimes similar to, or also called, sunshine laws. These refer to open meetings of government bodies and closely regulate what meetings must be open to the public.

Health Insurance Portability and Accountability Act (HIPAA)—This law regulates a number of privacy issues related to patient care. It also provides insurance guarantees for employees changing jobs.

Every organization should have an information release policy. Once this policy is in place (after consultation with agency lawyers), you should not initiate or change any aspect of your policy without consulting with your legal counsel. Some policies might be regulated by the state you live in. Police, fire, and medical agencies may have very different regulations to abide by. Some of the items covered by state legislation include public records regulations, freedom of information, and HIPAA. Your agency legal council may help you review case law as it applies to certain information release policies in your state.

In addition to the legal aspects of information release, there are other considerations. Sensitive information, if released at the wrong time, could compromise investigations or place people in harm's way. Information release policies walk a thin line between the public's right to know and the need to protect the agency's interest in making a strong case. For example, a law enforcement agency's statements or the release of certain information can affect a defendant's Sixth Amendment right to a fair trial. In certain areas, the county attorney (or the state's attorney) may have information release policies that have been tested, thus ensuring that everyone's rights are protected.

Media Access to a Scene

The media often cite the first amendment as their rationale for obtaining information. As discussed in earlier chapters, the media see themselves as the protectors of the public's right to know, based on the First Amendment, which covers the right of freedom of the press. Public safety officials who still believe that they can keep the media from getting a story are naive at best.

The worst violations of media access are often decisions made by first responders who have little or no understanding of the law. A common issue is allowing the public into an area where the press is forbidden. Aside from the Constitution, the right of the media to have access to certain scenes is often spelled out in state laws. Some are very specific about media access, others are more open ended. (See Box 10-1.)

A California statute says that police cannot prevent journalists from entering areas at disaster scenes that are closed to the general public. Although police can bar the general public from the scenes to protect public health and safety, they can deny media access only if the disaster may have been the result of a crime and the police need to seal the area off to protect evidence.[1]

In Ohio, the disorderly conduct law prohibits interference with the police at the scene of an emergency, but states that "Nothing in this section shall be construed to limit access or deny information to any news media representative in the lawful exercise of his duties."[2]

Oregon law states that military or state police personnel may restrict access to a search and rescue area, but provisions "shall" be made for reasonable access by members of the media in the performance of newsgathering and reporting.[3]

Hospitals or other entities have no right to restrict photographers who are on public property from taking photos.[4,5]

Box 10-1

Virginia

CODE OF VIRGINIA

TITLE 15.2. SUBTITLE II. CHAPTER 17.

POLICE AND PUBLIC ORDER. ARTICLE 1. GENERAL PROVISIONS.

15.2-1714 Establishing police lines, perimeters, or barricades.

Whenever fires, accidents, wrecks, explosions, crimes, riots or other emergency situations where life, limb or property may be endangered may cause persons to collect on the public streets, alleys, highways, parking lots or other public area, the chief law-enforcement officer of any locality or that officer's authorized representative who is responsible for the security of the scene may establish such areas, zones or perimeters by the placement of police lines or barricades as are reasonably necessary

Personnel from information services such as press, radio and television, when gathering news, shall be exempt from the provisions of this section except that it shall be unlawful for such persons to obstruct the police, firemen and rescue workers in the performance of their duties at such scene. Such personnel shall proceed at their own risk.[1]

[1]*How to Conquer Public Speaking Fear*, Morton C. Orman, M.D., © 1996–2002, M.C. Orman, MD, FLP.

The right of the media to access a scene regularly undergoes court challenges. Most cases cite the press' right to be where the public is allowed.[6] PIOs should understand any laws that govern how and when they release information to the media and allow access to emergency scenes. Developing a formal media relations policy for your agency may be the best way to uniformly manage media access to scenes. The U.S. Department of Homeland Security's Federal Emergency Management Agency (FEMA) has a formal policy for media access to scenes,[7] and variations of that policy may be applicable to other public safety agencies.

When developing a policy for your agency, consultation and "buy-in" of the leadership is crucial. No policy can be enforced if the leadership does not appreciate the aspects of the policy. Policy development should include input from the agency's legal counsel as well as key agency personnel. Some agencies have encouraged the media to be involved in the developing a policy. There are distinct advantages to this partnership. It allows the issues of media access to be discussed openly, and while there may not be 100 percent agreement on all points, the discussions should open a better line of communication between private industry and public service personnel.

Health Insurance Portability and Accountability Act (HIPAA)

When it comes to medical operations, understanding HIPAA and how it affects your agency is extremely important. HIPAA, among other things, guarantees a patient's right to privacy. **Protected health information (PHI)** must not be released by certain organizations. The University of Miami Miller School of Medicine says PHI is "any information, whether oral or recorded in any form or medium" that "is created or received by a health care provider, health plan, public health authority, employer, life insurer, school or university, or health care clearinghouse"; and "relates to the past, present, or future physical or mental health or condition of an individual; the provision of health care to an individual; or the past, present, or future payment for the provision of health care to an individual."[8]

Some organizations that are not bound by HIPAA use the federal law as a means to limit information being provided to the press. This is not an acceptable interpretation of the statute, and an agency's legal council should be involved in making decisions as they apply to HIPAA. If a paramedic and police officer are at the same incident, the police may release nearly any information that would not compromise an investigation; however, the paramedic is often bound by HIPAA and other state regulations to protect that same information.

HIPAA was passed in 1996, but the most significant privacy provisions did not take effect until April 2003, showing the complicated nature of rule making involved with HIPAA. HIPAA regulates the use and release of a patient's PHI by "covered entities." In order to determine whether your agency is a covered entity, you should refer to the latest information available from the Centers for Medicare and Medicaid Services (CMS).[9]

The Radio-Television News Directors Association (RTNDA) says a "covered entity must be a health care provider, such as hospitals, physicians, emergency medical or ambulance personnel, health and insurance plans and health care clearinghouses. These entities must also transmit (PHI) electronically. Business associates of these entities (such as accountants, consultants, lawyers, managers, etc.) are also required to keep **protected health information** confidential."[10] The RTNDA and other professional groups have a wealth of information available about HIPAA and how it applies to release of medical information. The PIO should review these sources, as well as any consultant resources available through his or her agency. Changes will occur as the law continues to be interpreted.

It is generally understood that police, firefighters, and other law enforcement agencies are NOT considered covered entities under HIPAA.

Police and fire department incident reports, court records, records of agencies that do not provide or insure healthcare and autopsies are not covered by HIPAA. Additionally, any patient has a right to indicate certain personal medical records may be disclosed.

There are many complicated "what if" scenarios pertaining to HIPAA. One such scenario is a public safety agency, such as a fire department or police department, which also provides emergency medical services. These are sometime referred to as "hybrid entities." These hybrid entities are generally considered covered entities by many experts on HIPAA; however, you should verify your agency's HIPAA status with the HIPAA compliance officer or consultant. Many public safety agencies are first responders, or the first responders might be **Good Samaritans** or family members. These responders are generally exempt from the provisions of HIPAA.

Documents such as one from the Maryland–Delaware–D.C. Press Association provide talking points to journalists who encounter HIPAA issues while attempting to gather information about stories.[11]

Court rulings have upheld certain HIPAA claims. In a Louisiana case, the State Supreme Court upheld the right of an EMS agency to withhold certain emergency dispatch audio in order to protect a patient's right to privacy.[12]

HIPAA regulations can be confusing for PIOs releasing information to journalists. Various consultants have interpreted the regulations and come away with differing opinions. Until one of these opinions is tested by a review of an alleged violation, we may never know where we truly stand in regard to HIPAA information release.

As an example of this confusion, some consultants have advised agencies as follows:

- Your agency responds to a motor vehicle crash in which one victim and one vehicle are involved. A covered entity may not release any information about this incident because the patient could be easily identified. However, other consultants have said that releasing the condition a patient is in and the hospital the patient was transported to does not constitute a release of protected health information.
- Your agency responds to a motor vehicle crash where there are multiple victims in multiple cars transported to multiple hospitals. In this case, it may be considered permissible for a covered entity to release a general statement Such as "Five people were taken to area hospitals as a result of a motor vehicle crash at the corner of "Walk Street and Don't Walk Avenue." The rationale is that no individual patient can be identified by this information.

These restrictions seem to make it impossible for covered entities to tell the news media the good stories about lives saved. However, an information officer can release protected health information with a patient's consent. Getting that consent may not be as easy as it sounds. Since protected health information is only supposed to be shared within an organization by those directly related to treatment or billing, there are questions as to whether an information officer has a right to know the information. As such, when a PIO is told, "we saved a life today," policies may exist which prevent the PIO from getting the rest of the story.

When writing your media policies, you would be well advised to address situations such as this. The best solution may be to have the people who were directly involved with the patient contact him or her to obtain written permission that allows for the sharing of PHI. Then the PIO may get involved and not run afoul of HIPAA regulations. Of course, if your agency is not a covered entity, obtaining permission from a patient may be slightly less complicated.

In certain circumstances, protected health information may also be released to law enforcement, public health, and disaster agencies. The specific circumstances involve the type of treatment, law enforcement operations (investigations), reimbursement, legal requirements, and listing in a directory of information.

Release of information regarding the treatment of the patient indicates sharing normally protected health information, such as disease or previous surgeries, in order to provide further treatment of a current problem.

Operations refers to such items as allowing EMS dispatchers to pass on information about a patient or patients so proper transportation can be completed.

When it comes to reimbursement, the HIPAA regulations allow providing information to an insurance company so proper payment can be made.

Some information release is required by law. For instance, under strict HIPAA interpretation, a paramedic could not reveal information about a patient's injuries, even if a child abuser inflicted them. However, many states have enacted mandatory reporter laws, which require this information be divulged to certain authorities under specific conditions such as child abuse.

There are additional rules governing hospitals. They may maintain a directory of information that includes a patient's name, the patient's location in the hospital, and his or her general condition and religious affiliation; however, the patient must be given the opportunity to object to or restrict the use or disclosure of this information. When it comes to religious affiliation, that information can be released only to the clergy. Most hospitals require media organizations to have a patient's name prior to releasing information. Patients have an option to refuse to allow information release.

Hospitals can disclose general condition information that is not specific about the patient. The American Hospital Association recommends certain condition codes be used by hospitals:

- Good: Vital signs within normal limits. Patient is conscious.
- Fair: Vital signs are within normal limits. Patient is conscious but may be uncomfortable.
- Serious: Vital signs not within normal limits. Patient is acutely ill.
- Critical: Vital signs are not within normal limits. Patient may be unconscious.
- Treated and Released: Patient received treatment but was not admitted.

Information that is not classified as PHI may be released to the media in a manner that is consistent with company policy and state law.

HIPAA violations can be expensive. The U.S. Department of Health and Human Services' Office of Civil Rights investigates HIPAA violations. Civil and criminal penalties up to $50,000 and/or imprisonment for as long as 1 year can be imposed. If PHI is disclosed under false pretenses, the maximum fine is $100,000 and/or imprisonment for as long as 5 years. Other penalties for specific HIPAA violations can be as much as a fine of $250,000 and/or imprisonment for as long as 10 years.

While journalists are not bound by HIPAA, they may have ethical considerations in releasing protected health information. Because news organizations are not covered entities, journalists would not be subject to the stiff penalties to which covered entities and their employees are.

Law Enforcement Disclosures

When it comes to releasing information in a law enforcement setting, a PIO must take several issues into consideration. Various laws require the release of certain information; however, some jurisdictions hold information that might compromise investigations. This is a policy decision and should not be used as an excuse. Strong media relations can help bolster an understanding of the use of this policy.

Of course, there are some disclosures that will assist in the apprehension of suspects, but care must be used not to compromise the ability to prosecute the suspect.

There are laws that will restrict the PIO's ability to release the name of juveniles and certain crime victims, such as those who have suffered abuse, neglect, or domestic violence.

Police are often the source of decedent names or those involved in motor vehicle crashes. Next of kin should always be notified prior to release of names.

Media Policies

Media policies can be a PIO's guide through the twists and turns of the potential legal implications of information release. The policies must be complete and cover a full range of communication issues, but not be too detailed. Flexibility must be maintained in order to adapt to various scenarios while at the same time maintaining consistency. These policies must be kept up-to-date, must be in line with changing regulations, and must be based on relevant court decisions.

The policy should be clear to employees who read it and not be in conflict with other policy statements or procedures.

Freedom of Information

The concept of the public's right to know has evolved into freedom of information programs at all levels of government, schools, and even corporate America. Freedom of information implies there is a free flow of information for anyone requesting it. However, this freedom has not come easily for individuals and reporters. Web sites abound addressing freedom of information issues. The Society for Professional Journalists[13] (SPJ) as well as the Radio-Television News Directors Association (RTNDA) have entire sections of policy dealing with issues related to the release of information. Federal and state laws exist outlining how information can be requested and distributed. These pieces of legislation are known as the Freedom of Information Act (FOIA) or **Freedom of Information Laws (FOIL)**.

PIOs may be placed in a position to handle the numerous inquiries allowed by FIOA. It is incumbent on the PIO to review and understand how FOIA will affect the agency. There are some issues that, once opened to public and media scrutiny, will create negative opinions about the agency. This may require the PIO to put into action a crisis communications plan (see Chapter Seven). The potential for negative publicity is not a reason to circumvent required information release. PIOs should consult with agency legal council about FOIA issues.

Summary

The PIO has a responsibility to the agency and the constituencies served by the agency to provide accurate and complete information. Some information is required to be released by law; other information must be withheld by law. Understanding the legal responsibilities related to information release will ensure that the PIO can accomplish the mission to provide accurate and timely information.

REVIEW QUESTIONS

1. A law enforcement agency can always withhold the names of people arrested in a raid
   a. True
   b. False

2. Any agency that deals with a sick or injured person is bound by HIPAA
   a. True
   b. False

3. A Freedom of Information Act allows newspapers to print nearly anything they want.
   a. True
   b. False

ENDNOTES

1. Cal. Penal Code § 409.5
2. Ohio Rev. Code Ann. § 2917.13
3. Or. Rev.Stat. § 401.570
4. http://www.rtnda.org/pages/media_items/rtndas-guide-to-health-coverage-under-hipaa427.php
5. *Communications Lawyer,* Volume 21, Number 2, Summer 2003, p.13
6. http://www.firstamendmentcenter.org/Press/topic.aspx?topic=journalist_access
7. http://www.fema.gov/media/resources/ground_rules.shtm
8. http://privacy.med.miami.edu/glossary/xd_protected_health_info.htm
9. http://cms.hhs.gov
10. http://www.rtnda.org/pages/media_items/rtndas-guide-to-health-coverage-under-hipaa427.php
11. http://www.mddcpress.com/mdaccess/hipaaletter1.04.pdf
12. Hill v. East Baton Rouge Parish Department of Emergency Medical Services, 05–1236 (La. App. 1 Cir. 12/22/05), *writ denied.* http://www.la-fcca.org/Opinions/PUB2005/2005-12/2005CA1236Dec2005.Pub.11.pdf
13. http://www.spj.org/foi.asp

Emergency Public Information and the Four Phases of Emergency Management

Mitigation

Mitigation actions try to eliminate or reduce the degree of risk to human life and property from any type of hazard, as well as from its effects. Examples of mitigation activities related to public information include the following:

- Develop/update agreements with local media.
- Coordinate with and develop agreements with media and emergency management personnel in adjacent counties (in the event of multicounty emergencies).
- Develop an agreement with the Emergency Management Agency PIO to coordinate news releases during emergencies.
- Develop agreements with local emergency response organizations for the coordinated release of public information through the County Public Information Office.

Preparedness

Preparedness activities, taken before a disaster occurs, aim at making a coordinated response more effective. Examples of preparedness activities related to public information include the following:

- Maintain and update lists of media contacts and capabilities.
- Keep hazard-specific public information up to date and available to news media contacts.
- Maintain an adequate supply of hazard-specific pamphlets and brochures that can be distributed to the public in an emergency.
- Train Emergency Management Agency staff and emergency responders to distribute emergency public information in the event of a power failure.
- Make media contacts aware of the location of the joint information center (JIC).
- Make sure that the JIC has the proper equipment needed for media briefings.
- Present regular emergency preparedness programs to local government agencies, businesses, and residents.

Response

The response to an emergency includes actions taken immediately before, during, or just after the emergency occurs. Besides trying to save lives and minimize property damage, responders hope to reduce secondary damage and make recovery efforts faster and easier. Examples of response activities related to public information include the following:

- See that approved information is released according to plan as soon as an emergency has been declared. (Use door-to-door notifications if necessary.)
- Coordinate with Emergency Operations Center (EOC) officials and site officials for information about emergency services available at the site.
- Direct the release of emergency public information through the joint information center.
- Brief the EOC executive group regularly.
- Brief the State Emergency Management Agency about local activities.
- Provide constant official news, through the media, in order to prevent panic and rumors.

- In general, relay information that will save lives and protect property.

Recovery

Recovery is the work required to return vital life-support systems to operating standards (in the short term) and to return society to normal or improved levels (in the long term). Examples of recovery activities related to public information include the following:

- Keep citizens informed about disaster assistance.
- Provide PIO representation at the Disaster Recovery Center.

During and Emergency

- Do take a deep breath to get control of yourself first. Crises are emotional by nature. You must calm yourself before you can address others calmly.
- Do tell the truth. This is the most important communication rule to follow, but it is also the most difficult. It is our natural tendency to cover up mistakes and defend ourselves even when we are wrong. However, the truth allows you to control the flow of information and start the recovery process sooner.
- Do ask the reporter's name. Log it for future reference.
- Do release only verified information.
- Do alert the press promptly to relief and recovery operations. The media can provide you an opportunity to communicate with citizens in your jurisdiction.
- Do escort the press.
- Do have a designated spokesperson.
- Do stick to the facts. Refuse to deal with hypothetical situations—"what ifs." Stick to the briefing sheets and steer the communication back to your specified message.
- Do use talking points.
- Do keep accurate records and logs of all inquiries and news coverage.
- Do try to find out and meet press deadlines.
- Do try to return media calls within two hours. Make yourself available whenever you can.

- Do be direct. A direct question deserves a direct answer.
- Do be brief. Your performance is measured in 30-second sound bytes. If you ramble on, the reporter or editor will be forced to select only portions of your answer.
- Do have a clear idea of what can and cannot be released. Rely on the briefing sheets.
- Do ask for clarification of any question you do not understand before you begin to answer the question.

Additional Readings

Visit the following Internet sites for further readings:

http://www.abacon.com/pubspeak/index.html

http://www.akdart.com/ebs.html

http://www.assignmenteditor.com/

http://www.cooperativeresearch.org/timeline.jsp?timeline=complete_911_timeline&startpos=800#a903

http://www.dartcenter.org

http://www.dhs.gov

http://www.emediawire.com/

http://www.Fema.gov

http://www.free-press-release.com/

http://www.icisf.org/

http://www.Newseum.org

http://www.nimsonline.com

http://www.Nioa.org

http://www.poynter.org/

http://www.prsa.org

http://www.rtnda.org

http://www.safekids.org

http://www.spj.org

http://www.stateofthenewsmedia.org/2006/index.asp

http://www.toastmasters.org

http://training.fema.gov

http://www.usfa.fema.gov/safety/

http://www.vocus.com

Answers to Case Study Questions

Chapter 1

1. What key messages were provided by these public information officers?

   The PIOs in this scenario provided alternate commuter routing information, as well as telling the public that there was no toxic hazard.

2. How would these messages potentially save lives?

   Providing alternate routes for commuters prevents a panic or disorganized reaction when they encounter the blocked roads.
   The message that there are no toxins can help suppress panic.

3. What skills do these PIOs need to provide this information to the public?

   The PIO needs an understanding of (1) the incident command system, (2) how to achieve cooperation with other agency PIOs, (3) local media deadlines and news preferences, and (4) the habits of local residents.

Chapter 2

1. What are the different needs of the media to deliver a story?
   a. **The television stations need parking space in the lot near the incident for the live trucks.**
   b. **The newspaper will need historical information, which should be developed in advance of the event.**
   c. **The PIO could assign another staff member to provide the radio reporter with the natural sound needed for his or her story.**
2. Does the PIO benefit from assisting the media in getting the story?
   a. **Yes. Lead stories were generated from this event.**
3. What is the importance of lead story coverage?
   a. **The lead story is the first story covered during a newscast. It often gets promotional play prior to the news, as well as a recap at the end of the newscast.**

Chapter 3

1. When should a PIO schedule a news conference?
   a. **When information needs to be released to everyone at the same time**

b. **To announce an event or incident**
c. **Mid-morning or mid-afternoon**

2. What types of questions should a PIO expect reporters to ask during an interview?
   a. **Challenging questions**
3. When should a PIO end a news conference?
   a. **When there are no further questions**
   b. **When the news conference begins to cover topics that are off limits**
   c. **When the topic has been covered**

Chapter 4

(Correct answers are in boldface type.)

1. This press release represents an accurate review of the fatal incident.
   a. True
   b. False
   c. **Unable to determine**
2. In the introductory sentence to the case study, the noun is
   a. **chase**
   b. a
   c. results
   d. none of the above
3. A press release should be written in a format called
   a. Aggressive and accurate
   b. Objective and benign
   c. **Inverted pyramid**
   d. Technical writing

Chapter 5

1. Would this situation qualify as a 'critical incident'? Why/why not?
   Yes, this would correctly be termed a critical incident, because of the serious injury and death of a child, an event that is out of the ordinary and that evokes strong emotional reactions.
2. What factors should be taken into consideration when Derek writes his press release?
   Derek, the PIO, should be mindful of the state of mind of the ambulance crew and should decline to interview them publicly. There may be legal repercussions to his agency from the accident, so his comments should be chosen wisely to avoid blame. He should also monitor his own reactions to this powerful scene.
3. What would be the general standard of care for the ambulance crew?
   The standard of care for this ambulance crew would be to have an initial defusing and, potentially, a debriefing, with follow-up and referral following these interventions.

4. What signs/symptoms of critical incident stress are evident in the case study?

   The visual impact of seeing a seriously injured child and pronouncing that child dead, the anguished cry of the mother for her child, and the distraught looks on the paramedics' faces are all signs/symptoms of critical incident stress.

5. What critical-incident stress management services should be available to the PIO, if any?

   Ideally, the same services should be provided for the PIO as are common practice for emergency workers: a defusing, possibly a debriefing, and follow-up/referral as needed.

Chapter 6

1. How can a PIO control information flow within a command post?

   Establishing a joint information system policy and training personnel in who has the authority to release information to the media can assist with this mission.

2. What harm can be done to public trust when incorrect information is reported?

   Once incorrect information is reported, all subsequent information released will be suspected of being inaccurate. If people are suspicious, the ability of a PIO to convince people to take lifesaving action can be undermined.

3. How do media deadlines influence the release of information?

   Information should be released with deadlines in mind, because some media outlets will not be able to update their information easily. The print media may not be able to change a newspaper run once it has started, allowing a long cycle of incorrect information to be absorbed by the public.

Chapter 7

1. How did the PIO in this case study benefit from this presentation?
   a. **The PIO's ability to showcase important programs managed by the agency allowed the local political leaders to hear of the acceptance of the programs by constituents, which resulted in pledges of budgetary increases for these programs.**
2. What are three tools the PIO might have used to make this presentation?
   a. **The PIO could have used**
      i. **Handouts**
      ii. **A PowerPoint presentation**
      iii. **Stories of program successes**
3. Did the presence of the public help influence politicians attending the luncheon?
   a. **Yes. Politicians respond to public opinion. Although you may believe that your program is important, convincing the public as well as politicians improves the chances that the program will be approved.**

Chapter 8

Marketing involves promoting and selling a product an audience needs. Match the product with the audience as depicted in this case study.

Product	Audince
__c_ 1. Neighborhood Watch groups	a. Mayor
__a_ 2. Positive publicity for police	b. Media
__b_ 3. News stories promoting a decrease in crime	c. Citizens

Chapter 9

(Correct answers are in boldface type.)

1. Emergency scenes are dynamic and
   a. Require PIOs to wait until all information is in before holding a press conference
   b. Require PIOs to hide the incident from the media until all the facts are known
   c. Require PIOs to provide frequent updates to the media
   d. Therefore the media will not be interested until all work is complete
2. Fact sheets, press conferences, and community meetings should not be used during emergencies.
   a. True
   b. False

Chapter 10

(Correct answers are in boldface type.)

1. Which agency cannot confirm a response to the residence?
   a. Police
   b. Fire
   c. EMS
   d. 9-1-1
2. The agency in question 1 cannot release the information because of which regulation?
   a. HIPAA
   b. FOIL
   c. FOIA
   d. RTNDA
3. The media can be kept in a separate area from the public so that they can't take pictures in a public venue.
   a. True
   b. False

Answers to Review Questions

(Correct answers are in boldface type.)

Chapter 1

1. Public information is used by people to make decisions and take actions to
   a. **Saves lives**
   b. **Avoid harm**
   c. **Protect property**
2. Public information can be used to
   a. **Inform**
   b. **Educate**
   c. **Persuade**
   d. **Get people to make lifesaving decisions**
3. In an ideal structure, the public information officer (PIO) reports to
   a. **The chief executive (CEO) or an organization**
4. The PIO should always attempt to stage a show for the press at emergency scenes.
   a. TRUE or **FALSE**
5. The PIO should determine which reporters are trouble and ban them from the organization.
   a. TRUE or **FALSE**

Chapter 2

1. The media are referred to as the big three plus one. This means
   a. ABC, CBS, NBC, and the Associated Press
   b. **Radio, television, newspaper, and the Internet**
   c. CNN, FOX, MSNBC, and C-SPAN
   d. Cable, print, over-the-air, and blogs
2. Public affairs programming
   a. **Often provides a longer interview to tell a story better**
   b. Deals with politics
   c. Allows broadcast outlets to editorialize
   d. Is run by FEMA during disasters

3. The Internet now has many Web-only newspapers.
   a. **True**
   b. False
4. Reporter deadlines
   a. Are of no consequence to a PIO
   b. **Should be observed whenever possible**
   c. Can be changed by reporters
   d. Do not apply to public information
5. The definition of news is the same for everyone.
   a. True
   b. **False**

Chapter 3

1. Before an interview, a PIO should do all of the following except
   a. Be early
   b. Mentally prepare for the interview
   c. **Eat something spicy and have an adult beverage; it will calm your nerves**
   d. Talk with reporters
2. During the interview, a PIO should do all of the following except
   a. **Use the reporter's name during an interview**
   b. Not look into the camera lens
   c. Be cautious of background noise
   d. Watch your posture
3. A dead-air question is
   a. A question that is caused by a technical malfunction
   b. **Designed to keep you talking even though you have completed your thought**
   c. Inevitable with the complexities of live broadcasts
   d. Your chance to make your point more completely
4. When doing a live "TV Remote Booth" interview,
   a. **Look into the camera, just as if the person was standing in front of you.**
   b. Look to the left.
   c. Look to the right.
   d. Make sure that it is conducted inside a small booth.

Chapter 4

1. Sentences are composed of two parts.
   a. Predicate and antecate
   b. Noun and verb
   c. **Noun and predicate**
   d. Purpose and action

2. The inverted pyramid style of writing places the most important information last and leads up to it with minor details.
   a. This entices the reader to go deeper into the release to find its true meaning.
   b. This is an incorrect statement.
   c. This style is preferred by news departments because editors will have to read the entire news release in order to comprehend its meaning.
   d. Both a and c
3. A media advisory is a form of a news release
   a. That provides only basic information
   b. That is often used to announce a media event
   c. That is written in a format of who, what, when, where, why, and how
   d. All of the above

Chapter 5

1. What are the components of Critical Incident Stress Management?
   a. Pre-incident education,
   b. defusings,
   c. debriefings,
   d. demobilization,
   e. pastoral care,
   f. one-on-one consultations,
   g. briefing
2. What are the seven phases of CISD?
   a. Introduction,
   b. fact,
   c. thought,
   d. reaction,
   e. symptom,
   f. teaching,
   g. reentry
3. Name the three stages of the human stress response.
   a. the alarm stage,
   b. resistance or adaptation,
   c. resolution or exhaustion stages
4. Identify at least seven types of critical incidents.
   a. Loss or serious injury to a child,
   b. loss or serious injury to a coworker,
   c. event drawing extensive media coverage,
   d. victim resembling or being someone you know,

e. **event during which prolonged rescue fails,**
f. **mass casualty incident,**
g. **workplace violence**

5. What is the definition of a critical incident?
A critical incident is a serious, out-of-the-ordinary event that produces the human stress response.
6. Define the terms 'eustress' and 'distress' and give examples of each.
Eustress is a positive stress that motivates, energizes, or inspires a person—a positive or happy event or news that elicits the human stress response. Distress is a negative or unhappy event or news that elicits the human stress response. Distress is sometimes viewed as a "crushing or oppressive" form of stress.

Chapter 6

1. Which federal document outlines the PIOs responsibility in a disaster?
   a. The Constitution
   b. **National Incident Management System**
   c. The Stafford Act
   d. None of the above
2. Within a joint information center, agency PIOs maintain their autonomy, while still providing coordinated incident information.
   a. **True**
   b. False
3. Reporter errors can occur because of
   a. A misunderstanding during an interview
   b. Incorrect information provided by a PIO
   c. Editing by superiors within the new department
   d. **All of the above**

Chapter 7

1. List three common causes of stress for a public speaker.
   a. **Covering too much in a short presentation**
   b. **Expecting to receive something from the audience**
   c. **Negative outcomes**
2. List three suggestions to ease the nervousness that is common with public speaking.
   a. **Learn about the audience in advance.**
   b. **Walk around the room prior to the program.**
   c. **Learn the material.**

3. A standard method of making a presentation includes the following:
   a. Tell the audience what you will tell them.
   b. Tell them.
   c. Tell them what you told them.
   __X__ **TRUE** ____ **FALSE**

Chapter 8

1. Public information, public relations, and marketing are different terms for the same thing.
   ____ True __X__ **False**
2. A marketing plan should include objectives and measurement tools.
   __X__ **True** ____ False
3. List three projects for which you could develop a marketing plan.

Chapter 9

Chapter 9 has no review questions.

Chapter 10

1. A law enforcement agency can always withhold the names of people arrested in a raid.
   a. True
   b. False
2. Any agency that deals with a sick or injured person is bound by HIPAA.
   a. True
   b. False
3. The Freedom of Information Act allows newspapers to print nearly anything they want.
   a. True
   b. False

Glossary

AAA The American Ambulance Association, a professional membership organization working on education, legislative advocacy, and other issues related to the ambulance industry.

Adjective Word in a sentence that describes something or someone.

Adrenalin An internal hormone, also called epinephrine, that stimulates the "fight or flight" response as part of stress.

Adverb Word in a sentence that answers the question "how?"

Advertising Bringing a product or service to the attention of potential and current customers. Advertising is typically done with signs, brochures, commercials, direct mailings, e-mail messages, personal contact, etc.[i]

Archive A filing system that maintains historical records of media work performed by a PIO.

Assisting agency In the National Incident Management System (NIMS) and National Interagency Incident Management System (NIIMS) Incident Command System (ICS), an assisting agency provides tactical support during an incident.

Assumptions Circumstances and environment predicted to exist during a marketing project.

Beat reporter A reporter who concentrates on writing stories about specific subjects, such as police, schools, or business.

Body The main part of a news release between the lead and the closing.

Briefing A presentation of material before a gathering of media members. A briefing can be spontaneous at an emergency or planned as part of a marketing program or for some other purpose when the media need a rapid situational update.

Broadcast media Media that use the public airwaves.

Broadcast Operations The area within a joint information center specializing in producing or providing segments for broadcasting on television and radio.

B-roll Video used as background material for new reports.

---

[i]http://www.managementhelp.org/ad_prmot/defntion.htm, Carter McNamara, MBA, PhD, Copyright 1999.

Bullet points Short statements or paraphrases of major points being discussed in a presentation.

Chief executive officer The leader of an organization.

Chroma key effect That which allows one video image to be superimposed upon another. The main subject is shot with a blue or green background. When the final cut is made, the background replaces the color.

Citizen journalist Citizen whose reports about news events are broadcast or reported as facts.

Close The end point of a news release, often containing standard information about the organization issuing the release.

Community relations A program that integrates an organization with community members.

Community relations lead The individual in charge of the community relations area of a joint information center.

Comprehensive critical incident stress management A form of crisis intervention that includes a range of services and techniques provided to prevent or minimize the effects of critical incident stress.

CONELRAD Control of Electronic Radiation; the first system established by the federal government providing the President with a method of communicating with all citizens in an emergency. CONELRAD was later replaced by the Emergency Broadcast System (EBS) and more recently by the Emergency Alert System (AES).

Confidentiality An ethical and legal issue requiring no transmission of information or data from one person to another.

Conflicting research Research studies that found different results on identical issues.

Constituencies Groups of people to whom an individual or group is responsible.

Cooperating agency In the National Incident Management System (NIMS) and National Interagency Incident Management System (NIIMS) Incident Command System (ICS), a cooperating agency provides support other than tactical during an incident.

Cortisol An internal hormone, sometimes called the "stress hormone," that is part of the human stress response.

Cost effectiveness The financial price of a program in terms of its results. Often, two programs are compared to learn which is more cost effective.

Crisis communications plan The plan that guides an organiz through communications issues relating to a crisis it is involve

Critical incident A serious, out-of-the-ordinary event that pro the human stress response.

Critical incident stress debriefing A group intervention used t mitigate the effects of critical incident stress following a critical incident.

DART Center for Journalism and Trauma An online global resou for journalists who cover violence. At the site are publications and training housed at the University of Washington. http://www.dartcenter.org.

Defamation The harming caused to a person by a statement made by another person.

Direct marketing A promotion mechanism that allows focused messages to be received by a targeted audience. The main difference between direct marketing and other promotion mechanisms is that, because the audience is known, the marketer can deliver a message that appeals to its specific needs.[ii]

Disaster Recovery Centers (DRCs) Locations that allow victims to receive important information about programs aimed at assisting their recovery during a disaster.

Dispatcher The person working in a dispatch or communications center who is responsible for assigning emergency crews to assist during incidents for which help is needed.

Distress A negative or unhappy event or news that elicits the human stress response. Sometimes viewed as a "crushing or oppressive" form of stress.

Diuretic A chemical compound, such as caffeine, that increases urination and the elimination of water from the body.

Editorial production A team of personnel within a joint information center who are assigned the task of developing written material for release to the media, the public, and the staff of the center.

Embargo A request by a PIO to hold the release of information until a specific time. An embargo allows the news media to prepare story content on a subject, but requests that they not run the story until a specific time.

[ii]http://www.l10creative.com/kb/terms/direct_marketing.php, Copyright © 1999–2005 Lorentz Consulting, LLC., Dallas, Texas.

Emergency Alert System (EAS) The system currently in use to warn the public about an actual or impending emergency. The EAS is the successor of the Emergency Broadcast System.

Emergency Broadcast System (EBS) The system, now defunct, designed for use by the President or his or her designees to communicate with the public during emergencies. The EBS also allowed for warnings to be issued. The EBS succeeded CONELRAD and was replaced by the Emergency Alert System.

Emergency Declaration A local, state, or federal designation allowing certain additional assistance to be provided. A local government may declare an emergency that allows the state to provide assistance normally not available (e.g., the National Guard).

Emergency manager The individual responsible for conducting community or business hazard analyses and risk assessments and for managing disaster response and recovery programs.

Emergency medical services Traditionally thought of as an ambulance service, emergency medical services (EMS) encompass much more than just the transportation of ill or injured people. EMS includes the equipment, personnel, and physician oversight of medical care and training programs needed to support emergency response in a community. Thus, EMS also consists of dispatchers, first responders, ambulance services, emergency medical field protocols, hospital services, and initial training, as well as continuing education.

Emergency Operations Plan (EOP) The plan developed to guide an organization, government entity, or business through various emergencies. The EOP consists of hazard analysis, as well as outlines of methods of operation during specific emergencies.

Emergency Public Information (EPI) Information provided to the public during emergencies.

Emergency Public Information Annex The section of an Emergency Operations Plan outlining specific methods of communication used during emergencies.

Emergency Response Plan A plan that outlines an organization's response to an emergency.

Emergency Support Function (ESF) The National Response Framework (NRF) outlines 15 emergency support functions (ESFs), while some states have as many as 18. ESFs consist of groups of similar organizations, usually governmental, that work together during disasters or emergencies to complete specific tasks. ESFs are often referred to simply as functions.

Equal access A policy established to ensure that all media representatives have the same information available to them.

Eustress A part of everyday life that motivates, energizes, or inspires; a positive or happy event or news that elicits the human stress response.

Exclusive A story released or printed by only one news outlet.

Extemporaneous Spontaneous, without prior planning.

External affairs The Emergency support function charged to work with the media, the public and with government and legislative leaders during emergencies and disasters.

Fact sheet A document outlining specific statements of fact on a subject.

Federal Emergency Management Agency (FEMA) The federal agency charged with implementing various aspects of the Stafford Act, the nation's main disaster relief legislation. In 2001, FEMA became an agency of the U.S. Department of Homeland Security.

Field Operations The function within a joint information center charged with providing public information to media and citizens at or near the site of a disaster.

Five "P's" of Marketing people, price, product, promotion, place.

Five W's and an H Main components of a news release: who, what, when, where, why, and how.

Freedom of Information Laws (FOIL) Laws that provide for the release of information to the press or the public by certain government agencies.

General assignment reporter A reporter assigned to cover many different stories, rather than concentrate on a specific subject.

Go kit Equipment, reference material, and personal items stored in a convenient location for immediate deployment and use during an emergency.

Good Samaritan Legally defined, a person who assists another without expectation of compensation and performs to a certain level of knowledge without negligence.

Government relations A program that ensures open lines of communication between government entities and between those entities and individual private, not-for-profit (NFP) and nongovernmental agencies.

Health Insurance Portability and Accountability Act (HIPAA) A federal law outlining rights to privacy for individuals receiving health care services.

Health promotion Activities and strategies used to assist people in maintaining and improving their level of physical, emotional, and social wellness.

Human stress response The normal physiological response to a perceived threat or stressor.

Incident Command System (ICS) Also referred to as the Incident Management System, the system used to set objectives, develop tactics, and manage resources in an effort to solve a problem such as injuries caused by a natural disaster, a fire in a house, or multiple victims involved in a motor vehicle crash.

ICS-209 Incident Summary An Incident Command System form providing information summarizing resource utilization, tactics, and strategy in use at an incident.

ICS-214 Unit Log An Incident Command System form completed by personnel and describing their work during an operational period.

ICS-221 Demobilization Checklist An Incident Command System form providing an individual with guidance through a check-out process when leaving an incident.

Incident Action Plan (IAP) The plan developed by an incident command team or incident commander that directs the operation for a specific period of time.

Incident Command System (ICS) A system of organization and policies outlined in the National Incident Management System as the command and control system to be used when managing an incident in the United States.

Incident Commander (IC) The person who sets the objectives for managing an incident and who is responsible for all incident management activities.

Industry-specific jargon Terminology common to an industry, but rarely understood by others.

Interagency coordination The liaisons established between multiple responding entities at an emergency.

International Critical Incident Stress Foundation An international organization founded in 1989 to establish a framework for practice, provide basic and advanced training, and form a network of CISM teams throughout the world.

International Fire Service Accreditation Congress (IFSAC) The agency responsible for accrediting (certifying) fire service training programs.

Investigative reporter A reporter (or a group of reporters) who looks in depth into stories, often taking weeks or months to develop a complete story.

Joint field office (JFO) The main command and operations location used by federal responders when managing a disaster.

Joint information center (JIC) Entity whose mission is to contribute to the well-being of the community following a disaster by ensuring the dissemination of information that is timely, accurate, consistent, and easy to understand. The JIC explains what people can expect from their government and demonstrates clearly that FEMA and other federal, state, local, and voluntary agencies are working together to provide the services needed to rebuild communities and restore lives.[iii]

Joint Information System (JIS) Set of policies and procedures used by PIOs when releasing information during an incident.

Key messages The most important topics in a conversation, a presentation, or an interview

Lead The term used for a person within a JIC who supervises certain personnel and functions.

Lead congressional liaison The person responsible for those working with congressional personnel during a disaster.

Lead public affairs officer The person responsible for all public affairs functions during a disaster.

Lead public information officer The person responsible for public information functions during a disaster.

Lead story The top story of a broadcast, newscast, newspaper, or magazine. This is the story that gets the most publicity.

Libel Written words that cause harm to someone.

Live truck A vehicle used by news media to broadcast news events as they happen.

Major Disaster Declaration Announcement of a determination by local or state governments or the federal government that damage from an incident is severe and/or significant.

[iii]http://www.fema.gov/plan/ehp/noma/public-involvement3.shtm.

Marketing Promoting and selling a product an audience needs.

Maximum disclosure, minimum delay A policy for providing information without delay or "cover-up."

Media advisory A short note distributed to the news media to provide basic information about an event, an incident, or a planned news conference.

Media kit A collection of material, often assembled in folders, for presentation to the media. Media kits often contain issue-based documents. Many times, media kits are distributed at news conferences.

Media Monitoring The process of reviewing broadcast, print, and web-based news presentations for coverage of a specific agency.

Media plan A formal document outlining an agency's policy and procedures as they relate to the media.

Media pool A group of media members chosen by other media members to cover a certain aspect of an event and share the material with all other media members present at the event. For instance, a pool may go to a crash site, while the other media members may wait at a nearby media staging area.

Media relations An agency-established program that ensures open lines of communication between the agency and the media. The program includes the agency's media contact policy, public relations, and press releases as a few of its elements.

Media relations plan The formal document that implements the media relations program or a spontaneous plan developed to manage the release of information at an incident.

Mission statement A statement that summarizes an organization's purpose and future direction.

Mult box An electronic device that allows more than one microphone to plug into it. A mult box provides the same audio feed to several news outlets using just one microphone.

Multilingual group A joint information center's group that performs translations, multilingual interviews, and other functions necessary to enhance communications with non-English-speaking disaster victims.

National Highway Traffic Safety Administration (NHTSA) The organization responsible for traffic safety policy in the United States. This organization should not be confused with the National Transportation Safety Board (NTSB), which investigates transportation crashes.

National Weather Service (NWS) The organization officially responsible for weather forecasting in the United States.

News A term that has many definitions, including this from the *Merriam-Webster Online Dictionary*: "A report of current events."

News conference An event, often formal, that announces a program. Also, a planned gathering of news reporters at which questions are asked and answered on nearly any subject. News conferences can also be held during emergencies as a method of providing vital information to all media members at the same time.

News Desk As defined by the Federal Emergency Management Agency (FEMA), the group of personnel who answer media inquiries. Often established as a function within a joint information center.

News release Official information provided by an agency to news media. A news release (also known as a press release) is written in a specific style and contains facts relevant to a specific topic.

National Incident Management System (NIMS) System that will provide a consistent nationwide approach for federal, state, and local governments to work effectively and efficiently together to prepare for, respond to, and recover from domestic incidents, regardless of cause, size, or complexity. To provide for interoperability and compatibility among federal, state, and local capabilities, NIMS will include (1) a core set of concepts, principles, terminology, and technologies covering the incident command system, (2) multiagency coordination systems, (3) a unified command, (4) training, (5) identification and management of resources (including systems for classifying types of resources), (6) qualifications and certification, and (7) the collection, tracking, and reporting of information and resources having to with incidents.

National Information Officers Association (NIOA) Professional organization that supports public information officer activities.

National Interagency Incident Management System (NIIMS) System sponsored by the National Wildfire Coordinating Group (NWCG) that provides a universal set of structures, procedures, and standards for agencies to respond to all types of emergencies. NIIMS is compliant with the National Incident Management System (NIMS).

National Response Plan (NRP) Plan that establishes a comprehensive all-hazards approach to enhance the ability of the United States to manage domestic incidents. The NRP was recently replaced by the National Response Framework (NRF), which is a similar document.

Noun A person, place, thing, or idea, which may or may not be specifically referenced in a sentence.

Operational period A specified period during an incident for which objectives and tactics are developed and carried out by personnel.

Package A longer news story containing more than one interview and various video clips.

Personal data assistant (PDA) An electronic device used to track names and addresses, appointments, and documents for use in the field or to track preliminary damage assessment (a survey of damage conducted after a natural or human-made incident prior to a disaster declaration.)

Planning Section The Incident Command organization component tasked with planning future management activities, resource allocation, and tracking, as well as situational awareness and documentation of an incident.

Police beat Reports are assigned to work with public information officers covering law enforcement, fire and emergency medical service incidents.

Position statement Statement that officially aligns an agency with a specific position.

Post-traumatic stress Acute stress reactions that last more than four weeks, with uncomfortable accompanying signs and symptoms.

Predicate Action word or phrase that "tells the rest of the story" about the preceding noun.

Preposition A word that describes a relationship between two things referenced or described by two words or two phrases in a sentence.

Print media News media that use the printed word to present their information.

Program liaisons Personnel within a joint information center who are responsible for establishing a relationship with citizen and public relief program entities for the purpose of sharing information.

Pronoun A word that substitutes for a noun.

Protected health information Information that a patient has an expectation of being protected under the Health Insurance Portability and Accountability Act (HIPAA).

Public Affairs personnel (Coast Guard) (PAs) U.S. Coast Guard personnel functioning in a role similar to that of a public information officer.

Public affairs programs Television or radio programs that tackle issues of public interest.

Public information Information that causes people to take action that will save lives, reduce injury, and protect property.

Public information officer (PIO) Person responsible for releasing emergency information, as well as nonemergency information, to the media and other constituencies.

Public relations The promotion of rapport and goodwill between an organization and some segment or all of the public. Public relations helps an organization and its public mutually adapt to each other.[iv]

Public service announcements Radio, television, or print advertisements for which there is no charge. Presenting the announcement is determined to be for the public good.

Publicity A mention in the media. Unlike the situation with advertising, with publicity, organizations usually have little control over the message the media present. Instead, reporters and writers decide what will be said.[v]

"Push/pull" system A system that provides information to the media and citizens by releasing it in traditional ways (the "push") and making it available on the Internet so that it can be retrieved (the "pull")

Recovery The emergency management phase during which a community begins the process of returning to normal after a disaster. Recovery can take hours, days, or years.

Recovery Times A FEMA publication, published during a disaster, that outlines assistance programs for disaster victims.

Relations Understanding, assistance, and cooperation developed between parties.

Remote site A site that is away from a news studio and at which a news story is often broadcast live.

Research and Writing The function within a joint information center that is responsible for researching and writing material for internal and external use.

Response The emergency management phase in which actions are taken to save lives and protect property while work goes on in a safe environment.

Sample size The number of respondents necessary for a survey to provide usable information.

Scoop An exclusive story discovered by a reporter before anyone else discovers it or given to someone for various reasons.

[iv]Public Relations Society of America (PRSA).

[v]http://www.managementhelp.org/ad_prmot/defntion.htm, Carter McNamara, MBA, PhD, Copyright 1999.

Sidebar story A story, usually in a newspaper, related to the main article, but set to the side.

Situation Unit The unit within the Incident Command Planning Section that gathers and displays situational intelligence.

Slander Spoken words that cause harm.

Slug line An explanation of the content of a news release.

Sound bite A short statement spoken for use during an interview with a reporter.

Spot news Immediate reporting of events.

Stafford Act Legislation that provides for specific disaster relief programs, as well as an orderly method for the provision of disaster aid.

Stakeholders Individuals, politicians, organizations, and companies affected by, or partners in, the delivery of public information or disaster management.

Standard of care The expected norm of customary services provided to people.

Stressor An event, a person, or an object that initiates the human stress response.

Talking points A specific set of facts approved for release. Talking points are often the primary points of discussion in an interview.

Tense The time frame referenced by a verb in a sentence.

The big three plus one FEMA's reference to print, television, radio, and Internet news delivery methods.

The five "C's" Crime, corruption, catastrophe, conflict, and color.

Town crier A town officer who makes public proclamations.[vi]

Trade magazine Publication read by specific industry workers.

Verb A word that denotes action or state of being.

Vision statement A statement made by an organization setting forth its direction for the future.

Web based Material based on the Internet.

Web Surfer A person who looks at a Web site seeking information.

Word of mouth Oral communication. An example is an audience passing on a message to those who did not attend a presentation.

[vi]*Merriam-Webster Dictionary.*

Index

Note: Locators in italics indicate figures, tables, or boxes.